PENDERYN PLACE-NAMES

I Rowland gyda phob
dymuniad da

Deric Meidrum.

16 . 9 . 21

ISBN: 978-1-84524-399-9

Cover design: Eirian Evans

Published by Gwasg Carreg Gwalch 2021
12 Iard yr Orsaf, Llanrwst, Wales LL26 0EH
☎ 01492 642031
books@carreg-gwalch.cymru
website: www.carreg-gwalch.cymru

Published and printed in Wales

Penderyn Place-names

Deric Meidrum John

"So that evening the name was still pure music, perhaps more earthy than before, more definitely mountainous, perhaps the sweetest place name in the world."

From *Penderyn* by Edward Thomas, 1878-1917

I. Selected Abbreviations and Bibliography

AA   The Arthurian Allusions in the Black Book of Carmarthen, A. O. H. Jarman

AB   *Atlas Brycheiniog/Breconshire Atlas*, Breconshire Education Committee, 1960

ADG   Gwynedd O. Pierce, Tomas Roberts, Hywel Wyn Owen, *Ar Draws Gwlad*, Llanrwst, 1997

AL   The Aberdare Leader

AMR   Archif Melville Richards

ART   John F. Mear, *Aberdare The Railways and Tramroads*, Aberdare, 1999

AS   Ann Selwood

AZSA   AZ Street Atlas 2010, Basingstoke, 1996

B   The Bulletin of the Board of Celtic Studies (Cardiff, 1921-)

Bartrum   Peter Bartrum, Welsh Genealogies 1 & 2. Disc.

BCT   The Brecon County Times

BFE   The Briton Ferry Estate Records, WGAS

BHO   British History Online

Blaeu   Johan Blaeu, Wallia Principatus, Vulgo Wales [map 1645] (facsimile of 1648 ed. GAS)

BMW   Catalogue of the Manuscripts relating to Wales in the British Museum

BWS   K.M. Evans, *A Book of Welsh Saints*, Penarth, 1959

CA   Ifor Williams, *Canu Aneurin*, Caerdydd, 1938

Cartae   Cartae et alia munimenta quae ad dominium de Glamorgancia pertinent, ed. G.T. Clark (Cardiff 1910). 6 vols.

CCRV   Calendar of Chancery Rolls Various BHO

CIPM   Calendar of Inquisitions Post Mortem (London 1904-)

CL   Cardiff Library

CMG   Cardiff and Merthyr Guardian

CRD   Records of the County Borough of Cardiff

CVAI   Raymond Grant, *Cynon Valley in the Age of Iron*, Aberdare, 1991

CVPN   Deric John, *Cynon Valley Place Names*, Llanrwst, 1999

D/D BF/E   164 'A Book of the Estate of George Venables Vernon in County Brecon Surveyed by E.Thomas 1776'. West Glamorgan Archive Service

DPNW   H. W. Owen, R. Morgan, *Dictionary of the Place-Names of Wales*, Llandysul, 2007.

ds	datestone
DWB	The Dictionary of Welsh Biography, NLW online.
DYB	Gwynedd Pierce, *Dan Y Bargod*, Prifysgol Cymru, 1990
EANC	R. J. Thomas, *Enwau Afonydd a Nentydd Cymru*, Cardiff, 1938
ELl.	Ifor Williams, *Enwau Lleoedd*, Liverpool, 1945
EllSG	J. Lloyd-Jones, *Enwau Lleoedd Sir Gaernarfon*, Cardiff, 1928
Enwau	Bedwyr Lewis Jones, *Enwau*, Llanrwst, 1991
ERB	Electoral Registers of Brecknock, 1836-79, PNDH
ERSD	Episcopal Registers of St. Davids, online
FJN	F. J. North
G	J. Lloyd Jones, *Geirfa Barddoniaeth Gynnar Gymraeg*, Prifysgol Cymru, Cardiff, 1931-63
GAS	Glamorgan Archive Service
Gaz	*A Gazatteer of Welsh Place-Names*, ed. Elwyn Davies, Cardiff, 1957
GFB	J. Lloyd, *The Great Forest of Brecknock*, 1819, online
GGF	George Grant Francis
GC	Glenda Carr
GM	Gwrgant Morgannwg, Melincryddan, Castell Nedd. Cymru, Vol. 44, 1913.
GMBG	The Glamorgan, Monmouth and Brecon Gazette and Merthyr Guardian
GOP	Gwynedd O. Pierce
GPC	Geiriadur Prifysgol Cymru, online
Griffiths MT	Place-Names in Merthyr Tudful and District by Griffiths Brothers, 2002. CD
GRO	Glamorgan Record Office, Cardiff
gs.	gravestone
HB	Theophilus Jones, *History of the County of Brecknock*, 1805-9), online
HEF	Glenda Carr, *Hen Enwau o Feironydd*, Caernarfon 2020
HMB	Historical Memoranda of Breconshire, ed. J. Lloyd,1903, online
HPP	Dewi Davies, *Hanes Plwyf Penderyn*, Aberdâr, 1905.
HVHR	Nansi Selwood, *A History of the Villages of Hirwaun and Rhigos*, 1997.
HVN	D. Rhys Phillips, *The History of the Vale of Neath*, Swansea,1925
IW	Ifor Williams
IWm	Iwan Wmffre
JGE	J. Gwenogvryn Evans
LC	Lewis Cymer – Lewis Davies (1863-1951) Eisteddfod Essay and Map 1919

Leland	*The Itinerary in Wales of John Leland, in or about the years 1536-9*, ed. Lucy Toulmin-Smith (London 1906)
LL	*The Book of Llan dav, Liber Landavensis* ed. J. G. Evans and John Rhŷs,, Oxford, 1893
LME	Lizzie Mary Evans, Pomprenllwyd, late 1960s.
loc. dial	local dialect
LYH	Lewis Davies, *Lewsyn yr Heliwr*, Wrecsam,1923
Malkin	Benjamin Heath Malkin, *The Scenery, Antiquities, and Biography, of South Wales*, 1803 (London 1804; second ed., 1807)
ME	Merthyr Express
MT	The Merthyr Telegraph
NA	National Archives
NCPN	B. G. Charles, *Non-Celtic Place-Names in Wales*, London, 1938
NLS	The National Library of Scotland
NLW	The National Library of Wales
NS	Nansi Selwood
NSPNB	Deric John, *Notes on Some Place-Names in and around the Bont*, Aberdare, 1999
OA	Old Aberdare, Vols 1-10, Cynon Valley History Society, 1976-2008
op.cit.	*opera citato*, in the work already quoted
OS	Ordnance Survey
OSLR	Ordnance Survey Landranger
OSPF	Ordnance Survey Pathfinder
PA	Powys Archives
Paroch	Edward Lhuyd, Parochialia, ed. R.H. Morris (AC supplements 1909-11)
PCC	Penderyn Community Centre
Pen	Nansi Selwood, *Penderyn a History*, Penderyn, 1990.
Penderyn Notes	Written by Edward Thomas on his walk between Pontneddfechan and Penderyn in 1914, generously reproduced by the Berg Collection, New York Public Library.
PENM	A Descriptive Catalogue of the Penrice and Margam Abbey Manuscripts (Series I-IV. London 1893-1905), online
Penpont	Penpont Estate, NLW
PHS	Penderyn Historical Society
PM map	Penmailard Estate Map, GRO
PNDH	R. F. Peter Powell, *The Place-Names of Devynock Hundred*, Brecon,1993
PNDPH	Gwynedd O. Pierce, *The Place-Names of Dinas Powys Hundred*, Cardiff, 1968

PNG	Gwynedd O. Pierce, *Place-Names in Glamorgan*, Cardiff, 2002
PNP	B.G. Charles, *The Place-Names of Pembrokeshire*, Aberystwyth, 1992
PPS	Celia Morgan, *Pigion Penderyn Snippets*, Hirwaun, 2011
PR	Parish Registers
PRME	Parliament Rolls of Medieval England; (BHO)
RCAHMW	Royal Commission on the Ancient and Historical Monuments of Wales
RCT	Rhondda Cynon Taf
RM	Richard Morgan
RMR	Rhys Morgan Rees, Gellidafolws, interview 1974.
RISW	The Royal Institution of South Wales
RSHVN	F. J. North, *The River Scenery at the Head of the Vale of Neath*, Cardiff. 1962
RWM	Report on Manuscripts in the Welsh Language, London, 1896-1910
SAPN	Some Aberdare Place-Names, Brynley F. Roberts, *Old Aberddare Vol. 7*, 1993.
Saxton	Christopher Saxton, *An atlas of the counties of England and Wales...* (London 1579, 1607)
SBPN	R. Morgan, R.F. Peter Powell, *A Study of Breconshire Place-Names*, Llanrwst, 1999
SEHPP	The Social and Economic History of the Parish of Penderyn Breconshire, 1500-1851, A.M.Selwood, unpublished PhD Thesis, Aberdare Library.
SM	Siscelia Morgan
SWB	South Wales and the Borders in the XIVth cent. map (1933) William Rees
SWCHPP	Rev. E, L, Jones *Spotlight on Welsh Church History with special reference to the Parish of Penderyn*, 1950
SWVSA	South Wales Valleys Street Atlas 1996
TAG	Melville Richards, *Enwau Tir a Gwlad*, Caernarfon, 1998.
TAS	Tithe Appointment Schedules
TCT	The Cardiff Times
TJ	Theophilus Jones
TL	Penderyn Timeline by Siscelia Morgan
TM	Tithe Map
TMR	Gwyn A. Williams, *The Merthyr Rising*, London, 1978.
TR	Tomos Roberts
Tred. Est.	The Tredegar Estate Records, NLW
TYG	Tarian Y Gweithiwr

TYR	Tafodiaith y Rugos. Astudiaeth o Dafodiaith Cymraeg Cylch y Rhigos, Olwen Samuel, unpublished MA thesis 1970, UCL
Vaynor	Elwyn Bowen, *Vaynor a Study of the Welsh Countryside*, Merthyr Tydfil, 1992.
viz.	videlicet, 'namely'
W	Wills NLW
WG3	*Welsh Genealogies, AD 1500-1600*, M. P. Siddons, Aberystwyth, 2017, plus disc.
WGAS	West Glamorgan Archive Service
WP	Welch Piety (Account of the Circulating Welsh Charity Schools) London 1740 ff.).
WPNB	Dewi Davies, *Welsh Place-Names of Breconshire*, Brecon, 1971.
WS	T.J. and Prys Morgan, *Welsh Surnames*, Cardiff, 1985
YEE	Bedwyr Lewis Jones, *Yn Ei Elfen*, Llanrwst, 1992.
YG	Y Gwladgarwr
YPN	Ystradfellte Place Names, Richard Powell.
YPP	Nansi Selwood, *Ysgol Pontbrenllwyd Penderyn, Portrait of Life in a Welsh Village School 1874-1906*, Neath, 2003

Location

Penderyn is the name of a village and parish, which was at one time in the south west of the old county of Breconshire.

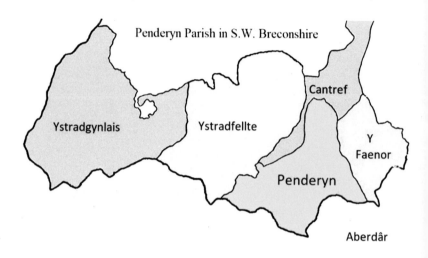

Map based on *Y Plwyfi, Atlas Brycheiniog, p52.*

The 1974 County changes saw Penderyn leave Breconshire and enter into the new county of Mid Glamorgan, while in 1996, further transformation of the Welsh counties made Penderyn Village and Parish part of the County Borough of Rhondda Cynon Taf. Indeed, the rivers Taf Fawr and Cynon form parts of the parish boundary, the former separating Penderyn Parish from that of Vaynor (Y Faenor), and the latter partly, along with Nant Hir etc., with the parish of Aberdare (Aberdâr).

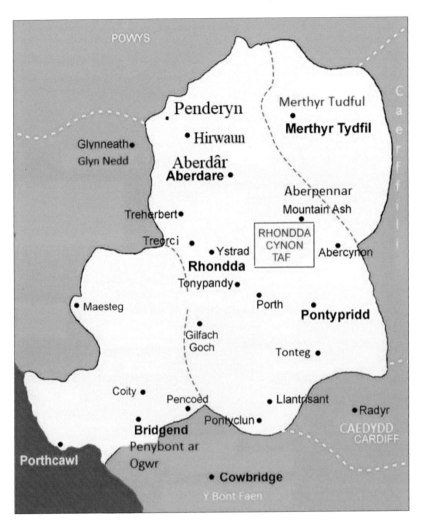

Some place-names in Rhondda Cynon Taf and neighbouring authorities

Introduction

Place-name etymology is a discipline that involves set procedures with an established method of investigation. This discipline is based mainly on written evidence of early forms of place-names within a given location. Early forms are important because of the tendency of some place-names to change over the years. This evidence is assessed and evaluated for language, spelling, pronunciation and meaning. Having collected and recognised names, it is essential that the toponymist knows the area's topography in order to properly interpret the given place-name elements. Fanciful guesses and onomastic tales may be entertaining but play no part in modern place-name etymology.

Main sources used are named in Abbreviations and Bibliography above. Special mention must be made of local historians, mother and daughter Nansi and Ann Selwood, Dewi Davies (Dewi Cynon), Jenkin Howell, Lewis Davies (Lewis Cymmer), and toponymist R.F. Peter Powell whose works and publications have been most valuable and informative. Siscelia Morgan, chair of the Penderyn Historical Society has been of great help and encouragement. Place-name author and authority Richard Morgan has also been most supportive. I am grateful to The Glamorgan Archive Service, The National Library of Wales, The National Library of Scotland, The Berg Collection, New York Public Library and Aberdare Library for allowing the use and reproduction of certain maps and images. A special thank you to the National Library of Wales and West Glamorgan Archive Service, for allowing use of the 1840s Tithe Maps and Schedules and the 1776 George Venables Vernon Estate Maps and Schedules respectively.

This survey is of place-names in the Parish of Penderyn in the old county of Becknockshire. In 1974 the Parish was incorporated into the new county of Mid Glamorgan. Further reorganisation in 1996 created the county borough of Rhondda Cynon Taf by the merger of the former Mid Glamorgan districts of Rhondda, Cynon Valley and Taff-Ely (apart from Creigiau and Pentyrch, which were joined to Cardiff). The place-names examined were all located in the old county of Brechnockshire.

As place-names reflect the language of the community, it is not surprising that most names recorded in this study are Welsh. Many were written in local dialect form and include expected spelling inconsistencies and changes over the passage of time. The earliest recorded Penderyn parish names occur in Liber Landavensis *c.* 1150, as part of the boundary of the episcopate of Llan Daf in the time of Bishop

Oudoceus (Euddogwy) LL p134, and they exemplify these changes. The names, original and commented upon are melltou (Mellte), Hepstur (not Hepste but Hesbddwr, later Sychryd), Guyragon (Gwrangon), Gauanauc (Gavannog, poss. Trebannog, but questionable), Deri Emreis (poss. Deri Hir), Cecin Clysty (poss. Sychbant or Mynydd y Glog), Frut y guidon (Nant Ffrwd) and Taf maur (Taf fawr). Later sources reveal the names of farms and landholdings with their borders and owners. Again, many of the farm-names have changed and some are difficult to locate in today's parish. Later material includes estate maps, parish registers, census returns, OS maps etc., as well as local historical publications (see Abbreviations and Bibliography). Nansi Selwood's local history books, as well as daughter Ann Selwood's publications and unpublished thesis have been invaluable. Books and articles by toponymists Gwynedd Pierce, Melville Richards, Richard Morgan, Ifor Williams, Brynley F. Roberts, R.J. Thomas, Glenda Carr and others have been most informative and supportive. I am also grateful to Dr Guto Rhys and D. Geraint Lewis for their contributions. The formation of Cymdeithas Enwau Lleoedd Cymru/The Welsh Place-name Society has been a positive influence on the standing of place-names in Wales while its articles and newsletters have been interesting and enlightening. I must express my sincerest thanks to Dr. David Thorne, Cadair Cymdeithas Enwau Lleoedd Cymru, Welsh Place-Name Society Chair, for kindly proofreading the work and advising before publication.

Each name is followed by early forms where possible, accompanied by an explanation and a meaning. The name heading is the latest form for that name, usually taken from late 20th cent. OS maps. Some names are noted as 'Lost' indicating that their location is unknown. Where possible, farms include maps as well as field-names listed on available schedules.

Some names are topographical, describing features in the landscape eg. Torfoel, Penycae, Pentwyn, Cefn-y-don, Gellidafolog, Wernlas, Hirwaun, Garwdyle, Bertlwyd, Maesyrhydiau etc., some name people long forgotten eg. Llety Rhys, Cae Hywel, Dolgynog, Pant Cynferth, others name animals and birds eg. Penderyn, Gelli Tarw, Tyle'r Morgrug, Pwll y dylluan, Llwyn y Moch etc. Occasionally certain buildings and manmade structures are involved such as Coedcae'r felin, Ynysyfelin, Beudy bach, Troed rhiw'r llan, Y Pandy, Tai Cyplau, Ysgubor Fawr, Gelli Neuadd, Pontbrenllwyd, Penpont, Penyrheol, Heol-las, Penpownd as well as names of rivers and streams or parts of them eg. Sychbant, Cilhepste, Ffrwd Uchaf, Ffrwd Isaf, Camnant, Blaen Nant-Hir, Sgwd yr Eira, Pwll Taf, Blaen Nant-Melyn, Y Naint, Garwnant, Llygad Cynon, Cefn Cadlan and Ceunant du. Trees, shrubs and plants are also named in Y Dderi Hir, Gelli

Dafolog, Beilihelyg, Berthlwyd, Pen yr Eithyn, Y Gelli, Llwyn Onn, Onllwyn and Yr Eithyn. There are 'colourful' names such as Pwll Coch, Wernlas, Heol-las, Coedcae-du, Llwyn-coch, Penyglog-fanddu and Pontbrenllwyd, plus past occupations and pastimes in Brynprydydd, Cae'r Arlwydd, religious activities in Pontycapel, Jerusalem, Siloam, Soar, Church Road, Chapel Road, Bethel and Penderyn Church dedicated to Saint Cynog, and not so religious places as Y Tafarn Uchaf, Y Tafarn Isaf, The Lamb Inn, The Red Lion/Y Llew Coch, The Brecon Arms, The Butchers Arms, The Railway Inn and The Three Oaks. There are difficult names including Bodwigiad, Trebannog, Ynyswendraeth, Gellidiafolws, Pantcefnyffordd and lost names such as Erw'r crydd, Cwrt yr Eithyn, Ynysfelin, Ynys-Daf, Tyn-y-ton, Troed-y-rhiw, Nant Melyn Uchaf, Penmailard, Cwt y Gwter, Clwyd Rhyd Fan, Cilhepste-cerrig and Abernant. Relatively new names have appeared as Court Farm, Llwyn-coch, Woodland Park and Beacons Park. Industry, businesses and education have left their mark in the various Quarry names, Mill names, Breweries and Distilleries, as well as the names of old and modern Schools.

Any shortcomings in this work are all of my own making and I apologise for them. Gratitude is also expressed to the staff at Aberdare Library, the National Library of Wales, the National Library of Scotland, Cardiff University Library, the Glamorgan Archive Service, West Glamorgan Archive Service, National Archives, Penderyn Historical Society, Cadw, British History Online, Old Maps Online, Cronfa Ddata Melville Richards, Ancestry. Co. UK., Geiriadur Prifysgol Cymru Arlein, Cymdeithas Enwau Lleoedd Cymru as well as others too numerous to mention.

I would like to extend a special thanks to Anita my wife for excusing me of so many household duties so that I could spend time collecting, evaluating, assessing and explaining the numerous place-names involved, as well as accompanying me on visits to different locations within the parish and reading much of the work.

Diolch yn fawr iawn i bawb.

Deric Meidrum John

Penderyn

Parish and village

Penderyn is the parish and village name. *Penderyn* village has a lower and upper part called *Pontbrenllwyd* and *The Lamb, Pentref y Lamb* in Welsh, respectively.

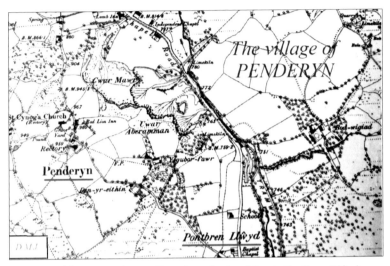

Late 19th cent. Penderyn Village from the Lamb Inn to Pontbren Llŵyd.

Penderyn is one of those names that needs historical examples to ascertain changes or otherwise. Certain earlier attempts at explaining the meaning have suggested that the name changed to *Penderyn* from Penydarren, Penyderi, Penderwen or Pendeuryn (see HPP pp. 9-10).

The following list will show that the name has not changed from any of the suggested forms and that the name has always been Penderyn or Penyderyn establishing *pen* and *aderyn* as the main elements, giving English 'bird's head' or 'the bird's head'.

Pennyderyn 1291 PRME; Penderin 1372 CIPM; Penyderen 1468 BMW iii.140; Penyderyn 1535 VE; Parish of Pennyderyn 1547 MWBM; Penyderyn 1628 Milbonne, AMR; Penderin 1729 E Bowen Map; Village of Penderyn 1765 WP; Penyderyn 1832 OS Map.

Penderyn is Welsh, *pen, y,* and *deryn,* or *pen, aderyn.* The significance of the 'bird's head' may be topographical, referring to the shape of a feature in the landscape such as *Moel Penderyn.* It may on the other hand be totemistic in nature, related to that family of place-names that contain *pen* followed by an animal name, eg. Penychen (ox), Penmarch (stallion), Pentyrch (boar), Penhydd (stag) etc. where such a head would have been placed on top of a pole to mark a point of assembly and boundary marker.

The late Bedwyr Lewis Jones wrote (translated) 'Many centuries ago, the people of a district or hundred would assemble in one particular place in order to hold meetings in the open air. In those meetings it was the custom to place the head of an animal on a pole - as a totem pole. It seems most likely that a boar's head on a pole would mark the early meeting place for each of the four Pentyrch('s) or Bentyrch('s) in Wales' (*Enwau* p. 37).

It is possibly a combination of both, where the topographical feature influenced the choice of totem. (see CVPN pp. 76-78).

Moel Penderyn – the likely topographical feature that resembles a bird's head.
© DMJ

Penderyn was recorded as a 'village' in 1765 when Lewelin John was named as a teacher in a Welch Charity School "in the Village of Penderyn" (WP). It had previously been recorded as a 'parish' (see 1547 above). From *c.* 1800 the Parish of Penderyn was popularised by the much-loved Welsh folk song "Y Ferch o Blwyf Penderyn" (The Girl from Penderyn Parish).

"Very little is known presently about the young man and girl mentioned in the song. She lived in the farmstead known as Tre Banog Fach, Brycheiniog and the boy lived in Ty Newydd – a farmstead in Glamorganshire. The county boundary lay between the two farmsteads.

The girl's father's oxen strayed on to the boy's father's farmstead, while the boy himself was driving them home, one of them happened to fall and break its leg. That brought on the wrath of the girl's family, and little by little, the two families became hostile to each other. In the end the girl was persuaded to end her amorous dealings with the boy, which resulted in the song's creation." (Translated from Dewi Cynon's 'Hanes Plwyf Penderyn' p.81).

The legendary Richard Lewis, alias *Dic Penderyn*, was reputedly born in 1808 in *Penderyn* Cottage, Aberafan, hence his alias according to *Y Bywgraffiadur Cymreig*. I can find no evidence of that cottage name on any historical document. Historian Gwyn A. Williams casts doubt on *Penderyn* Cottage as the source of his alias, preferring *Penderyn* parish, Brecs. He states that as a youth, Dic is said "to have run away to Penderyn parish" (TMR p. 173), and that "Richard Lewis seems actually to have worked in Penderyn parish in 1828;" (op. cit. p. 174). He was buried in St. Mary's churchyard Aberafan on August 14, 1831 aged 23.

Vaynor and *Penderyn* Rural District Council was operational between 1896 and 1974, while Vaynor and *Penderyn* Comprehensive School catered for *Penderyn* secondary school pupils until 2004. Ysgol Pontbrenllwyd, *Penderyn* opened in 1874, educating younger pupils. It is known today as Ysgol Gynradd Gymuned *Penderyn* Community Primary School. Canolfan Cymunedol *Penderyn* Community Centre was built nearby in the 1980s and extended *c.* 2010.

Penderyn is also a brand name used by the local Welsh Whisky Company. *Penderyn* single malt whisky was launched on St David's Day 2004. In 2007 the distillery introduced Vodka, Gin and a Cream Liquer to its products. In 2008 a visitor centre was opened at the distillery in *Pontbrenllwyd*, Penderyn, by H.R.H. Charles, The Prince of Wales.

There is also a *Penderyn* Mansion and estate on the River Wye in Queenstown, Baltimore, Maryland, USA. It was built in 1989 by the late Mario Baiardi and named *Penderyn* by his wife Maureen, nee Howard, born in Treorci, Cwm Rhondda. She named it *Penderyn* "which is Welsh for 'bird's head'." "Penderyn is on the Wye River and is home to thousands of birds of many species." *The Baltimore Sun* 1990.

Pen, aderyn; 'bird's head'

Abernant SO 0011

Former Farm, Stream
Abernant 1911 Census; 1833 Will of Herbert Jones NA; 1768 Will of Joan John NLW; 1696 ; Tyr Abernant, 1613-26 Cymorth, Tredegar NLW; Tir Abernant 1617 Will of John Llewellin David NA;

A former farm of between 113 and 147 acres, Abernant was located at the mouth of the stream named *Nant Abernant* as it flowed into Taf Fawr. The farmhouse and land were submerged under the Llwyn Onn Reservoir prior to its opening in 1926.

The valley was called Cwm Dyrys 'tangled, dense valley' and the stream itself was known earlier as Nant Dyrys (Nant Duris Brook 1780

Tred. Est.). Cf. other streams named Nant Dyrys at Llangeinwyr, Blaengwrach, Llanwrthwl, Brecs. and Rhondda (see AMR).
The farm took the name of the generic *Abernant*.

1841 Tithe Appointment Schedules [henceforth TAS], Abernant (103 acres):

Landowner Sir Charles Morgan Bart. Occupier David Davies

1256 Coed cae (grazing enclosure), 1257 Cae Newydd (new field), 1258 Wern Isha (lower wet meadow; note the mutated Wern for Gwern, following an assumed def. art. and the loc. dial. isha for standard Welsh isaf), 1259 Hendre (main farm),1260 Cae Newydd (new field), 1261 Close bach (small courtyard), 1262 Ynis Isha (lower river meadow), 1263 Ynis Ucha (upper river meadow),1264 Homestead 1265 Wern Nessa (next/adjacent wet meadow), 1266 Waun fach (small meadow) 1267. Tyle bach (small hill) 1268. Wern Ucha (upper alder swamp) 1269. Wern fach (small alder swamp) 1270. Caer Waun (the meadow field) Waun fawr (big meadow).

Aber, nant; 'mouth (of the) stream'

Afon Cynon

SN 9508

River

Afon Cynon 1991 OSPF 1108; Ynys Kynon 1638 CFL; river Kynon 1622/3 Plymouth; Glin Kynon 1578 RM/BGA; Forest glyn Kynon 1568 Plymouth; o lwytcoet cynon *c.* 1500 B. AMR.

The earliest forms of the river-name written as *Kynon* or *Cynon* are noted above. The river emerges from a pool in *Llygad Cynon* and flows south eastwards towards Hirwaun. It forms the parish boundary with Aberdare, from the mouth of Nant y Bwllfa until it reaches the confluence with Nant Hir. It then continues towards *Trecynon*, Aberdare and Mountain Ash/Aberpennar before joining the River Taf at *Abercynon*.

For its meaning, the renowned academic Aberdarian Dr Brynley F Roberts, CBE, MA, PhD, FSA writing on *Some Aberdare Place-Names* (Old Aberdare Vol. 7) states that "Cynon may be a personal name containing the element cyn as in 'hounds, dogs'. There are many personal names in Welsh which have -on as a final syllable and it is generally agreed that many of these are in origin names of Celtic gods and goddesses, Mabon, Modron, Teyrnon, Rhiannon, Gofannon, Amaethon. Cynon may be the name of the river deity, perhaps a 'hound goddess'. Incidentally, there are streams called Cynon, in Cardiganshire, and in Montgomeryshire."

Cynon is also the name of a brave warrior of the Old North, named in Y Gododdin, a 6th cent. poem written by Aneurin. He (*Cynon*) is also reputedly one of the many sons of Brychan, the eponymous ruler of Brycheiniog (Brecknockshire). Brycheiniog is formed from the personal name Brychan, plus the territorial suffix -iog, cf. Pebidiog, Pembs., Cyfeiliog, Mntg., Rhufoniog, Dnbs. etc. The river-name is probably the name of a deity or a personal name. Many Welsh river-names are also personal names eg. *Alun, Dewi, Meurig, Pedran, Beuno, Cynfael, Einion, Machno* etc.

The river *Cynon* gives its name to *Llygad Cynon, Glancynon, Bryn Cynon, Maescynon, Trecynon, Ynyscynon, Cwm Cynon* and *Abercynon* all in the *Cynon* Valley.

Afon Cynon, 'hound-goddess river'

Afon Hepste   SN 9309

River

Afon Hepste 1988 OSPF 1084; 1919 River Hepsta LC map; Duffryn Hepste 1503 Penpont.

The river Hepste rises at Llygad Hepste Fechan on Waun Tincer in the parish of Ystradfellte. It flows towards the parish of Penderyn, forming part of the Penderyn/Ystradfellte parish boundary from Tai Hirion to its confluence with the river Mellte just southwest of Sgwd-yr-eira.

Hepste contains Welsh hesb and teu/te (alternative forms of tam and taf). Hesb is the feminine form of hysb that has become hesp through metathesis plus the hardening of the letter b to a p. The local Gwentian dialect river-name pronunciation is hepsta as seen in the verse

A dry Hepste riverbed from the Pont Hepste bridge early November 2016. © DMJ

below, as well as Pont Hepsta (LYH p. 20) and 1919 above.

Hesb means 'dry' and refers to a river or stream whose riverbed is dry in places. The limestone part of the riverbed is porous resulting in water seeping through it and often emptying the riverbed. The rivers and streams named Sychnant, Sychryd, Beusych, Hepstwr, Hesb, Hespin, Hafesb and Hepste all belong to that family of rivers whose beds are dry in parts at certain times. Here is a verse written by Gwrgant Morgannwg (GM) in Cymru, 1913, translated by DMJ:-

Rhodio glanna'r Hepsta'n unig *Roaming Hepste's banks alone,*
Sydyn trodd yn afon gerrig, *It suddenly turned a river of stone,*
Mynd am filltir hyd ei gwely, *A mile I went along the stream,*
Cyn câ'l dwr i ymolch ynddi *Before some water washed me clean.*

The second element teu/te is present in the sister rivers Hepste and Mellte. The root (tam, taf) is found in rivers in Britain and the continent. See Afon Taf below.

Hepste; 'dry, dark (river)' or 'dry river'

Afon Mellte   SN 9209

River

Afon Mellte 1991 OSPF 1108; Melte 1578 HMB1, 162; ; r. Mellte 1482 Tred.MSS 114/10 AMR; Melltou 12th. cent. LL.

The Mellte river begins at the confluence of Afon Llia and Afon Dringarth at Castell Mellte. It flows southwards to Ystradfellte village and on to Porthyrogof and Craig-y-Dinas before joining the Nedd Fechan at Abermellte. From its junction with the Hepste to its meeting with the Sychryd it forms part of the boundary between the parishes of Penderyn and Ystradfellte.

 Afon Mellte could contain Welsh mellt 'lightning' or could figuratively be for something that moves swiftly and flashes perilously. This may be linked to the many waterfalls along its course. For the te, teu suffix, see Afon Hepste above. Mellte is also found as a personal name. The eminent historian and toponymist Gwynedd Pierce refers to a thirteenth century document called De Situ Brecheniauc, in which one of the many daughters of Brychan Brycheiniog is said to be buried in an unknown grave 'under the stone of Meltheu' (a written form of Mellteu, locally Mellte). The same personal name occurs in Bedwellty (bod, Mellte) Monmouthshire, (See PNG pages 19-20; SBPN p. 155.). The personal name Mellt also occurs in Culhwch and Olwen as Mabon am Melld. Professor A. O. H. Jarman suggests a possible Celtic root *meldo- meaning 'gentle, mild, pleasant' (AA p. 108). The river Mellte may contain an identical personal name. For personal names and river-names see Afon Cynon above.

Afon Mellte; 'Mellte's river' or 'lightning, flashing river'

Afon Taf Fawr

River

Afon Taf Fawr 1989 OSPF 1109; Taf-fawr 1830 OS; Taffe River 1759 Penmlrd Map;
Tav vawre 1676 Penpont; tafmaur *c.* 1150 LL.

The earliest recorded forms Taf maur, along with Tafbechan are listed as
part of the boundaries of the Episcopate of Llan Dâv in the 12th century
Book of Llandav (LL). Afon Taf Fawr starts its journey on the slopes of Y
Gyrn in the Brecon Beacons, just north of the Storey Arms. It enters the
parish of Penderyn at its junction with Nant-y-geugarn, now part of
Cantref reservoir, north of Llwyn-onn reservoir, previously near the
hamlet of Ynysyfelin. It flows from the reservoir southwards along Cwm
Taf, leaving the parish at its junction with the Ffrwd stream at Pontycapel.

Taf Fawr and Taf Fechan have two distinguishing second elements
'large' and 'small' respectively. The two rivers meet at the confluence
(cymer) at Cefncoed-y-cymer, 'mountain ridge (near) the woods (of the)
confluence' thereafter to be called Afon Taf, Anglicised as the River Taff.

The river-name Taf has been discussed by many toponymists with
early writers suggesting it meant 'dark'. Gwynedd Pierce believes that
modern opinion favours 'to flow, to melt'. He notes that Welsh Taf is
related to British *Tam, and that this British element is also found in the
rivers Tame, Tamar, Teme, Thame, Thames, Team (England), Tambre
(Spain), Tammaro (Italy), Demer (Belgium), Tamaran (France) and Tawe
(Wales), (PNG pp. 25-26). Today, Afon Taf Fawr forms part of the
Penderyn parish boundary.

Afon, Taf, mawr; 'large Taf river'

Beacons Park

Housing Estate

Beacons Park 1996 SWVSA; 1983, 1982, 1979 PR;

Beacons Park is the name of a housing estate opposite the Lamb Hotel. It
was opened in 1976. It takes its name from its location as part of the
Brecon Beacons National Park. Its Welsh equivalent would be Parc y
Bannau.

Beacons is the plural of English beacon 'a fire on an eminence lit as a
signal' also 'a hill on which it could be lighted'. It occurs as the second
element of the Brecon Beacons, 'peaks of Brecon' and it is this estate's
location near to those peaks that probably resulted in its inclusion when
the name was chosen. The second element park is also English with a
number of meanings including 'a piece of ground for public recreation' as

well as 'a tract of land surrounding a mansion, kept as a pleasure ground' which could account for its popularity as the name of an estate, street or district.

Beacons, park; 'pleasure ground (near the) Beacons'

Beili Helyg
SN 969104

Farm

Beili-Helyg 1988 OSPF 1084; Beilihelyg 1905 OS6"; Beilihelig1911-1841 Census; Baili-helyg 1832 OS1".

Beili Helyg sign and farmhouse 2017. © DMJ

Beili Helyg is the name of a farmstead in Cwm Cadlan located between Wernlas and Nant Maden. The first element beili is from Eng. bailey cf. motte and bailey castle. Welsh beili is used for a farmyard or fold usually located alongside the farmhouse. The second element helyg describes the willow trees that would once have grown in or around the beili.

Baily Helig of the 1840 Tithe Map is named Blaen Cadlan on the 1841 Tithe Schedules. The lands of Blaencadlan Uchaf, purchased by Reynold Davies in 1820 went to Baily Helyg. See Blaen Cadlan.

For the 1841 Tithe Schedules: see Blaen Cadlan.

Beili, helyg; 'courtyard (of) willows'

Berthlwyd

Earlier Farm, now afforested

Berthllwyd 1841 Census Upper Penderyn; 1828 Will Thomas Jenkins NLW.

There was a *Berthlwyd* in Cwm Taf (now afforested) and another *Berthlwyd* as well as a *Berthlwyd* Cottage near Cefndon in Cwm Cynon. It appears that *Berthlwyd* (Cwm Taf) was changed to *Glanyrafon* 'the riverbank', sometime between 1891 and 1901, prob. to avoid confusion with *Berthlwyd*, (Cwm Cynon).

1841 TAS for Berthlwyd and Penycoed (107 acres):

1429. Road & Waste 1430. Seven Acres Meadow 1431. Cae bach (small field) 1432. Coed Newydd (new wood) 1433. Cae Drussy (drysi; brambles field) 1434. do & Wood 1435. Ynis Isha (lower river meadow) 1436. do ucha (upper river meadow) 1437. Cae bryn cenol (middle hill field) 1438. Coed bach (small wood) 1439. Bryn Ucha (upper hill) 1440. Homestead &c. 1441. Cae Glas (green field) 1442. Coed cae Bedw (birch trees enclosure) 1443. Erw Llwyd (poor acre) 1444. Waun pen y garn (top of the cairn meadow) 1445. Waun (meadow) 1446. Building 1447. Blank 1448. Y nerag (hanereg; half acre) 1449. Worlod cae Mawr (y weirglodd; Cae Mawr meadow) 1450. Road and Waste 1451. Blank 1452. Ynis y coed (wood river meadow) 1453. Cae ffynnon ddu isha (lower black well field) 1454. do ucha (upper black well field) 1455. Cae Newydd (new field) 1456. Cae wrth r heol (field near the road) 1457. Homestead &c. 1458. Cae Gwennith (wheat field) 1459. Cae dan y coed (field below the wood).

Berthlwyd

Farm and Cottage

Berth-lwyd 1991 OSPF 1108; Berth-lwyd Cottage 1920 OS25"; 1911 Census; Berth Lwyd 1851 Will of Wm. David NA; Berthllwyd 1813 BFE; 1691 HVHR 36; Tir y Berth Lwyd 1665 HVHR 42; Tyr y berth llwyd 1626 Tred. Est.

Berthlwyd farm near Cefndon and Court farms, was at one time a one storeyed building with one large living room (Hall/Neuadd) and a loft under a steep-pitched, thatched roof. The farmhouse was much altered during the 19th and 20th centuries to include front doors, a ground floor and first floor (upstairs) as well as a slate roof. (HVHR 125, 126.)

Berthlwyd has mutated from *Perthlwyd* due to a redundant definite article viz. (Y) *Berthlwyd*. *Perth* is Welsh feminine singular noun, for a row of small trees or bushes that form a hedge; also 'thorn bush, brake, thicket, copse, coppice'. GPC. *Llwyd* can refer to the colour grey or to the pers. name *Llwyd* (Lloyd).

1841 TAS Berthllwyd (77 acres):

Landwoner Morgan Morgan Occupier William David.

438. Erw Wen (white acre) 439. do fclan fach (small yellow acre) 440. Craig y Ty (rock near the house) 441. Cae dan y ty (field below the house) 442. Cae ar yr heol (field on the road) 441a. Homestead &c 443. Caer Odyn (the kiln field) 443a. Erw felan fawr (big yellow acre) 444. Wernlass (sic) (green alder swamp) 445. Llwyn y crychyddod (the herons' bush) 446. Cae bach (small field) 447. Coed caer crychyddod (the herons' grazing enclosure) 448. Do 449. Old Building &c. 450. Caer Ysgubor (the barn field) 450a. do 451. Waun fawr (large meadow) 452. do Ucha (upper large meadow) 453. Cae pen y waun (top of the meadow field).

Perth, llwyd; 'Grey or Lloyd's hedge/copse/wood'

Bethel

SO 0011

Chapel

Capel Bethel 1905 OS6"; 1851 Census; Bethel, Ynysyfelin 1905 (1799) HPP p103; Bethel 1847 Will of Jeffrey Morgan, NLW;

The early *Bethel* Baptist chapel located in Ynysyfelin was built in 1799 (see HPP pp102-104). This was the chapel frequented by Baptists of the Hepste and Cadlan farms before Siloam was opened in Pontbrenllwyd in 1823. In his will of 1847, Jeffrey Morgan of Neuadd, Nant ddu, bequeathed £1 to his friend "the Reverend David Davies, minister of the Gospel at Bethel, Ynisyfelin." The Reverend David Davies was a son to the Rev. D. Owen Davies, the chapel's first ordained minister. This chapel is now submerged under the Llwyn-onn reservoir. New Bethel Baptist Chapel, sited across the valley opposite the old chapel, was opened in 1914.

Chapel name: Bethel is the name of the place where Jacob rested.
It is said to mean 'The house of God'. (Genesis 28:19).

Beudy Bach

SO 0011

Smallholding

Beudy-bach 1905 OS6".

The building located in Ynysyfelin is now submerged under Llwyn-on Reservoir. There is a *Beudy Bach* on the opposite side of the valley. *Beudy* is Welsh 'cowshed', an outbuilding where cows are kept and milked. *Bach* 'small' is the adjective that describes the noun.

Beudy, bach; 'little cowshed'

Blaen Cadlan

SN 976108

Farm

Blaen-cadlan-uchaf 1988 OSPF 1084; 1884 OS6"; Blaen-cadlan-isaf 1884 OS6"; Blaen Cadlan 1841 TS; 1793, 1770 PR, 1739 HPP 52; Blaincadlan 1841 Census; Tyr

Blaen Cadlan (two tenwments) *c.* 1626 Tredegar NLW; Tyr blan cadlan 1619 Will of Rees William Price NA.

Blaen Cadlan was divided into *Uchaf* and *Isaf* with *Blaen Cadlan-isaf* shown as a ruin on the 1884 OS map. Dewi Cynon describes the eviction of "Old Jem" and two old bachelors from Blaen Cadlan in 1864, and the ensuing fire at the cottage. (TYG 31/8/1899). He further recalls Blaen Cadlan as "a smallholding enough to sustain two or three cows on the mountainside." (AL 1/7/1905) trans. The 1861 Census has William Davies aged 72 as "farmer of 2 acres" at one of the two "Blaen Cadlan" properties. James Thomas, Labourer aged 27 born at Ferwig, Cardigan and family inhabited the other. 1861 was the last time that Blaen Cadlan was listed on the Penderyn census returns. The farmhouse was left uninhabited and allowed to become a ruin.

"The lands of Blaencadlan Uchaf, having been purchased by Reynold Davies in 1820 went to Baily Helyg". SEHPP p. 257. The 1793 PR entry is for Lewis Lewis, son of Jenkin and Margaret Lewis of Blaencadlan. Lewis was better known as Lewis yr Heliwr, of the 1831 Merthyr Risings.

Blaencadlan has two elements, blaen 'source of river, headwater; front,; upland', plus the name of the *Cadlan* stream, giving 'source of (the) *Cadlan* (stream)'

1841 TAS Blaen Cadlan (73 acres):
Landowner Morgan Morgan Esq. Occupier William Morgan
984, 985. Waun Goch (red meadow) 986a. Cae Crwm (bent, crooked field) 986. Coedcae (grazing enclosure) 987. Homestead 988 Weirglodd (pasture) 989. Coedcae y Berth (grazing enclosure of the hedge) 990. Waun (meadow) 991. Blaen Cadlan (source of the Cadlan stream) 992. Cae bach (small field) 993. Cae dan y Berth (field under the hedge) 994. Cae Shams (James's field).
Blaen, Cadlan; 'Head (of the) Cadlan (stream)'

Blaen Nant hir SN 985071

Residence

Blaennanthir 2016 visited; 1905 OS6"; Blane Nant Hire 1841 Census D20; Blaen nanthir 1830 Will of Morgan Jenkins (John Rees of BNH) NLW; Blaen Nant Hir 1778 PR; 1776 BFE Schedules; 14th cent. SWB.; Blan Nanthir 1749 PM Map; Blane Nanthir alias Derlwyn 1738 CL.

Blaen nanthir is the name of a modern residence (built *c.* 2008) located between *Nant Hir* and *Nant Moel* Reservoirs. The old *Blaen Nant Hir* farmstead was so named as it was situated at the head of the *Nant Hir* brook. It was ruinous and used as an animal shelter in the early 1990s (PNDH 7.8). It had an alias of *Derlwyn* (derw, llwyn, 'oak grove') in 1738, which also appears as 603. *Derwlwyn Mawr* in the 1841 TAS. For *blaen* see the previous entry plus *Nant Hir*, a stream name.

1841 TAS Blaen Nant Hir (68 acres):

Landowner Morgan Morgan, Occupier John Rees.

592. Waun (Meadow) 593. cae bach (small field) 594. Cae dan ty (field below the house) 595. Wood 596. Homestead &c. 597. Cae Uwchlawr ty (field above the house) 598. Coed Cae (grazing enclosure) 599. Do 600. Road & Waste 601. Cae Cwm (valley field) 602. Cae bach (small field) 603. Derwlwyn Mawr (large oak grove).

1776 Schedules [D/D BF/E 164]:

1. Cae dan y ty (field below the house 2. Garden 3. Cae bach (small field) 4. The wood under the house 5. Cae uchlaw'r ty (field above the house) 6. Coed cae (grazing enclosure) 7. The Road that leads thro' the Farm 8. Cae Carn (cairn field) 9. The Meadow.

Blaen, Nanthir; 'Head (of the) Nant Hir (stream)'

Blaen Nant Melyn   SN 9807

Previously a farm

Blane Nant Melyn 1841 Census; Blaen nant melin 1807 Will of Thomas Rees NLW.

Blaen Nant Melyn farm is submerged under *Nant Moel* Reservoir, built 1898. For *blaen* see *Blaen Cadlan*. *Nant Melyn* 'yellow brook' is a stream name.

Blaen, nant, melyn; 'source (of the) Nant-melyn (stream)'

Bodwigiad   SN 9508

Estate, farm

Bodwigiad 1991 OSPF 1108; Bodiced 1923 LYH p9; Plas Bodwigiad 1923 LYH p55; Bod-wigiad 1904 OS25"; Bodwigiad Farm 1861-1881 Census; Bodwigiad House 1871-1911 Census; Bodwigiad and Glogue 1853 CMG; Bodwigiad Lodge 1851 - 1911 Census; Bodwigiad Arms 1851 - 1911 Census; located in Station Road, Hirwaun. Burnt down 2003; Boduigiad 1733 Reynold Davies Will.; Bodwiggiad 1797 Will of Morgan Watkins NLW; Bodwiggiate 1705, 1744/45 BFE, NLW; Bodwicced 1748 WP; Tyr Modwigiad 1691 Court Baron; Bodiwiggiad 1646 Will of Richard Games, NA; Bodigwiad 1646 Sentence of Richard Games; Bodwigiad 1652 Will of Mary Games, NLW; 1646 Will of Richard Games; 1841 Census UP;

The earliest document containing the *Bodwigiad* name is the 1646 will of Richard Games, husband of Mary Games nee Prichard. Ann Selwood informs us in her NLWJ article 'The Games Family of *Bodwigiad*, Penderyn, Breconshire', that in 1622 Mary Prichard was to become Richard Games's second wife and that she was the granddaughter and

Bodwigiad House   Courtesy of Gareth and Celia Morgan

heiress of John Gwyn, *Bodwigiad*. John Gwyn is recorded as John Gwyn of *Bodwigiad c.* 1570 in Bleddyn ap Maenyrch 20(C8), Welsh Geneologies A.D. 1500-1600 [2013].

In the middle of the 17th cent. the estate became part of the Mansel family's Briton Ferry Estate through the marriage of Elizabeth Games, daughter of Edward Games, to Thomas, son of Bussy Mansel. At the end of the 18th cent. the Briton Ferry Estate was purchased by Lord Jersey. Following Lord Jersey's death, the Rev. Reynallt Davies bought the *Bodwigiad* Estate in 1815. The Morgans family of the Van were the owners in the middle of the nineteenth century, and by the end of that century Captain E. M. Whitting held the property.

Note the local dialect pronunciation *Bodiced* in LYH, written in 1923 by local author Lewis Davies as well as *Bodwicced*, 1748 in Welsh Piety, which records 24 pupils attending one of Gruffydd Jones's Circulating Schools there.

Many attempts have been made to explain the meaning, including a clumsy Bodwaun-y-gâd 'mansion of the battlefield' and a fanciful 'mansion of the wigs'. Others have linked the second element wigiad to Wesh gwig 'wood, forest, grove' plus the adjectival suffix -iad giving gwigiad 'a dwelling of the woods'. One relatively recent etymology is that of the late Tomos Roberts, who suggested *bod* and *ewigiaid*, contracted to wigiad giving *Bodwigiad*, 'the dwelling place of hinds or female deer', cf. Nant yr Ewig, 'the hind's stream', near Blaen Pergwm, Glyn-neath. The deer related etymology is not without precedent. An article in the

Monmouthshire Merlin, dated 19th May 1838 states "There is Bodwigiad (the lair of the Deer) in the parish of Penderin".

The first element bod 'homestead, dwelling', is more prevalent in the north of Wales than the south. Gwynedd Pierce (PNG 19) states that it is followed normally, but not exclusively, by a personal name. In this case however, *Gwigiad* does not appear to be a personal name and *ewigiaid* seems to be a more likely element. *Bodwigiad* could contain *bod* and *ewigiaid*, with the final element contracted to *wigiaid* and *wigiad* in local parlance. The probable etymology is the "lair or dwelling place of hinds".

1841 TAS Bodwigiad (1,330 acres);
Landowner Morgan Morgan Esq. Occupier John Jones.
690. Coed y Glynos (small valley wood – glyn & dimunitive suffix -os; or poss. scribal copying error for Gurnos, see A 24 BFE below) 691. Cae Newyddu (renewed field) 692. Pasture 694. Ynis (river meadow) 697. Plantation 698. Cae drain Nant drain (bramble) is probably a copying error for draw'r (over/by the) see A 5 BFE below, (field near the brook) 699. Plantation 700. Cae dan ty (field below house) 701. House, Plantations, Garden etc. 702. Plantation 703. Worlod (y weirglodd; meadow) 704. Cae deol dial Isha (lower punishing field; cf. fields A 3 & 4 in 1776 BFE below) 705. Cae deol Ucha (upper punishing field) 706. Coed cae (grazing enclosure) 707. Coed cae'r Glog (Glog grazing enclosure) 708. Cae Ddysgwylfa (look out field) 709. Glogue (sic) barn & Plantation (Glog barn & plantation) 710. Cae Glog (Glog field) 711. Cae Lodes fain Ucha (lower slim girl's field. In 1776 BFE it is B7 under Glogue Farm and called 'Cae Lewis fain uchaf'. Prob. a copying error Lodes for Lewis.) 712. Cae Lodes fain Isha (upper slim girl's field. Again 1776 BFE B8 has Lewis for Lodes.) 713. Latch (poss. wet ground) 714. Cae Gwyn (white field) 715. Tri Pedwere (three quarters) 716. Cae Tyle (hill field) 717. Cae Tyle Gwenith (wheat hill field) 718. Caer Odyn (kiln field) 719. Cefn caer odyn (back of the kiln field) 720. Erw fawr (big acre) 631. Gwaun y Deri (oak meadow) 631a. Mynydd y Glog (the Glog mountain) 695. Tram road.
1776 Schedules [D/D BF/E 164]:
A.1. The Farm House Yard & Gardens 2. Banwen (cotton grass) 3. Cae'r Dial uchaf (upper punishing field) 4. Ditto isha (lower punishing field) 5. Cae draw'r Nant (field near the Nant) 6. The Brake in ditto 7. Ynis Cwrt y Gwtar (Cwrt y Gwtar river meadow; gwtar is loc. dial. for gwter) 8. Cwrt-y-Gwtar House & Garden 9. House & Garden by the smith shop 10. Coed y Staple (stapal; wood near the stable) 11. Cae'r cerig (field of the stones) 12. The Brake in do 13. Tree tri pudwran (pedwaran; three quarters) 14. Ynis ddu (black river meadow) 15. The Brake in do 16. Cae'r Tyla (the hill field) 17. Coed cae bach (small enclosure) 18. Worlod (meadow) 19. Cae gwyn (white field) 20. Cae'r otin (otin is loc. dial. for odyn;

kiln field) 21. Erw fawr (big acre) 22. Cae'r Gwenith (the wheat field) 23. Garden by do 24. Coed cae'r Gurnose (enclosure near the small tumps, hillocks and depressions cf. Y Gurnos p. 89 PNG) 25. Part of the great meadow 26. Part of do 27. Narrow strip 28. Half of part of Heol y Moch.

Bod & prob. ewigiaid; 'hinds' dwelling'

Bolgoed　　　　　　　Lost

Wood, Mansion

Bolchoyth 1253 Cartae; Bolgoyth 1256 Cartae; Bolgoyd 1362 BMW 1043; Bolgoid 1536-39 Leland.

Gwynedd O. Pierce states that the early records locate Bolgoed (in modern orthography) "on Hirwaun in the parish of Aberdâr" (PNG 21). Nansi Selwood (HVHR 33) is more specific, quoting records from the 1630s naming 'Tir y bolcoyd vedowe lying in Hirwen wrgan right against nant moel'. If Bolgoed and Bolgoed Fedw refer to the same place, then the 17th cent. location was more exact but unfortunately the name does not appear on modern OS maps.

The first element in *Bolgoed* is Welsh *bol*, bola 'belly', which can be interpreted in two ways. Firstly, as a protruding belly (hillock or mound), and secondly, as an incurved belly (a depression, hollow or swamp). The *Bolgoed* of Glyn Tarell, Brecs. is preceded by bryn 'hill' (Brynbolgoed) which confirms the swollen nature of the belly, while Rhos-y-bol (the belly moor), Anglesey indicates a flat or hollow belly. Because its exact location is unknown, one cannot determine with conviction whether the Hirwaun Wrgan *Bolgoed* is a wooded hillock or a wooded depression. However, it is worth noting that birch trees (*bedw*) favour light, well-drained soil, so that *Tir y Bolged Fedw* may well be better suited to a dryer hill or hillock rather than a wetter hollow or depression.

Bol & coed, 'belly of the wood'

Brecon Arms　　　　　　　SN 948081

One-time Public House

Brecon Arms 1851-1911 Census; 1857 PR; 1869 YG; 1904 OS25"; 1921, 1934 OS6"

The *Brecon Arms* was opened between 1842 and 1850 and closed *c.* 1940s. It became the site of the Post Office and is now a private residence. It was probably named the *Brecon Arms* as it was located on the Brecon road in Breconshire. Arms are frequent elements in the names of public houses, often indicating the coat-of-arms of a particular district, county, town, dignitary, or profession.

Bryn Cynon

SN 963057

Housing Estate

Bryn-Cynon 2010 AZSA; 1920 OS25"; 1911 Census; 1884 OS6".

A small estate located on the Merthyr Road south-west of Berth-lwyd Cottage. *Bryn* is Welsh 'hill', plus the *Cynon* river-name, indicating that the estate is on a hill near the river *Cynon*.

Bryn, Cynon; 'Cynon Hill'

Bryn Onnen

SN 949077

Housing Estate

Bryn Onnen 1996 SWVSA.

Bryn Onnen is the name of a road at the end of *Llwyn Onn* Road. The houses were built in 1964. (TL) *Bryn* is Welsh 'hill' while *onnen* is Welsh fem. sing. noun 'ash-tree', giving 'ash-tree hill'.

Bryn, onnen; 'ash-tree hill'

Bryn Prydydd

SO 002125

One-time Farm

Brynprydydd 1911 Census; 1887 Senghenydd AMR; 1840TM; Bryn Prydydd 1905 HPP p16; 1832 OS; Brynprydith 1841 Census UP; Tyr Bryn y Prydith 1691 Court Baron; Tir bryn y prydydd 1673 Will of Roger Symond NA.

Bryn Prydydd was the name of a small holding in *Cwm Taf Fawr* now a ruin in Coed Taf Fawr. There is also "cae'r prydydd" field 980 on Wernlas TM & S 1840. The earliest recorded form is in the will of Roger Symond, 1673, in which he leaves Tir bryn y prydydd in Penderrin to his wife Janett Powell. Tyr Bryn y Prydith of 1691 has *Prydith*, an anglicised spelling of Welsh *prydydd*.

Bryn is Welsh 'hill' while prydydd is Welsh 'bard, poet', usually trained in the art. We may not know the poet's name, but we can deduce that the poetic art was prevalent in old Cwm Taf. Dewi Cynon (HPP 142-160) names a number of poets with Cwm Taf connections, including the famous Gwilym Harri, whose ancestors may well have been linked with *Bryn Prydydd* "the poet's hill".

1841 TAS Brynprydydd (45 acres):
Landowner William Williams Esq. Occupier Thomas Hughes
1403. Coed cae Garw (rough grazing enclosure) 1404. Waun (meadow) 1405. Cwm y Waun (the meadow valley) 1406. Pen y cae (top of the field) 1407. Brest y cae (the field mound) 1408. Cae Garw (uncultivated field) 1409. Glaes Homestead

&c. (Glaes is glais – 'stream') 1411. Cae'r ffenest (the window field) 1412. Gorof (wooded precipice by a stream) 1413. do 1414. Ynis (river meadow) 1415. Cae Brynprydydd (Brynprydydd field) 1416. Cae Ganfa (stile field) 1417. Ddigoed (without trees/deforrested).

Bryn, prydydd; 'poet's hill', from earlier Tir Bryn y Prydydd 'land of the poet's hill'

Butchers' Arms   SN 9407

One-time Public House

Butchers Arms 1999 Brecon Beacons National Park plan; Douglas Rees, Publican 1977, Gazette obit.; 1871- 1911 Census; 1870 MT.

The *Butchers' Arms* opened in the 1860s and closed in 1993 when it was converted into a private dwelling. The MT 1870 above, has John Williams of the *Butchers Arms Beerhouse*. *Butcher* 'one who slaughters animals for food' would not be an uncommon occupation in this rural community. The tavern's name is probably the plural butchers with an apostrophe s, indicating that the coat of arms belonged to butchers. The full name would probably have been *The Butchers'Arms*.

Bwa Maen, Y   ST 9108

Large rock, geological fault

Bwa Maen 2020 Fforest Fawr Geopark, 1852 Mon. Mrln.,1804 LWDTSW; Bwa Maen or Bow Rock 1907 Weekly Mail; Gwaith grafel Bwa Maen 1909 TYG; Bŵa Maen 1905 HPP p44.

Y *Bwa Maen* is the name of a warped 70 ft high limestone formation on the banks of the Sychryd stream in Glamorganshire, near Craig y Dinas. The earliest recorded form, 1804 above, is from Letters Written During a Tour Through South Wales 1803 by John Evans. He translates *Bwa Maen* as 'the Curved Rock' and reports that its polished Marble Lime is in great demand in London. A century later, Tarian y Gweithwyr reports of Gwaith grafel Bwa Maen 'the Bwa Maen gravel works', while Dewi Cynon writing in 1905 also mentions the *Bwa Maen* works.

Y *Bwa Maen* contains two elements as well as the def. art. *Bwa* is Welsh 'bow' and *maen* Welsh 'stone' giving 'the stone bow' which is a realistic description of this geological fault.

Y, Bwa, maen; 'the stone bow'

Bwllfa   SN 9506

Farm

Bwllfa 1905 OS6"; 1841 Census D20; 1720 HPP 65; Y Bwllfa, before 1750 Pen.;

Bwllfa vach 1771 PR; Tyr y Bullva 1691 Court Baron; Tyr y Byllva 1626 Tred. Est. (Sr Henry Willi Kt.)

The former farm was occupied by three different people in the 1841 Tithe Appointment Schedules. By the 1990s the site was "evidenced with substantial ruins of a house and other buildings, shown as Bwllfa Cottage (OSM), occupied until the middle of this century (20th) ...", PNDH 7.11. The ruins are adjacent to Llety Rhys.

The original name would have been Pwllfa, listed and mutated as Y *Bwllfa* before 1750, later Bwllfa, with a redundant def. art. Cf. *Bwllfa Dare*; *Bwllfa Aman* etc. *Pwllfa* can denote a basin or hollow as well as the source of a river or stream. *Nant y Bwllfa* may well be the stream indicated in *Tir y Bwllfa* 1841 TAS:

1841 TAS Tir y Bwllfa (60 acres):
Landowners Rev. Richard Davies & William Payne. Occupier Watkin Watkins. 307. Coed cae Isha (lower grazing enclosure) 308. Waun fach (small meadow) 309. Cae Clyniage (cluniog? haunch shaped? field) 310. Pentwyn r ynis (top of the river meadow hill) 311. Bedw (birch trees) 312. Cae Pentwyn (top of the hill field) 313. Ynis (river meadow) 314. Cae Odyn (kiln field) 315. do 316. Buidings &c 317. Wern (alder trees) 318. Waun fach (little meadow 319. Buildings &c. 320. Road & Waste 321. Cae Bach (small field) 322. do 323. Waun Dwyn (stolen/reclaimed field) 324. Cae Nant y Deri (Nant y Deri field) 325. Wood 326. Wern Ucha (upper alder trees/marsh) 327. Coed cae Mawr (large grazing enclosure) 328. Cae Groben (gravel end? Field 329. Waun (meadow) 330. Dwy Erw (two acres) 331. Cae Bresla (Priscilla's field?) 332. Cae Dderwen (oak tree field) 333. do 334. do 335. Cae Melyn (yellow field) 336. Bedw (birch trees) 337. do 338. do 339. do

Bwllfa; 'basin, hollow; also, as the source of a river or stream'

Bwllfa Cottage   SN 9506

Bwllfa Cottage 1991 OS PF1108;1911 Census (Evan Thomas, Gamekeeper, Ystradfellte, Both.); 1904 OS25".

Bwllfa Cottage is now in ruins.

Cadair Arthur   not located on map; in Penderyn parish
Hill
Cadair Arthur 1905 HPP p20.
Dewi Cynon locates *Cadair Arthur* 'Arthur's Chair' to the north of the parish at 1,225 feet near the foot of the Beacons. "Cadair Arthur. - This mountain lies on the northern side of the parish, near the foot of the "Bannau" (Beacons). It is a high ridge, with limestone outcrops. There

was previously much burning of lime here, its kilns were well known in the countryside. Its height is 1,225 feet above sea level. Jenkin Howell maintains that this was the location of one of "Arthur's Chairs"." HPP p. 20; (trans.) Cf. Cadair Idris, Mid. Wales. Cadair is a reasonably common element in Welsh place-names, as explained by Tomos Roberts in ADG p. 82. It occurs in *Pencader, Cadair Idris, Cadair Ferwyn* etc. and represents a hillock or a chair-shaped hill. The latter is certainly the meaning in the listed names as well as in *Cadair Arthur*. One can only assume that the second element *Arthur*, refers to King Arthur.

Cadair, Arthur; 'Arthur's chair'

Cadair Fawr   SN 9712

Hill

Lewis Cymer Map; Y Gadair vaur 1526 Tredegar Est. Rec.; Carn Pen Cader Bella 1840 TM.

Cader and *Y Gatar* are dialectic forms of cadair 'chair', ie. a mound or hill shaped like a chair; it may also indicate a fort or camp. *Carn Pen Cader Bella* 'cairn (on the) summit (of the) furthest chair', suggests another (lost) local *Pen Cader*.

Cadair Fawr is the highest point on *Cefn Cadlan. Pant-y-Gader* lies at the bottom of the hillside.

Cadair, mawr; 'Large chair (shaped hill)'

Cadlan   SN 9509

Stream name

Cadlan 1905 HPP p10; Cadlan 1705 BFE; Kadlan 1448 Penpont.

The 15th cent. Penpont document has "Grant of three messuages in parish of Penderyn in breadth between the river there called Kadlan on one side, and the land of David Lloyd ap Jake on the other, and in length from the land of Jevan ap Rees Lloyd at one end, up to the land of Morgan ap David Game on the other. Latin."
In all probability, the last-named land of Morgan ap David Game, refers to Morgan son of Dafydd Gam of Agincourt fame.

There are several possibilities for the etymology:

1. Cadlan 'battlefield' from cad 'battle' and llan 'open land'. This is the traditional meaning as found in CA p. 168, where IW defines it as 'maes brwydr' (battlefield). Many have tried in vain to locate the site of a historic battle on the banks of this stream in order to explain the meaning. When two 18th century swords were found there in 1939, the

battleground theory gained credence. The weakness with this theory however is that the Cadlan name predates the swords by some 300 years (Kadlan 1448).

The 'battle' is more likely to be between the stream and its riverbank (cad & glan), with a full, fast flowing stream fighting against its banks, often succeeding in overflowing some banks to flood adjacent lands.

Glan and *llan* are often confused in Welsh place-names, usually where a mutated *glan* (lan) is assumed to have been an original *llan*, cf. *Llanbradach* < *Lanbradach* < *(G)lanbradach* < *Glanbradach*. The second element in this place-name is *glan* 'edge, brink; shore, bank; rising ground, hillside' with 'shore, bank' being the likeliest meaning.

2. Cad 'strength' and glan 'bank' indicating a stream with strong banks. Cad in Geiriadur Prifysgol Cymru has "enw nant fel Cadnant yn golygu 'cryf, nerthol, mawr' ", transl. 'in the stream name Cadnant, it means strong, powerful, big'. The Cad of Cadnant implying a strong, powerful stream, is likely to have the same meaning here in *Cadlan* giving a 'strong, powerful bank'.

Cad, glan; 'strong bank'

Cae'r Arglwydd
SN 965095

Farm name

Caer arlwydd 1905 HPP; 1843 Will William Morgan NLW; Cae y rarglwydd 1832 OS. Tyr y Gorwydd 1613-26 Cymorth, Tredegar NLW; SEHPP p. 19.

Cae'r Arglwydd or *Cae'r Arlwydd* is the name of a small holding in *Cwm Cadlan*. *Arlwydd* is a variation of *arglwydd*, cf. Waunarlwydd, Swansea. Mr B. Williams, Gellidafolws states that *Cae'r arlwydd* is known today as *Ty Fry* 'highland house'. An earlier name for *Cae'r Arlwydd* appears to be *Y Gorwydd*.

Cae signifies 'a field' while *arglwydd* 'lord' would be the landowner or the lord of the manor, rather than the religious master. *Y Gorwydd* or *tir, y, gorwydd* is 'land on the edge of the wood'.

1841 TAS Caer Arlwydd (41 acres):

Landowner Morgan Morgan Occupier, John Davies

951. Coed cae (grazing enclosure) 952. Caen bach (small covering/layer) 953. Cae bach (small field) 954. Coed cae (grazing enclosure) 955. Homestead &c. 956. Coed cae (grazing enclosure) 957. Cae bach (small field) 958. Caer Arlwydd (the lord's field) 959. 3 quarter 960. Waun (meadow).

Cae, 'r, arlwydd/arglwydd; 'the lord's field'

Cae'r Llwyn

SN 926071

One-time Farmstead

Cae'r Llwyn 1905 OS6"; 1911 Census; Carllwyn 1871 Census, 1808, 1783 PR.

This former farmstead had, by the 1840 TS become part of *Trebanog uchaf*, and is now an outdoor pursuits centre known as *Caer Llwyn House*. There is also a *Cae'r Llwyn bungalow*. (PNDH 7.15.) Note the dialectic ca for cae in 1783. *Cae'r Llwyn* contains two elements, *cae* and *llwyn* as well as the def. art. giving 'field (near or with) the bush'.

Cae, 'r, llwyn; 'field (near) the bush'

Caer Howel and Caerhowell Isaf

SN 945096

Previous and current farm names

Caerhowell Isaf Farm 2020 Sign; Caerhowell 1991 OS Pathfinder; 1974 OS First Series; Caer Howell 1841 Census D20; 1830 Will Morgan Jenkins NLW; Cae Howel 1833 GMBGM: Cahowell 1829 Will William Jenkins NLW; Cae Hywel 1805 Will Jenkin Morgan NLW; Cae Howell 1776 BFE; Tyre Cae Howell 1752 Will of Morgan John NLW; Kaye Howell 1719 Will John Williams NLW; Tyr Kae Howell 1691 Court Baron; Kaye Hoell 1537 BMW4; Kay Howel 1526 Tredegar Est. Rec.; Kaye Hoell 1468 MWBM;

The properties named *Caer Howel* and *Caerhowell Isaf* are located opposite *Pant Garw* on the A4059, a half mile north of the village of Penderyn. *Caer Howel* farmhouse was sold as a private house *c.* 2008, while the land is still farmed by Mr Glyn Bevan who resides at the nearby converted barn called *Caerhowell Isaf Farm*.

The 19th and 20th cent. *Caer Howell/Caerhowell* may be an attempt at upgrading the status to a 'fort' rather than a 'field'. R.F. Peter Powell suggests that a man-made mound adjacent to the farmyard may account for the change. However, the apostrophe r is more likely to be an intrusive definite article, often used with personal names in place-names, eg, Tir y Iorin, Aberdare; Coed y Cradock, Llancarfan; Tir y Barnard, Llantrisant etc.

The earlier forms, from *Cae Hywel* 1805, back to *Cae Howell* 1776 and *Kaye Hoell*

Cae Howell on the 1776

Map courtesy of SM and WGAS (D/D BF/E 164)

1468, clearly show that the first element in this place-name is *cae* 'field' rather than *caer* 'fort'.

1841 TAS Cae Howell (102 acres):

Landowner Penry Williams Esq. Occupier Richard Evans

787. Gwaun y Cor (fig. choir? meadow, as the field resembles the shape of a harp) 788. Cae Wain Isha (lower meadow field) 789. Waun Isha (lower meadow) 790. Garden 791. Coedcae (grazing meadow) 792. Cwm (small wooded valley) 793. Cae pen y Cwm (top of the valley field) 794. Cae Isha (lower field) 795. Cae Main (narrow field) 796. Ty Mawr (big house) 797. Cae dan ty bach (field below the little house) 798. Homenedd (?amynedd 'patience, suffering') 799. Coed cae bach (small grazing enclosure) 800. Cae Glas (green field) 801. Homestead &c. 802. Cwmbach (small valley) 803. Coed cae bach (small grazing enclosure) 804. Gwloscod (charcoal, burnt field) 805. Coed cae Mawr (large grazing enclosure).

Cae, Hywel; 'Hywel's field'

Camnant
SN 9207

Stream

Camnant 1905 OS6"; 1555 RISW/GGF/100;.

The *Camnant* brook flows past *Tai-cwplau* and *Trebanog Isaf* to join *Nant Wyrfa* near *Nant Llechau* to form the *Sychryd* stream. The *Camnant* forms part of the Penderyn parish boundary with Ystradyfodwg. *Camnant* has two elements *cam* 'bent, crooked' and *nant* 'brook, stream'. *Nant* originally meant 'valley' but later referred to the stream that flowed through the valley. *Dynfant* in the county of Swansea, originally *Dyfnant* (Dovenant 1650) dwfn and nant means 'deep valley'. The *Dyfnant* valley is very steep rising to three hundred feet in a few hundred yards. In that instance nant means steep valley rather than stream, but the nant in *Camnant* has the later and more usual meaning of 'brook, stream'.

Cam, nant; 'crooked stream'

Carn Pwll Mawr
SN 954109

Cairn

Carn Pwll Mawr   1905 OS6"; 1840 TM.

This cairn is located close to *Pwll Mawr* 'big pool' on *Cefn Cadlan* (PNDH 7.115). Carn means 'cairn, barrow, heap' and is generally seen these days as a heap of stones on a hillock or mountainside. *Pwll Mawr* was apparently a large pool of water formed in a geological sink hole.

Carn, pwll, mawr; 'Pwll Mawr cairn'

Cecin Clisti

Mountain ridge, lost name

Cechenclisti c1150 LL p42; Cecin clysty LL p134; Cecen Clisti LL p363; Cecin Clisti LL p391.

JGE (LL p367) suggests that Cecin Clysty is located on "? Mynydd y Glôg in Penderyn." Regarding the first element, GPC has cegin3 as "ridge, hog's back", which suits the location at Mynydd y Glog.

The second element *clysty* is difficult. It could be linked with Welsh *clust* 'ear', or possibly with an older, obsolete word. There is a river named *Clyst* in Devon which may be related to Welsh 'ear'. *Clisti* could also be an old, forgotten river-name possibly for the *Sychpant* or *Cadlan* that flow on *Onllwyn* near *Ogof Fawr*, close to *Mynydd y Glog*. It may be that the *Clisti* was the name for a river that was subterranean in places and could only be detected by the human ear. R. J. Thomas in EANC pp. 127-173 deals with the suffix -*i* in Welsh river-names eg. Brefi, Byrri, Cedi, Ceri, Cothi, Dyfi, Gafenni, Gwili, Llynfi, Rhymni, Teifi, Tywi etc. *Clust* plus the suffix -*i* could well connect with that category of Welsh river-names, as well as being related to the Devonshire river *Clyst*. It must be noted here however that GPC has *clust* (b) as a 'creek or inlet' and this may well apply to the Devonshire *Clyst*.

Cecin, clisti; 'Clisti ridge'

Cefn Cadlan

Mountain ridge

Cefn Cadlan 1905 OS6"; 1905 HPP p19; 1830 OS.

Cefn Cadlan has two elements, cefn 'mountain ridge' pronounced *cefen* in local parlance, and *Cadlan* the stream name, giving 'Cadlan mountain ridge'. *Cefn* is an element that belongs to those that are parts of the human body, *see esgair*. However, as a geographical term it means 'mountain ridge'. It is possible for a mountain ridge to resemble the shape of a human back.

Cefn, Cadlan; 'Cadlan mountain ridge'

Cefn Nant-y-geugarn

Mountain ridge

Cefn-Nant-y-Gougarn 1905 OS6".

The elements are *cefn* and *Nantygeugarn*. *Gougarn* is the local dialect form of *geugarn* – a hollow cairn. *Nant-y-geugarn* is a stream name. See *Nant-y-geugarn*.

Cefn, Nant-y-geugarn; 'Nantygeugarn mountain ridge'

Cefn-y-don

Farm

Cefn-y-don 1991 OS Landranger 160; Cefndon Cottages 1901 Census; Cefnydon Terrace 1881 Census; Cendon Terrace 1871 Cefnydon Isaf 1861 Census; Kendon 1841 Census; 1813 BFE; 1789 John Lloyd Coll.; 1689 Will of Wm Morgan NLW; 1662 Will of Edward Morgan NA; Cefn y don 1791 SAPNs; Cendon 1742 Will of Thomas Watkin; Tyr y Kendon 1691 Court Baron; Tyr y keven Done 1626 Tred. Est. (Sr Edward Lewis Kt.);

The earlier topographical name became the name of two farms, *Cefndon* and *Cefnydon Isaf*, as well as cottages and a row of houses *Cefndon Terrace*, plus the anglicised *Kendon Court*. *Cefn-y-Don* is listed as a 'gentry house' in Atlas Brycheiniog.

Ton, y don is the lay-land, ie. land left unploughed, grassland, green turf. The loss of the penultimate 'f' of *cefn* is not unusual (eg. Cendon, anglicised Kendon). Cf. *Cenfaes*, earlier *Cefnymaes* 'field ridge' (see below) and Cyncoed, Cardiff, earlier Cefncoed 'wooded ridge'.

1841 TAS Cefndon (114 acres):

Landowner Morgan Morgan. Occupier John Thomas

394. Caer Odyn hadan (adain; wing shaped kiln field) 395. Wood & Waste 396. 9 Erw (sic) (nine acre) 397. 9 erw Isha (lower nine acre) 398. Caer Lloi (calves' field) 399. 5 Erw (sic) (five acre) 400. Cae Stroni (?estroni; transferred field) 401. Wern fawr (large alder swamp) 402. Erw (acre) 403. do 404. Coed cae (grazing enclosure) 405. Wern Batty (sic) (Batty's alder swamp) 406. Homestead Garden &c 407. Caer Cefndon bach (little lay land field) 408. Waun dan ty (meadow below the house) 409. Cae Madin (fox's field) 410. Waun Newydd (new meadow) 411. Cefndon Mawr (big lay land ridge) 412. do Isha (lower do) 413. Cottage & Garden 414. Worlod (meadow) 415. Waun fawr (large meadow) 416. Garden 417. do 418. do

Cefn, (y), ton; '(the) leyland mountain ridge'

Cefn-y-maes

Mountain ridge/plateau

Cefn-y-Maes 1905 OS6"; Cenfaes 1905 HPP p17; 1794, 1780 PR; Tire y kenvas 1692 Will of Wm Morgan; Kenvase 1646/7 Tred. Est. Tyr kenvaes 1626 Tred. Est. (Sr Edward Lewis Kt.).

A former farm, now in ruins in *Coed Taf Fawr*, pronounced *Cenfas* in the local dialect, cf. *Cendon* (anglicised Kendon) for *Cefndon* and *Cyncoed* for *Cefncoed*. The *Nant-cefn-y-maes* stream flows into *Nant Abernant* and alongside the former *Cefnymaes* smallholding, which in 1626 was the property of Sir Edward Lewis, Knight. The stream and former smallholding take the *Cefn-y-maes* name from the topographical mountain ridge plateau.

The *cefn* element has already been explained as a 'mountain ridge'. The final element *maes* usually means 'open field', but in this case as a flat piece of land on the side of a hill, it could be a form of plateau.

1841 TAS Cefnmaes (77 acres) :

Landowner Sir Charles Morgan Bart. Occupier Thomas Jenkins

1272. Godre cae Isha (bottom of the lower field) 1273. Cae bach (small field) 1274. do 1275. Barn &c. 1276. Cae bach (small field) 1277. Cae Isha (lower field) 1278. Cae Rhyg Isha (lower rye field) 1279. Llwyn Rhos Goch (red moorland bush) 1280. Cae Rhyd Ucha (upper ford field – the ford was on Nant Cefn y Maes which flowed through Cwm Dyrys and entered river Taf Fawr at Abernant) 1281. Waun Rhos Goch (Rhos Goch 'red moorland' meadow) 1282. Cae bach (small field) 1283. Cae Ucha (upper field) 1284. Gwain ddufeting (burnt pared turf moor) 1285. Cae Ucha (upper field) 1286. Coed cae Garw (uncultivated grazing enclosure) 1287. Coed cae (grazing enclosure) 1288. do 1289. Waun (meadow).

Cefn, maes; 'field ridge or flat mountain-ridge'

Chapel Road   SN 9508

Chapel Road 1911 Census; 1904 OS25"

This is the name of the A4059 road leading from Pontbrenllwyd and branching first left beyond the Lamb Inn. The chapels named Capel Siloa, Capel Soar and Capel Jerusalem were located along the road, hence the Chapel Road name.

Church Road   SN 9408

Church Road 1996 SWVSA

Name of the road leading from Pontbrenllwyd via Penyreithin, The Rectory and Ysgubor Fawr to Penderyn Church.

Cilfach Rhydyfaen   SN 9208

One-time smallholding

Kilvach rhyd vaen 1643 Tredegar 8; ; Tyre Kylvach Rhydvaen 1589 Tredegar (8) NLW;

Cilfach is a fem. sing. Welsh noun for 'corner, nook; sheltered or secluded spot; a retreat', often close to a stream or river. In this case the river is *Afon Mellte*. See *Clwyd-rhyd-fan* and *Rhydfaen*.

Cilfach, Rhydfaen; 'Rhydfaen's little nook/sheltered spot'

Cilhepste

Cilhepste is a farm name that is usually followed by a distinguishing element viz. fawr, fach, cerrig or waelod (see below).

Cil is Welsh 'nook, corner, retreat', a secluded place; *Hepste* is the nearby river-name.

Cil, Hepste; 'Hepste's nook/secluded spot'

Cilhepste Fach

Former farm

Cilhepste-fâch 1991 OS Pathfinder 1109; Kilhepste Fach 1840 TM; Cil-Hepste-bach 1768 PR/PNDH.

Today *Cilhepste fach* is in ruins. It was formerly a Welsh long-house with enclosures which appear to have been occupied until the middle of the 19th century. The site has been afforested and is now a part of *Coed y Rhaiadr* (PNDH 7.24). The name is *Cilhepste*, plus the distinguishing element *bach* 'small'.

Cil, Hepste, bach; 'Little Cilhepste'

Cilhepste Fawr

Former farm

Cilhepste Fawr c1840 HPP 70; Kilhepste Fawr 1840 TM; Kilhepste 1833 GMBGM, 1771 PR.; Kilhepste 1827 Will Thomas Morgan NLW; Tyr killhepste waylodd 1626 Tredegar Estate.

It appears that *Cilhepste Fawr* became *Cilhepste'r Cerrig c.* 1830-40. Both *fawr* (large, big) and *cerrig* (stones) are distinguishing elements. It is likely that this was called *Cilhepste Waelod* (Tyr killhepste waylodd) 'lower/bottom Cilhepste' in 1626. *Kilhepste Fawr* and *Kilhepste Fach* were both occupied by Rhys Morgan in the 1841 TAS, covering an area of 576 acres extending from below the confluence of *Mellte* and *Hepste* streams to *Craig-y-Dinas* or *Dinas Rock*. This territory covered much of the area of the earlier *Clwyd Rhydfaen* (see below). The name is *Cilhepste* plus the distinguishing element *fawr* 'big'. The owners in 1905 were Messrs. William and Bevan, the occupier, Mr Evan Harries (HPP p. 17). The 1901 Census returns have Evan Harries at *Heol las. Cilhepste* is not listed on any of the census returns for Penderyn after 1841. Today the site is ruinous on the south-eastern edge of *Coed y Rhaiadr*.

1841 TAS for Cilhepste Fach and Cilhepste Fawr (576 acres):
Landowners John Bevan and William Williams, occupier Rhys Morgan
42. Waun Ucha (upper meadow) 43. do Isha (lower meadow) 44. Croft & Buildings

45. Cae bach (small field) 46. Coed Cae (grazing enclosure) 47. Cae Ucha (upper field) 48. Cae Isha (lower field) 49. Dinas Rock Piece 50. Graig (rock) 51. Caer Bedw (Birch trees field) 52. do Isha (lower birch trees field) 53. Caer Caidd (caith; poss. confined field) 54. Nuadd (neuadd; hall (small square field)) 55. Caer Breast (mound field) 56. Caer Lan (top field) 57. Cwm (valley) 58. Wern Newydd (new meadow) 59. Wood 60. Cae Newydd (new field) 61. Cae dan ty (field below the house) 62. do 64. Caer Pant (dingle field) 65. Wern fach (small alder swamp) 66. Erw (acre) 67. Cae bach (small field) 68. Gwern y Gwain (alder swamp of the meadow) 69. Wern (alder swamp) 70. Cae Main (narrow field) 71. Caer Yscall (thistle field) 72. Croft 73. do 74. Cae bach (small field) 75. do 76. Caer Lloi (calves' field) 77. Cae Ucha (upper field) 78. Cae Bach (small field) 79. do 80. do 81. do 82. Homestead etc 83. Cae dan ty (field below the house) 84. Coedcae (grazing enclosure) 85. Caer Coedcae (grazing enclosure field) 86. Graig (rock) 87. Coedcae (grazing enclosure) 88. Waun Newydd (new meadow) 89. Waun (meadow) 90. do

Cil, Hepste; 'secluded spot (near river) Hepste';
Cilhepste Fawr; 'large, main Cilhepste'

Cilhepste'r Cerrig   SN 9209
One-time farm
Cilhepste-cerig 1991 OS Pathfinder 1109; 1905 OS6"; 1830 OS; Cilhepsta y cerrig 1841 Census D20.

The farmhouse is in ruins and the site has been afforested as part of *Coed y Rhaiadr* (PNDH 7.23). The distinguishing *cerrig* 'stones' element probably describes the terrain, while the earlier fawr 'big' distinguished it from *Cilhepste fach*.
     Cil, Hepste (river-name), cerrig; 'Hepste's nook (near) stones

Clogfanddu   SO 9913
Farm and Hill
Clog fandu 1841 Census UP; Pen y Glogfanddu 1841 TS; Pen-y-Glog-Fan-Du 1780 Tred. Est.

The former farm, now in ruins was located at the top of *Clogfanddu*; since 1950, it has been part of *Coed Taf Fawr* near the *Sycamore Grove* picnic site. See *Penyglog-fan-ddu* below.
     Clog, ban, du; 'Cliff (of the) black peak/mountain'

Clun Celli   SN 9507
One time farmstaed
Tir Clyn Celli 1703 Maybery NLW.

41

Glyn Celli and *Ynys Llwyfog* later became *Trebannog Fawr* (HVHR p. 39). *Clun* 'meadow' and *glyn* 'valley' are often confused in Welsh place-names, with an early *clun* often changed to a more popular *glyn*.

Clun, celli; 'meadow (of) groves

Clwyd-rhyd-fan

One-time farm

Clwyd-rhyd-fan 1991 OS Pathfinder 1109; Clwyd-Rhyd-Fan 1905 OS; Clyn rhyd faen 1814 OS; Kilvach rhyd vaen 1643 Tredegar 8; Killvach y rhyd vaen alias Tyr Carne lloyn hyddoll 1631 Tredegar 8; Yr esker issa/ycha Rhyd vayne 1595 Tred. Est. NLW; dan garreg lloyn hyvol 1595 Tred. Est. NLW; Tyre Kylvach Rhydvaen 1589 Tredegar (8) NLW; Rydfaen 1482 Tred. Est. NLW; Rhydfaen 14th cent. SWB; Redevayn 1253, 1256 Cartae, 'per fluvium de Neth tendendo versus orientem usque ad Redevayn et a Re[devayn] usque ad fines Breconie.'

Clwyd-rhyd-fan, now in ruins, is a relatively modern name. Its location is near Afon *Mellte*, on the side of the old drovers' road south–west of *Moel Penderyn* and east of *Craig y Dinas*.

The 13th cent. documents naming Redevayn are agreements between the Abbots of Margam and Caerlyon respecting common of pasture at Hyrwenworgan. The early Rhydfaen probably occupied a large area between Afon Mellte and Nant Sychryd, (earlier Hepstwr) alongside the old route from Glyn Nedd to Craig y Dinas and on to the Foel and Penderyn Church. The 1482 document is a "Grant of a parcel of land in p. Penyderyn in the lordship of Brecon between a torrent called Mellte on the one side and the way leading from Rydvaen to a place called Pen lloyn Gruffyth' on the other side." It is not possible to identify Pen Lloyn Gruffyth but the 'way leading from Rydvaen' to it, is probably the old route from Craig y Dinas to the Foel. It is possible that the llwyn 'bush' in Pen lloyn Gruffyth is the same llwyn that occurs in Tir Carne Lloyn Hyddoll (1631 above), an alias for Kilvach y rhyd vaen.

Tyre Kylvach Rhydfaen 1589 includes the following areas of land: y koedkae issa (the lower coedcae), dwyerwr Bedwenni (the birch trees' two acres), dwyerwr Glwydfawr (the large gate's two acres), dwyerwr Deri Mawr (large oak's two acres), Erwr Wyddyn dewe (thick bindweed acre), Kae Newydd (new field), all part of *Tyre Kylvach Rhydvaen*.

It would appear from the above descriptions that *Cilfach Rhydfaen* occupied much of the land that is listed for *Cilhepste Fawr* in the 1841 TAS. Both *Cilfach Rhydfaen* and *Cilhepste Fawr* (as well as *Cilhepste Fach*) contain a cil 'corner, retreat, nook' element. The final element in *Rhydfaen* is maen 'stone', which matches the final element of *Cihlepste Cerrig* 'stones', the alias for *Cilhepste Fawr*. *Rhydfaen* and *Sychryd* have the same *rhyd* element. *Sychryd* 'dry ford' and *Rhydfaen* 'stone ford' could refer to the same ford across the *Sychryd* stream. It is also possible that the *maen* in *Rhydfaen* could refer to a ford close to the conspicuous *Bwa Maen* 'stone bow'. Unfortunately, these possibilities are circumstantial and more concrete evidence is needed for certainty.

It should also be noted here that *Sychryd* is the later name for the *Hepstwr* recorded *hepstur* (hesb, dŵr) as part of the boundary of the episcopate of Llandaf, *c.* 1150 in LL. This should not be confused with the *Hepste* stream, a tributary of *Afon Mellte*, (see *Afon Hepste* above). Any confusion occurred as both *Hepstwr* and *Hepste* contain the same *hesb* 'dry' element. They have carboniferous limestone riverbeds which tend to dry up in the summer. The *Sychryd*, *Sychnant* and *Sychbant* streams similarly have *sych* 'dry' as an element.

Rhydfaen appears as the primary name in *Cilfach Rhydfaen*, *Esgair Isaf/Uchaf Rhydfaen*, *Clyn Rhydfaen* and *Clwyd-rhyd-fan*. *Rhydfaen* has the elements *rhyd* 'ford' and probably maen 'stone' which indicates a crossing near the stone, possibly *Y Bwa Maen* 'the stone bow'. *Cilfach Rhydfaen* is the 'small nook' area of *Rhydfaen*. *Clyn Rhydfaen* is *Rhydfaen* meadow (clun). *Esgair Rhydfaen* is *Rhydfaen* ridge.

The *clwyd* (gate) element of *Clwyd-rhyd-fan*, was added to *Rhyd Faen* as a distinguishing element to mark the *Glwydfawr* part of the territory. The final element *faen* was later changed to *fan*.

Tir Carn Llwyn Hyddoll is an alias in 1631 but *llwyn hyfol* is recorded in neighbouring dan *garreg lloyn hyvol* in 1595. *Hyddol* and *hyfol* are identical as dd and f often interchange, cf. plwyf and plwydd, Eifion and Eiddon, Caerdyf and Caerdydd etc. The meaning of *hyddol*, *hyddoll* or *hyfol* is not known to this writer. One could hazard a guess at y *ddol* 'the meadow', but this is speculative.

Rhydfaen is 'stone ford', *Esgair Rhydfaen* 'Rhydfaen ridge', while *Cilfach Rhydfaen* is 'small nook (on) *Rhydfaen*'.

Clwyd Rhydfaen;'Rhydfaen gate or hurdle'

Coed Llwyn y Moch   SN 9606
Wood
Coed Llwyn-y-moch 1991 OS Pathfinder 1109; 1904 OS25".

Coed Llwynymoch is the name of a wood near Llwyn-y-moch farm and an earlier Heol-y-Moch Road. The elements are *coed, llwyn, y, moch*, see *Llwyn-y-moch*.

Coed, Llwyn-y-moch; 'Llwyn-y-moch wood'

Coed Penmailard

Wood

Coed Penmailard 1991 OS Pathfinder 1109; 1905 OS6".

See *Penmailard*

Coed, Penmailard; 'Penmailard wood'

Coedcaedu

SN 9510

Farm

Coed Cae Ddu 1991 OSPF; Coedcae-du 1974 OS; Coedcadu 1841 Census UP; 1771 PR.; Coed-cadu 1767 PR;

Coedcae or *coetgae* (local dialect *coedca*, *coitca*, *coica*) is Welsh 'land enclosed by a hedge or by a dry-stone wall'. IW (ELl 56) explains that the original coed in Coetgae was a living quickset hedge rather than a lifeless stone wall. Locally however, expedient Penderyn farmers and shepherds used abundant local stone for that purpose. Dewi Cynon (HPP 13) states that coedcae refers to rough, poor quality grazing land. The final element du, describes the colour of the ground. The local dialect pronunciation was Côdca-du (RMR).

1841 TAS Coedcae du (99 acres):
Landowner Griffith Jones. Occupier himself
880. Ynis (river meadow) 881. Wood 882. Groft Llwyd (poor quality small field) 883. Cae bach (small field) 884. Worlod (meadow) 885. Cae bach dan y Odwyn (sic) (odyn; small field below the kiln) 886. Cae bach (small field) 887. Tir Gwyllt (uncultivated land) 888. Odwyer (sic) (two acres) 889. Carne Isha (carnau? lower cairns) 890. Waun (meadow) 891. Coed cae (grazing enclosure) 892. Caer haidd ucha (upper barley field) 893. Caer haidd (barley field) 894. Cae Ysgubor (barn field) 895. Homestead &c. 896. Cae Newydd (new field) 897. Carne (cairns) 898. Coed dan y carne (woods below cairns) 899. Cae (field) 900. blank 901. blank 902. Coed ucha (upper wood) 903. blank 904. Waun dan ty (meadow below house) 905. Escyr (esgair; ridge) 906. blank 907. Cae bach y (sic for 'yr') ysgubor (the barn's small field).

Coetgae, du; 'black enclosed land'

Coedcae'r Felin

SN 956058

Housing estate

Coedcae'r felin 1905 HPP; 1881 Census;1861 Census; Coedcae'r felin 1841 TAS; Coedcarn Felin 1829 Iron works houses.; Heolyfelin 1814 OS; Coed car felin 1800 Penpont; Coedcar felin 1800 Bacon/Price;

The elements are *coedcae* and *melin*. The mill (*melin, y felin*) referred to in *Coedcae'r felin* is *Melin Rhydiau*. This was the corn grist mill. Y *felin* does not refer to the fulling mill. This is Welsh y *pandy*. *Coedcae* is a large, enclosed piece of land used for grazing animals, usually sheep.

After the ironworks opened *c.* 1758, the mill's earlier grazing land was used to build houses for the workers. In an 1813 sale of Hirwain Iron Works, *Coedcafellin* (sic) is listed as having 38 tenements, a school room and garden.

Heolyfelin was the road that led from the Ironworks to this corn mill. The 1841 TAS no. 424 on *Maes y Rhydia* is named *Mill Cottage* while numbers 422 and 423 are called *Coedcae'r felin*.

The same *melin* 'mill' is present in today's *Cae Felin Park*. For field names see *Maesyrhydiau*.

Coedcae, 'r, melin; 'the mill's enclosed grazing land'

Court Farm   SN 976058

Farm
Court Farm 1991 OS Pathfinder 1109; 1920 OS25"; 1911 Census; Court y Llacca 1861 Census; 1813 BFE; Court House 1851 Census; Court Lodge 1911 Census; Court Cottage 1901 Census; The Court 1789 J. Lloyd Coll.; Court y Llackae 1676 Plymouth.

Court Farm is located between *Berthlwyd* to the west and the A465 Heads of the Valleys Road to the east. *Court Lodge*, is recorded nearby on the 1920 OS25".

Nansi Selwood in a map titled *Penderyn before* 1750 has *Cwrt y Llaca* (*Methygen*); see *Meddygen* below. *Meddygen* (meddygyn – a violet plant known as 'self-heal') became *Cwrt y llacca*, and later *Court Farm*. *Court y Llacca* 1861 and *Court y Llackae* 1676 above represents Welsh *Cwrt y Llaca* literally 'the mud farmyard'. Dewi Cynon names it as *Y Cwrt* (HPP 15) and explains the meaning as "Y Llys" (The Court) "but it may refer to the porch or yard in front of the house" (trans.). Welsh cwrt can be translated as a 'court' but usually, when used in an agricultural context, it signifies a 'farmyard'. *Court Lodge* is a modern-day residence. Visited Nov. 2020.

1841 TAS Court (76 acres):
Landowner Morgan Morgan Esq. Occupier Thomas Rosser
454. Naw Erw (nine acres) 455. Llwyn Glas (green bush) 456. Erw las (green acre) 457. Cae Newydd (new field) 458. Wood 459. Ton bach (small lay land) 46 o. Erw fawr (big acre) 461. Wood 461a. Cae Isaf (lower field) 462. Wood 463. Cae Carna ucha (upper cairns' field) 464. Cae Gwyn (white field) 465. Homestead &c. 466.

3 Pedwan (pedwaran; 3 quarters) 467. Wern (alder swamp) 468. Pant Serw (bright dingle) 469. Cae Gwyn (white field) 470. Wern Newydd (new alder swamp) 471. Erw ddu (black acre).

Court; 'court', 'farmyard'.

Craig Penmailard ST 0109

Rock

Craig Penmailard 1991 OS Pathfinder 1109; 1905 OS6"

Craig Penamailard is the name of a rocky outcrop located near *Penmailard farm* and *Coed Penmailard*, west of *Afon Taf Fawr*. See *Penmailard* below.

Craig, Penmailard; 'Penmailard rock'

Craig y Dinas ST 9108

Rock; hillfort.

Craig y Dinas 1925 HVN p26; 1905 HPP p11; 1805 HB iv 65; Craig y Ddinas 1991 OS Pathfinder 1108; 1925 OSM; 1905 OS6"; Dinas Rock 1840 TM; Craig y dynas c1700 *1584) Paroch.; Caer Craic Dynas gawr c1600 Cymmrodor xxvii 142 (Peniarth 118/835).

Craig y Dinas is the name of an imposing limestone promontory which holds the remains of an iron-age hillfort.

The earliest form appears in Peniarth 118, *c.* 1600 AD, which lists the names of Welsh giants, recorded by Hugh Owen M.A., in Cymmrodor xxvii p142 as *Caer Craic Dynas* gawr. Here it is claimed that *Dynas gawr* 'Dynas the giant' was killed by Arthur at *Caer Craic Dynas gawr* 'the fort of *Dynas* the giant's rock'. This story is regarded as medieval mythology.

The element *dinas* here is masc. hence y *dinas* and means 'stronghold, fort, encampment'. The fem. *dinas, y ddinas* means 'city'. *Craig y ddinas* is erroneous and misleading. *Craig y dinas* is grammatically the more accurate, and means 'rock of the stronghold, fort, encampment'.

Craig y Dinas 2018 © DMJ

The '*Dinas Fire Brick Co.*' specialising in silica-based bricks, took its name from the adjacent *Craig y dinas* silica mines. *Dinas* village in the Urals, Russia, located near silica mines is also linked to *Craig y dinas* via the '*Dinas Fire Brick Co.*'.

Craig, y Dinas; 'Rock (of) the stronghold/fort, encampment'

Cross Bychan / Croes Bychan ST 982058

One-time Public House/Crossroads

Crossbychan Inn 1939 Vaynor & Penderyn Rural District official guide; Cross Bychan 1920 OS25"; Croes-bychan 1884 OS6"; Cross Bychan 1841 Census D20.

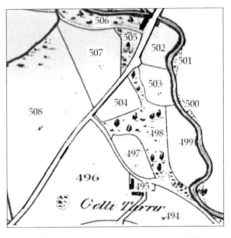

The word order in *Cross Bychan* is Welsh, with a later Cymricised Croes. Welsh croes would be pronounced *cros* in the local dialect (cf. *Nantygros* for *Nantygroes*). *Cross Bychan* (1841) may well be a written anglicised representation of the dialectic Welsh *cros*. Whether English *cross* or Welsh *cros*, it refers to the pub's location near the

The black rectangle on the extreme right on 1840 Tithe Map no. 506, near the bridge, bordering the road and Nant Hir is the Croes Bychan public house. TAS no.506 records 'Public House, Cottages and Wood'.

Llwydcoed junction of the old Hirwaun to Merthyr road. Cf. *Penygroes*, *Tycroes*, Carms. It may have acquired the adjective *bychan* 'small' because it was less active than other, busier crossroads on the old Hirwaun to Merthyr Road.

Croes, bychan; 'small cross'.

Cwar / Quarry

The parish is located geologically on strata of rocks that includes a predominant layer of carboniferous limestone which is rich in lime and silicone. This feature accounted for the many old local lime kilns as well as the early development of the quarrying industry here. Limestone is linked with agriculture while silicone has properties which suited the iron industry. Bricks containing silica are more able to endure the high temperatures of the iron furnaces. The quarries became connected to Hirwaun Iron Works, Aberdare, Abernant and Aberaman by early tramroads with horse drawn wooden trams, later to be replaced by metal trams pulled by steam and diesel-powered engines. A weighing machine (see *Machine House* below) was positioned just north of Hirwaun Iron Works to weigh the quarried stone. Three blacksmith's shops were kept busy along the early tramroad, shoeing horses, repairing trams etc.. The 1841 TAS locate three quarries, one at *Pantcynferth* no. 117 and two at *Ysguborfawr* nos. 157 & 161. Number 157 is probably *Cwar Crawshay* (opened 1818) with no. 161 likely to represent *Cwar y Gadlys* (opened 1827). By 1861 the quarries employed the majority of the village's adult male population. Today, only the Llwyn Onn quarry remains operational as a quarry. The company at *The Stuart Quarry* produces concrete products. For further details on QUARRIES see HPP pp. 44-47.

Horse drawn trams on the Penderyn tramroad. (Courtesy of PHS)

Cwar Aberaman   ST 9408

Cwar Aberamman 1919 LC essay; 1904 OS25";

Cwar Aberaman was opened in 1848 to supply Crawshay Bailey's Aberaman works. (LC essay). It was located between *Ysgubor-fawr* and *Chapel Road.* See HPP p46. Part of this quarry was also known as the *Stewart* or *Stuart Quarry* recorded at five acres in 1919 with *Aberaman Quarry* at eighteen acres, both owned by Mr T Jones J.P., (AL). For *Stuart*

Quarry see *Cwar Stuart* below and also *Cwar Crawshay*.

Aberaman consists of *aber* 'river mouth' and *Aman*, a river-name. Crawshay Bailey bought the old Aberaman Estate in 1835 and started the Aberaman Ironworks in 1846. He sold the estate, iron works and coalmine to the Powell Duffryn Steam Coal Co. Ltd. in 1867.

Cwar, Aberaman; 'Aberaman (Iron Works) quarry'.

Cwar Abernant   ST 9408

Cwar Abernant 1919 LC essay, 1905 HPP 44; Cwar Mt Fothergill Abernant 1904 TYG;

This quarry was opened in 1822 behind *Troedrhiw'r llan* beer house, to supply the Abernant Iron Works owned by the Fothergills (LC essay). By 1905, the lower part of the quarry was run by W. P. Powell & Co. Ltd. Hirwaun.

Abernant is a truncated form of the fuller *Abernant-y-wenallt* 'mouth of the *Wenallt* stream'. The ironworks were sited opposite today's Windsor Terrace roughly one mile east of the town of Aberdare. The Fothergills, originally from the north of England, lived in *Abernant House*, which later became an ecclesiastic college before being converted into Aberdare General Hospital.

Cwar, Abernant; 'Abernant (Iron Works) quarry'

Cwar Crawshay   ST 9408

Cwar Crawshay 1919 LC essay, 1905 HPP 44;

This was opened in 1818 by William Crawshay to supply his Hirwaun Iron Works (HVHR p. 61). It was renowned for the long arch or tunnel the tramroad went under as it connected the quarry to the main road. It also became known as the *Stewart Quarry*.

William Crawshay was descended from a Yorkshire family that gained prominence and wealth as ironmasters in Cyfarthfa, Merthyr Tydfil and the south Wales valleys. *Crawshay* is a variant of *Crawshaw*, a place-name meaning 'crows' wood'. Cf. *Crawshaw Academy*, Pudsey. Leeds; *Crawshaw Booth* Lancs. etc.

Cwar, Crawshay; 'Crwashay's quarry'

Cwar Dafis   ST 9408

Cwar Dafis 1919 LC essay, 1905 HPP 45;

This quarry was opened in 1842 by David Davies of Blaengwawr (formerly of London Warehouse, Hirwaun), in order to supply his Blaengwawr works. The quarry closed *c.* 1872. Dafis is the local Welsh language pronunciation of the surname Davis or Davies. Davis and Davies were formed from the Welsh Christian name Dafydd losing the final consonant to become Dafy. The anglicised Davy then acquired the English genitive, apostrophe s to produce Davys, Davis and Davies, becoming widespread in the 16th century via English administration. The anglicised Davis/Davies were soon re-cymricised to Dafis in Welsh orthography and speech.

Cwar, Dafis; 'Davies's quarry'

Cwar Llwyn-onn ST 9509

Cwar Llwyn-on 1991 OS Pathfinder 1109; 1904 OS25"; Cwar Llwynonn, 1919 LC essay. Cwar Llwyn Onn 1905 TYG.

Located between *Twyn-y-glog* and *Cwm Cadlan*, *Cwar Llwyn-onn* takes its name from nearby *Llwyn-onn* farm See HPP p. 47. It was opened in 1853 by William Powell Esq., *Maesydderwen*, Hirwaun. His eldest son W. P. Powell succeeded him and following his death, his younger brother, along with other local businessmen formed W. P. Powell & Co. Ltd. Today's owners are the Hanson Heidelberg Cement Group. For *Llwyn-onn* see below.

Cwar, Llwyn-onn; 'Llwyn-onn quarry'

Cwar Mawr ST 9408

Cwar Mawr 1904 OS25".

Located between the Red Lion Inn and Chapel Road, this 'big quarry' probably included a number of quarries worked by the different works' companies viz. *Cwar Crawshay*, *Cwar y Gadlys*, *Cwar Aberaman* and *Cwar Abernant*.

Cwar, mawr; 'big quarry'

Cwar Stuart ST 9408

Cwar Stuart 1914 y Darian; Stewart Quarry, Stuart Quarry 1914 AL;.

Today W. D. Lewis Ltd. operates its concrete product business from *Stewart Quarry*, Penderyn. In a sale of the freehold estate of *Ysgubor Fawr* and *Pantcefnyfford* in 1919, the five-acre *Stuart Stone Quarry* was sold to Mr T Jones J.P., for £725 (AL 20/12/1919). It had previously been leased to W. P. Powell & Co. Ltd. This company took over The Hirwaun Ironworks in 1880. "The ironworks site remained unoccupied until 1880 when the *Stuart Iron, Steel and Tin Plate Company* took it over. The Hirwaun Ironworks was renamed the *Stuart Ironworks* and some improvements were made to the furnaces." (Cadw). Crawshay's Hirwaun Iron Works became *the Stuart Iron Works*, so it seems likely that the *Crawshay Quarry* became the *Stuart Quarry*, as the ironworks continued to receive its silicone stone via the tramroad that connected the Hirwaun works to its Penderyn quarry.

Dewi Cynon reports an accident at *Cwar Stuart* in 1914 where Thomas Jones, a foreman "yng *Nghwar Stuart*" and a deacon of Siloam Baptist chapel fell to his death.

Cwar, Stuart; 'Stuart quarry'

Cwar Stuart   *Courtesy of the Penderyn Historical Society*

Cwar y Gadlys   ST 9408

Cwar y Gadlys 1919 LC essay, 1905 HPP 46;

Cwar y Gadlys was located opposite the entrance to *Llwyn-onn* quarry (HPP p46). It was opened in 1827 to supply Wayne's Gadlys Iron Works (LC essay). This company's tramroad joined the Aberdare Canal Company's tramroad to their Penderyn quarry.

Y Gadlys, originally a farm-name refers to the courtyard or enclosure within the farm. The iron works and resulting village adopted the *Gadlys* name, as did the works' quarry in Penderyn.

Cwar, y Gadlys; 'the Gadlys quarry'

Cwar yr Eithin

Cwar yr Eithyn 1907 AL;

Cwar yr Eithyn 'the Eithin quarry' is the old, small quarry located behind the present-day Community Centre.

Cwm Cadlan ST 9509
Valley
Cwm Cadlan 2017 Signpost; 1991 OS Pathfinder 1109; Cwm Cadelan 14th cent, SWB.

Cwm, Cadlan; 'Cadlan valley'. See Cadlan

Cwm Nant Hir ST 980
Valley
Cwm Nant-hir 1991 OS Pathfinder 1109; Cwm Blaen-nant-hir OS6"; (stream called) Nant hire 1546 Penpont.

Cwm, Nanthir; 'Nanthir valley'

Cwm Taf Fawr SO 0013
Valley
Cwm-Taf Vawr 1849 Will Edward Lewis NLW.

Cwm Taf, fawr; 'Taf Fawr valley'

Cwm Ynysmintan ST 9805
Valley/River-meadow/Road/Woods/Bridge
Cwmynysmintan Road 1996 SWVSA; Cwm-ynys-mintan Woods 1981 OS; Pont Cwmsmintan 1981 OS; Cwmynysmintan 1905 HPP 79; Cwmsmintan 1905 HPP 15; 1919 LC essay; 1923 LYH p38; Cwmynysmentyn 1833 OS1"; Cwm ynis y mintan 1802 PR; Ynis y mintan 1799 PR; Ynys Mintan 1787 PR.

Cwm Ynysmintan Road is the name of today's road leading from the red-bricked *St. James's Church* junction at *Llwydcoed* to the *Cross Bychan* junction en route to Llwydcoed Cremetorium. *Pont Cwmsmintan* crosses the *Nant Hir* stream near the old *Cross Bychan* Public House, while the Woods and river-meadow are on the stream's banks. Fiellds numbered 502, 503 and 499 on the TAS map for Gelli Tarw (see Cross Bychan above) would have been the location of Cwmynismintan, but unfortunately they are not named on the TAS. Note the local truncated pronunciation *Cwmsmintan*, 1905, 1923 and 1981.

Several possible meanings have been put forward regarding the final element, among them the personal surname *Minton* and the possible

Welsh verb *mintan* 'to gather mint (herb)'. Neither of these inspire confidence as there have been no examples of the *Minton* surname in the locality and the Welsh verb *mintan* is rare, possibly unknown.

It's interesting to note that GPC has "Ar lafar ym Morg. yn yr ystyr 'dadlau', 'Pwy fintan â'ch gilydd ichi', LlGC 1171 32." [Translated – spoken in Glamorgan meaning 'to argue', 'Why do you argue amongst yourselves'.]

This meaning would put *ynys mintan* 'disputed river-meadow' into the same category of names as *Tir y Dadlau* 'disputed land', Aberdare, *Tir Llwyn y Dadley* 1660, Pembs., *Trehwbwb* 'disputed farm', St Lythans, Glam., and *Cwmwbwb*, 'disputed valley', Caerffili. (PNDPH 269)

There were many disputes in the vicinity of Hirwaun Common over the centuries, between the religious houses of Llantarnam and Margam, between freeholders and the right to pasture, and industrialists with rights of access, as well as disputes regarding the enclosure of common land. Although without documentary evidence, it is reasonable that *Ynys y mintan* could have acquired its name from a past dispute.

Cwm, ynys, mintan; poss. 'valley (of the) disputed river meadow'.

Cwt y Gwter   ST 952083
Previously a small cottage
Cwt y Gwter 1905 HPP. p147; Cwt y gwttar 1841 Census D20; Cwrt y Gwtter 1808 PR; Cwrt-y-gwtar House & garden 1776 BFE; Ynis Cwrt y Gwtar 1776 BFE.

Cwtygwter was the name of a cottage on *Bodwigiad* land near the *Cadlan* stream. It was used as a school c1840-55 (HPP 114). The first element is shown as *cwrt* 'court, farmyard' in 1776, but by 1841 it had changed to *cwt* 'cottage, hut'. *Ynis Cwrt y Gwtar* refers to the river-meadow alongside the cottage.

Note the dialect form of *gwtar* for *gwter*. The gutter was probably a small water channel emptying into the nearby *Cadlan* stream. The cottage took its name from the location.

Cwt, cwter; 'cottage (of the) gutter, ditch'.
Earlier Cwrt, y, cwter; 'courtyard (near) the gutter'

Cwt yr Eithin   Lost   ?ST 9408
Previously a small farmstead
Cwt yr Eithin 1919 LC essay; 1841 Cens.; Cwrt yr eithin 1797, 1783, 1770 PR.

Poss. located near *Penyreithin*. In 1919 LC states that it was in ruins.

Cwt or cwrt, yr, eithin; 'the gorse cottage' from earlier
'the gorse courtyard'

Cwt yr Hytir   ST 9508

Previously a small farmstead in Pontbrenllwyd

Cwt yr Hit hir 1841 Census D20, Thos Rees. (poss. TS 693, 696).

The first element cwt is as the previous place-name, while the final element written as *Hit hir* in 1841 above, is probably Welsh *hytir* 'a length of ploughed land'.

Cwt, yr, hytir; 'cottage (of) the length of ploughed land'

Deri Hir   ST 9806

Farm name

Dderi-hir 1991 OS Pathfinder; Thery Hir 1841 Census; Dderi Hir 1808 Will Thomas Watkin NLW. Tyr-y-Derihir 1744/5 BFE; Tir y Deri Hir 1705 BFE.

Deri Hir farm is located east of *Cross Bychan* on the opposite side of the road to *Hendre Bailey* farm. The mutations on the 1991, 1841 and 1808 forms are not necessary although several other place-names in Wales show the same dderi mutation. The *hir* element refers to the unusual length or height of the oak trees. There may be a link between *Deri Hir* and *Deri Emreis* of LL. Both place-names have *deri* as a first element as well as being on the parish and episcopal boundaries respectively.

1841 TAS Deryhir (107 acres):

Landowner Earl Jersey Occupier Thomas Watkins

548. not named 549. Wood 550. Cae Cefn Coed Isha (lower field behind wood) 551. do Ucha (upper field behind wood 552. Coed cae bach (small grazing enclosure) 553. Waun Isha (lower meadow) 554. Gwaun y Borfa (pasture meadow) 555. Cae Waun y do (pasture meadow field) 555a. Wood 556. Erw Isha (lower acre) 557. P Bant (sic) (yonder P for pant? 'dingle') 558. Cae Cenol (middle field) 559. Erw Ucha (upper acre) 560. Wood 561. Cae Mawr (big field) 562. Cae dan ty (field below house) 563. Cae bach (small field) 564. Homestead &c. 565. Ynis (river meadow) 566. Cae Uwchlawr Ty (field above house) 567. Coed cair Lan (top enclosure) 568. Cae Glas (green field) 569. Pen y Wain (top of the meadow) 570. Wern (alder swamp) 570a. not named 571. Waun Goch (red meadow) 572. not named 573. Taurer (tairer; three acres)

1776 (D/D BF/E 164) Schedules:

L.1. The Farm House & Garden 2. Cae uchlaw'r ty (field above the house) 3. Ynis uchaf (upper river-meadow) 4.Cae'r Darren (the Darren field) 5. Ynis ishaf (lower river meadow) 6. The Wood 7. Cae main (narrow field) 8. Field by the house 9. Cae Mawr (big field) 10. Croft (small field) 11. Cefn y Coad (coed; back of the wood) 12. Wern (wetland) 13. Cae glace (glas; green field) 14. Coedcae'r Lloy (lloi; calves' grazing enclosure) 15. Wayn goch (red meadow) 16. Nerag green (green half acre. Not named in 1841 TAS no. 570a) 17. Nine acres 18. Tair Erw (three acres) 19. Wayn y Borva (the pasture meadow) 20. Wayn Hwynt (yonder meadow) 21. Coed cae bach (small grazing enclosure) 22. Cae pen y coed (field at the end of the wood) 23. Cae isha yn y coed (lower field in the wood) 24. Cefn y coed isha (lower Cefn y coed) 25. 'r Ynis (the river meadow).

Tir, y, deri, hir; 'land (of) the long/tall oaks'

Dôlgynog   ST 9408
Housing Estate
Dolgynog 1949 SWCHPP p54 (1950). 1949 ME; 1950 PR;

Dôlgynog is the name for an estate of houses erected by the Vaynor and Penderyn District Council, opened on Easter Monday 1949, (ME 23.4.1949; SWCHPP p. 54). "Happy Easter for Six Penderyn Families First Tenants of Dolgynog Estate", are headlines in the Merthyr Express, April 23rd 1949.

Dôl is Welsh 'meadow, dale, field, pasture, valley', while *Cynog* is the patron saint of Penderyn church.

Dôl, Cynog; 'Cynog's meadow'

Drain Bach   SO 0011
Former homestead
Abernant and Drain bach 1646/7 Tred. Est.

Drain, bach; 'small brambles'

Dyrlwyn   ST 9526
Former property near Nant-y-deri
Dyrlwyn 1705 BFE;

Dyrlwyn is almost certainly derlwyn 'oak-grove'

Eithin, Yr   SN 949080
Grazing enclosure, Cottage, Old Quarry, Community area
Yr Eithin 2019 PCC; 1905 HPP p14; ; 1785 PR Bapt.; Coedcae Eithin 1841 TAS.

In 1841, Tithe Appointment field numbers 140 and adjacent 175 are named *Coedcae Eithin*. Dewi Cynon states that the *Coedcae garw* (rough grazing enclosure) that lay below *Penyreithin* was called *Yr Eithin* because of the abundance of furze that grew on it. HPP p. 14. Tithe Appointment number 174 (the site of the present-day Community Centre) is described as 'Cottages and garden', occupied by William Thomas. The 1785 P.R. Baptismal records name William, son to Thomas and Margaret John at *Yr Eithin*. *Yr Eithin* is Welsh 'the furze, gorse'.

Clwyd yr Eithyn

Clwyd yr Eithyn 1919 LC essay; Glwyd yr eithin 1905 HPP p93.

Tri pheth sydd ym Mhenderyn	*Three things are in Penderyn*
Yn felltigedig drwyddyn,	*that people love to hate.*
Gwraig y ffeirad a'r hen gi llwyd,	*The vicar's wife, the old grey dog,*
Ac aethus glwyd yr eithin.	*and the eithin's frightening gate.*

Both 1919 and 1905 examples above refer to the same verse. *Clwyd-yr-eithin* is 'the eithin gate'.

Yr Eithin has been the centre of community activity recently, organised by the Community Centre committee. The 1884 OS 6" OS map has 'Quarry' marked at the location. Much of the old quarry is in the process of being reclaimed, "with paths being restored, new seating being put in place and water ways being managed" (Tracy Sweetland-Hodges). This voluntary work will hopefully result in a natural peaceful and attractive local amenity.

yr, eithin; 'the gorse'

Erw'r Crydd   Lost name   poss.SN 943085
Former property

Tyr Errow nup Rs ap Morgan 1626 Tredegar Estate (Watkin Philip gent.);
Tyr pant kyffnerth and erwr kridd 1609 RISW GGF 1/84.

Tyr Errow nup Rs ap Morgan is identified as *Torfoel* (SEHPP p. 19). *Erw'r kridd* 1609 above may be the same property as the 1626 entry. The lost *Erw'r Crydd* would have been located near *Tyr pant kyffnerth* known today as *Pantcefnyffordd*. If *Tyr Errow* and *erw'r kridd* are the same property, then *Torfoel* could well have been the location, as suggested by AS. This piece of land would have been owned by the cobbler (*y crydd*). *Tyr Errow* (tir erw) may be a contraction of *Tir Erw'r Crydd*, 'land of the cobbler's acre'.

erw, 'r, crydd; 'the cobbler's acre' from poss. tir, erw'r crydd;

Escar-y-Vedwan   Lost
Mountain ridge

Escar-y-Vedwan 1776 BFE Map

The location is north of *Heol-y-moch*, between present day *Llwyncoch* and *Coed Llwyn-y-moch*. *Escar-y-Vedwan* is written in the local Gwentian dialect. The elements are *esgair, y* and *bedwen*, 'the birch tree ridge'. *Esgair* is Welsh 'leg, shank', also a 'long mountain ridge'. Parts of the body are often used to describe topographical features, cf. *ael* y bryn 'brow of the hill', *bron* deg 'fair mound', *cefn* coed 'wooded ridge', *bol* goed 'belly of the wood', *troed* y rhiw 'foot of the hill' etc. The final element *bedwen* is Welsh sing. fem. noun 'birch tree', plural *bedw*. There may have have been just the one birch tree on the ridge, but it was probably conspicuous.

Esgair, y, bedwen; 'the birch tree ridge'

Esgair Cadlan
SO 966104

Mountain ridge and farm

Esgair Cadlan 1919 L C essay & map; Esgair-y-gadlan 1905 OS6"; 1874 OS6"; Esgairgadlan 1905 HPP; Ysgair Gadlan 1864 PR; Eskicatland 1841 TS; Yskir Cadlan 1808 PR; Esgyr Cadlan 1774 PR.

Esgair Cadlan was the name of a small farm, now in ruins, taken from its location on the ridge of the same name.

In HPP p13 Dewi Cynon has "Esgairgadlan – "Esgair" – a long ridge; a spur of land jutting out.* "Cadlan" was a soldier of old."

The last statement is incorrect. For 'cadlan', GPC has "battlefield, battle". *Cadlan* is Welsh for 'battlefield'. It is also the name of the nearby stream (see *Cadlan* above for a detailed explanation). The *esgair* 'ridge' has *Cadlan* the stream-name as its second element with the whole, *Esgair Cadlan* meaning 'Cadlan ridge'.

Note the anglicised *Eskicatland* form of 1841, with the misleading and misunderstood final two elements 'cat' and 'land'. Note also, the local dialect pronunciation, written as *yskir* (yscir) for *esgair* of the 1808 parish register.

1841 TAS Eskircatland (37 acres):
Landowners Rev. Richard Davies & William Payne Occupier Gwenllian Meredith Charles Meredith
934. Coedcae (grazing enclosure) 935. do 936. Homestead &c. 937. Erw Pant y Maes (acre of the field with a hollow) 938. Ysgir fach (esgair; small ridge) 939. Cae Ysgubor (barn field) 940. Ysgir fawr (esgair; great ridge) 941. Cae Cam (crooked, distorted field) 943. Wern Dafydd (Dafydd's alder swamp) 1007. Cae blaen Catland (Blaen Cadlan field) 1008. Old Cottage & Gardens

esgair, Cadlan; 'Cadlan ridge'

Ffrwd

Stream name

Cwm Ffrwd, Nant Ffrwd 1989 OS PF1109; Nant y Frood 1749 PM Map; frood c1700

(1584) Paroch.; Ffrwd (Cwm Tâf) 1533 GRO (SEHPP p. 22); Frut y guidon c1150 LL.

Ffrwd is the name of a stream rising on *Onllwyn*, flowing through *Cwm Ffrwd* and entering *Taf Fawr* at *Pontycapel*, south-west of *Cefn-coed-y-cymer* and forming part of the boundary between the parishes of Penderyn and Merthyr Tydfil. This was probably the *ffrwd* of *Frut y guidon c.* 1150 above. (also see Introduction). *Gwidon* is *gwiddon*, "giantess, female monster; hag, witch, sorceress." GPC.

The Ffrwd stream joining the Taf Fawr below Pontycapel. © DMJ

'swift stream, brook'; earlier prob. 'of the giantess etc.'

Ffrwd Fach Uchaf   Lost

Former farm

Ffrwdfach-uchaf 1879 ERB

Ffrwd, bach, uchaf; 'higher Ffrwdfach'

Ffrwd Ganol Fach   SO0208

Former farm

Ffrwd-ganol-fâch 1991 OSPF 1109; Ffrwd-Ganol-Fach 1905 OS6"; Ffrwdganolfach 1851 Census; Ffrwd-genol-fach 1840 TM; Frwd-ganol 1830 OS6"; Frwod Genol Vach 1818 Cambrian; Frood Genol vach 1749 PMoel. map;

The earlier name of the larger farm was *Ffrwd Ganol* (1830). It was later divided into two with *fach* and *fawr* added as distinguishing elements.

"This small farm ceased to exist as a separate holding in the second half of the 19th cent. and today the barn remains with ruins of the house alongside." PNDH 7.41. Note the dialectic *genol* of the 1840 form.

1841 TAS Ffrwd Genol Fach (102 acres):
Landowner Edward Vaughan Nash Esq. Occupier Thomas Williams
1063. Gwaun ffrwyd (ffrwd; meadow near the stream) 1064. Waun Newydd (new meadow) 1065. Coed cae ffa'r Palog (stick bean grazing enclosure) 1066. Waun

caer Lluest (the temporary shelter field meadow) 1067. Erwr Drainen (bramble acre) 1068. Cae Lluest (shelter/booth field) 1069. Nerer Fach (hanerer; small half acre) 1070. Ceven cae Lluest (behind cae lluest) 1071. Erw Garw Wen (white uncultivated acre) 1072. Cae Scallog (ysgallog; thistle field) 1073. Cae Tyle Ucha (upper hill field) 1074. do Cenol (middle hill field) 1075. do 1076. Gelli fach (small grove) 1077. Cae Main (narrow field) 1078. Cae Tyle Isha (lower hill field) 1079. Homestead &c. 1080. Cae bach (small field) 1081 & 1082 Cae ffynnon (well/spring field) 1083. Cae dan ty (field below the house) 1084. Pen y Graig (top of the rock) 1086. Graig (rock)

Ffrwd, canol, bach; 'small Ffrwd-ganol'. (middle Ffrwd)

Ffrwd Ganol Fawr   SO 0207
Former farm

Ffrwd-ganol-fawr 1991 OSPF 1109; 1920 OS6"; 1841 Census; Ffrwd-genol-fawr 1840 TM; Ffrwd-ganol-fawr 1836 Will Phillip Jones NLW. Frood Genol 1749 PMoel. map;

"Today the site is evidenced with extensive ruins of a house, barns and enclosures with records indicating occupation for the first half of the 20cent." PNDH 7.42. Note the dialectic *genol* of the 1840 form.

1841 TAS Ffrwd Genol Fawr (126 acres):
Landowner Edward Vaughan Nash Esq. Occupier William Jones
1039. Cwm dur (sic) (dŵr; water valley) 1040. Caer Pant (the dingle field) 1041. Cae Main (narrow field) 1042. Digod fach (small deforestation) 1043. Erw hir Isha (lower long acre) 1044. Caer Coed (field of trees) 1045. Cae ffynnon Rhos (moorland well field) 1046. Erw hir ucha (upper long acre) 1047. Frasgoed Isha (lower stout trees) 1048. do Ucha (upper stout trees) 1049. Caer Scybor (barn field) 1050. Homestead &c. 1051. Caer ffrynddy? (sic) (y fron ddu? field of the black mound) 1052. do 1053. Cae dan ty (field below the house) 1054. do 1055. Cae dan y Buarth (field below the farmyard) 1056. Caer coed cae bach (small grazing enclosure field) 1057. Waun Isha (lower medow) 1058. do Genol (middle lower meadow) 1059. Coed cae (grazing enclosure) 1060. Waun ceven y Coed cae (meadow behind the grazing enclosure) 1061. Waun Newydd (new meadow) 1062. do y ffynnon (the well's new meadow)

Ffrwd, canol, mawr; 'Large Ffrwd Ganol'

Ffrwd Isaf   SO 0207
Residence

Ffrwd-isaf 1991 OS Pathfinder 1109; Frwd Isha 1841 Census UP; Ffrwd Isha 1840 TM; Frwd isaf 1825 Will Robert Williams NLW; Frwod Isa 1818 Cambrian; Frood Issa 1749 PMoel. map;

"Today the site has a modernised dwelling house and ruined barns."
PNDH 7.43

1841 TAS Ffrwyd Isha (133 acres):
Landowner Edward Vaughan Nash Occupier William Williams
1011. Waun fach (small meadow) 1012. do Newydd (new small meadow) 1013.
Coed cae (grazing enclosure) 1014. Waun fach (small meadow) 1015. Cae Main
Ucha (upper field of stones) 1016. Cwm (wooded valley) 1017. Cae Newydd (new
field) 1018. Binkws (bunkhouse) 1019. Homestead &c. 1020. Caer Odyn (the kiln
field) 1021. Cwm Nant Iorath (Nant Iorath *Iorwerth* wooded valley)1023. Do 1024.
Cae Gwan (weak, poor field) 1025. Cyllgoed (hazel trees) 1026. Llwyn Gwan
(weak, poor bush) 1027. 1028. Wood 1029. do 1030. Bryngoll (hazel nut? Hill)
1031. do 1032. Brest (mound) 1033. Caer Dderwen (the oak tree field) 1034. Cae
Mawr Isha (lower big field) 1035. Wood.
Landowner & Occupier Edward Vaughan Nash (5 acres):
1036. Tyle ban (lofty hill) 1037. Mill Cottage Road &c. 1038. Cae Poth (poeth; hot
field). This is named Mill field on the TM, referring to the Pontycapel Mill (see
below).

Ffrwd, isaf; 'Lower Ffrwd'

Ffrwd Uchaf
SO 0208

Farm
Ffrwd Uchaf 1991 OS Pathfinder 1109; Frwd ycha 1841 Census UP; Frwod Ucha
1818 Cambrian; Frood Ycha 1749 PM map;

One of the highest of the *Ffrwd* farms on the lower slopes of Penmoelallt.
The second element *uchaf* 'upper' is a distinguishing element.

1841 TAS Ffrwd Ucha (115 acres):
Landowner Edward Vaughan Nash Occupier Jenkin Williams
1087. Erw Pwll Taf (acre near Pwll Taf) Pwll Taf was pronounced Pwll Tev by
pupils in Vaynor and Penderyn Comprehensive *c.* 1970-90. 1088. Tri ffydwen ? for
mutated *pedwen* (three fields of a quarter?) 1089. Cae dan yr Hewl (field below the
road) 1090. Graig Isha (lower rock) 1091. Cae dan yr Odin (field below the kiln)
1092. Graig Ucha (upper rock) 1093. Cae Pentwyn (top of the hill field) 1094. Cae
Scybor (barn field) 1095. Caer Ellen (Ellyn; the razor shaped field) 1096.
Homestead Croft &c. 1097. Cae Perwood? Isha (lower pear-wood? field) 1098.
Naer (uncertain poss. nawer; nine acres) 1099. Cae Pentwyn (top of the hill field)
1100. Calon Goch Isha (lower red heart *shaped*) 1101. do Ucha (upper red heart
shaped) 1102. Cae Coedcae (field near grazing enclosure) 1103. Coedcae (grazing
enclosure) 1104. Pasture & Wood 1105. Coed cae bach (small grazing enclosure)
1106. Waun Grion (greon; flock/herd meadow).

Ffrwd, uchaf; 'Upper Ffrwd'

Ffrwd Uchaf Fach

Farm

Ffrwd Ucha Fach 1840 TM; Frood ycha vach 1749 PMoel. map;

This small farm was at one time owned by Ffrwd Uchaf. PNDH 7.98.1

1841 TAS Ffrwd Ucha Fach (87 acres):

Landowner Edwards Vaughan Nash Esq. Occupier David Thomas

1107. Gardir (garw & tir) Mawr (big rough/uncultivated land) 1108. Gardir (rough/uncultivated land) 1109. Cottage & garden 1110. Barn 1111. Cae Main (narrow field) 1112. Road & Waste 1113. Cae dan ty (field below house) 1114. Graig Yscallog (thistle rock) 1115. Cae Pant (dingle field) 1116. Graig (the rock) 1117. Cae bach Ucha (upper small field) 1118. Graig Isha (lower rock) 1119. do Genol (middle rock) 1120. Talion y Graig (rock heights) 1121. Graig fawr (large rock) 1122. Erw (acre) 1123. Pedwen bach (small quarter) 1124. Llwyn Isha (lower bush) 1125. Bachlain ty (small strip ? *bach*, *llain*, near the house).

Ffrwd, uchaf, bach; 'little upper Ffrwd'

Ffynnon Ddu

Spring, well

Ffynnon Ddu 1905 OS6" 1897 OS6".

The well is located between the river Mellte and Clwyd Rhydfaen.

Ffynnon, du; 'black/dark well'

Garwdyle

Garw-dyle 1991 OS PF1108; Y Garwdyle 1923 LYH p. 8; Cwrwdylan 1844 Cambrian (obituary, Wm, Harry Williams age 82 Weaver & Bard); Garwdyle 1841 Census UP; Garwdyla c1762 HPP 153; 1905 AL; Tyr Vadocke ddy 1626 Tred. Est. (Sr Edw Lewis Kt.).

Located on the hillside behind Cwar Llwyn-onn, Garwdyle was the birthplace and one-time home of local poet Gwilym Harri, 1762-1844. He later moved to Llwyn Onn, and then to the weaver's cottage on the banks of the Cynon at Pontbrenllwyd. It was here that his friend Iolo Morgannwg used to visit him (HPP p. 154). Gwilym wrote about Garwdyla in one of his verses:

'O fewn y Garwdyla	*Within the Garwdyla*
Y rhoes f'anadliad cynta'	*I drew my first breath*
Nis gwn ym mhle na pha ryw lun	*I know not where or in what shape*
Y chwithau'r un ddiwetha'.	*I'll puff my final one.*

Note his local dialect pronunciation of Garwdyla, confirmed as Garwdila (RMR). The name is misprinted as an inappropriate *Cwrwdylan* (Dylan's beer) on his obituary notice, 1844 above.

Garwdyle the birthplace of poet and weaver Gwilym Harri. Courtesy of SM

Tyle is Welsh for "steep road or path;" GPC, while *garw* is Welsh for "rough, rugged, craggy, uncultivated" GPC. In this case, *Garwdyle* would have referred to a rough, unsurfaced, steep path leading from present-day Cwar Llwyn-onn to the farm that took its name from the difficult footpath leading to it. (see 1903 OS6" map). In the twentieth century, the lower part of the path was converted to a metal surfaced road suitable for motor vehicles.

1841 TAS Garw Dyle (38 acres):

Landowner Rev. David Jones Occupier Catherine Jones

944. Gellir March (the stallion's grove) 945. do Gwayr (grass grove) 946. do Drain (bramble grove) 947. Cae Mawr (big field) 948. Homestead &c. 949. Coed cae (grazing enclosure) 950. Cau (sic) Haidd (barley field).

Garw, tyle; 'Rough, difficult, steep path/road'

Garwnant   SO 9913

Stream name, farm name & visitor centre

Garwnant 1905 HPP 16; Garnant 1841 Census UP; Car-nant 1830 OS; Carnant 1740, 1739 WP

Garwnant is the name of today's visitor centre in Coed Taf Fawr on the edge of Llwyn-onn Resevoir. The old farmhouse has been converted to a visitor's centre. This farmhouse, known as *Carnant* in 1739/40, is recorded as having 60 pupils attending the Charity School in 1740.

It is possible that the early *Carnant* was lenited to (y) *Garnant* and later 'corrected' to *Garwnant*. The stream name became the name of several smallholdings viz. *Garnant Fach, Garnant Fawr*. *Garwnant* indicates a 'rough, wild stream', probably referring to the rocky nature of its bed, but also poss. describing the flow of water. It should be noted that *nant* had an original meaning of 'valley, ravine, glen' and later developed to 'stream, rivulet, brook.'

The original name may be *Carnant*, containing the two elements *car* and *nant*. *Car* occurs in several stream names viz. *Nant Car*, and can be translated as the 'dear, kind stream'. Coincidentally *car* also occurs in *Nant Car* and the submerged *Abercar* on the opposite side of the reservoir. Likewise, *Rhydycar* in Merthyr Tudful has *car* as a final element, but here it means 'cart' giving 'the cart ford'.

1841 TAS Garnant (77 acres):
Landowner Rev. Richard Davies & William Payne Occupier William Jones
1370. Waste 1371. Coed cae (grazing enclosure) 1372. Waun (meadow) 1373. Ddi Goed (treeless) 1374. Erw fawr (big acre) 1375. do Lluyd (sic) (grey/poor/Lloyd's acre) 1376. Caer Ciroi (*curo?* the thrashing? field) 1377. Wood &c. 1378. Homestead &c. 1379. Cae dan ty (field below the house) 1380. Coed cae bach (small grazing enclosure) 1381. Cae ffynnon (well/spring field) 1382. Caer Guire (cae'r gwair; the hay field) 1383. Cae Lloi (calves' field) 1384. Caer Guire Isha (cae'r gwair isaf; lower hay field) 1385. Ynis (river meadow) 1386. do Coed (river meadow wood)

Garw, nant; 'Wild, rough stream'; Car, nant; 'dear, kind stream'.

The Garnant stream flowing over rough terrain and under the old road bridge to Garnant Farm. ©DMJ

Gate House

SN 945092 SN 948075

Tollgate

Gate House 1841 Census; Penderin and Trebanog Gates 1840, 1822, 1814, 1813 etc. The Cambrian; Pantgarw Gate 1813 The Cambrian; Trebanog Gate 1857, 1855, 1852, 1848, 1827 PR.

There were two *tollgates,* one on the Brecon road above the Lamb Inn called the Penderyn Gate, (replacing the Pantgarw Gate in 1814) the other on the road below Trebanog Fawr known as the Trebanog Gate. The Pantgarw or Penderin (sic) Gate was sited below Pantgarw while the Trebanog Gate was located near Ynys fawr field on Trebanog Fawr land. The Brecon Turnpike Road Act was passed in 1809 and by 1813 two gates were operating on the outskirts of Penderyn village on the Turnpike road between Hirwaun and Brecon.

Both Gates were regularly advertised for rent in *The Cambrian* and other local papers. The 1813 advertisement also lists the Newbridge Gate (Blaentaf) along with the Penderin (sic) and Trebanog Gates on the Brecon and Hirwaun Road. Adverts after 1814 do not include the Newbridge Gate; they only name the Penderin and Trebanog Gates on the Brecon and Hirwaun road. The Penderin Gate continued to be advertised until 1865. The Local Government Act of 1888 gave the responsibility for roads to County Councils.

Gavannog   Lost

Gavannauc, gauanauc c1150 LL; Gavannog 1893 LL; 14th cent. SWB.

This is one of the earliest place-names associated with the parish of Penderyn. It occurs in the 12th cent. Gwynasey Manuscript of Liber Landavensis, published by J. Gwynogvryn Evans with the cooperation of John Rhys, Oxford 1893 (along with place-name contributions by Egerton Phillimore). Page 42 quotes the Latin boundaries of the episcopate of Llandaf which includes "meldou, adgauannauc ad deriemris" (Melldau, Gavannauc, Deri Emris). Page 134 has the boundaries in Welsh, "Guayragon hyt y blayn, Oy blayn hyt gauanhauc, o gauannauc bet deri emreis" (Gwrangon hyd 'i blaen, o'i blaen hyd gavanhawc, o gavannawc hyd Deri Emris). Page 363 provides a translation of the Welsh boundaries "upwards to the Mellte to Gavannog to Deri Emris". Two of the places mentioned relate to present day Gwrangon (Guayragon) and Mellte (meldou), but *Gafannog* and Deri Emris are more difficult to explain in their modern contexts.

Some sources equate *Gavannog* with Trebannog, but the link seems tenuous. There is a problematic gap of some 400 years between *Gavannog* (c. 1150) and the earliest *Trebanog* (1555).

Gafanog could contain the Welsh noun *cafn* (pron. cafan in loc. dial.) meaning 'a trough' with *y gafanog* (*y* plus *cafan*, plus adj. suffix *-og*) giving a meaning of 'the corrugated, furrowed land'. Although *cafn* is a masc. noun, GPC shows an example of lenition in y *gafyn*, 14th cent. Llyfr Blegwryd. *Cafn, cafan* occurs as an element elsewhere, eg. *Caban Ygha* 1541 and *Cavan ycha* 1580 in Glynrhondda and *Glan y Cavan* 1751 NLW Probate BR/1751/40 in Llanddewi'r-cwm; *Cafnan* 1748 Anglesey and *Nant-y-cafn*, Meirioneth and Glamorgan (see EANC pp. 45-46). Unfortunately, there are no examples of *cafan* plus the adjectival suffix -og.

It is also possible that *Gavannog* is derived from a lost *Gavan* pers. name plus the territorial suffix *-og* giving the territory of *Gavan*, cf. *Defynog, Gregynog*.

It is not impossible for *gavannog* to have become *trebannog*, but the crucial evidence is not documented. The territory called *Gavannog* may have been prefixed with *tref* 'homestead' giving *Tre-gavannog*. *Tre-gavannog* could have contracted to *Trevannog*, cf. *Myfanwy > Fanw*, *Aberaman > Bremen, Pontaberdulais > Pontardulais, Cwmynysmintan > Cwmsmintan*, etc. *Trevannog* could then have changed, either through confusion with, or 'correction' to *Trebannog*.

Be that as it may, it seems likely that *Gavannog* contains Welsh *cafn* 'trough' plus the adjectival suffix *-og*, probably descriptive of 'furrowed' land.

Gelli Benuchel

SN 955066

Farm

Y Gelli 2017 Clochdar. GM. (William Gwyn Davies); 1905 AL; Gelli-ben-uchel 1991 OSPF1108; Gelli 1891 Census; Gelly 1871, 1851, 1841 Census; 1807 Will of Thomas Rees NLW; Gelli Benuchel 1849 Will of Morgan Rees NLW; Gelly Ben Uchel 1841 Census; Gelly Penychell 1807 Will of Thomas Rees NLW; Gelly Pen Ychaf 1768 CL/BRA; Tyr u Gelly pen uchell 1742 Will of Thomas Watkin; 1739 Will of Llewelin Meredith; Kelliben Ychal 1705 BFE; Celli Benychell 1700 Will Meredith Llewelin; Tyr Gelly Ben Ychell 1691 CL/BRA 745/5; Tir Gelly Benychel 1665 HVHR 42; Tyr Gelly Blennuchell 1626 Tred. Est.

The 1742 form of *Tyr u Gelly pen uchell* (tir y gelli pen uchel) shows the presence of the definite article which causes a lenition in *celli* (to gelli). In later forms, the def. article is redundant, but the lenition remains eg. *Gelli Benuchel.*

Kelliben Ychal 1705, has the loc. dial. *uchal* for *uchel*. The 1626 form of *Tyr Gelly Blen-nuchell* prob. contains a scribal error with *blen* (blaen) for *ben* in *Blennuchell*.

Penuchel is literally 'high-headed, haughty' (GPC); this would fit in with TAS field no. 362, 363 and BFE E34 and 35, *brenhinaidd* 'royal', or it could be used here figuratively for 'proud, conspicuous', as a descriptive and topographical factor. *Gelli Benuchel* is located on a small hillock and is visible from a distance. On reflection it is more likely to be the latter rather than the former, for 'the haughty (people/ones)' would require a definite article, viz. *Gelli'r Benuchel*, which is not evidenced in the examples given.

Gelli-fach was part of *Gelli Benuchel* lands (see 1776 BFE schedules) where *bach* appears as a distinguishing element. *Gelli Benuchel* is often abbreviated to *Y Gelli*, as seen in Clochdar, 2017 above and some 19th cent. census returns. For *Gelliau* and *Celliau* see *Pentre Celliau*.
Gelli Benuchel is also a farm-name near Creunant, Cwm Nedd.

1841 TAS Gelli Benucha (sic) (127 acres):
Landowner Morgan Morgan Occupier Morgan Rees

Gelly Ben Uchal BFE 1776 map. Courtesy of SM and WGAS (D/D BF/E 164)

341. Cae bach (small field) 342. do 343. Building, Road &c. 344. Cae draw (yonder field) 345. Ty Wern (wern house) 346. Isha (lower) 347. Worlod (gweirglodd; meadow) 348. Homestead, Gardens Road &c. 348a. Cae Cyd (kite field cf. *Cae'r Cude* 1776 BFE no. 21) 349. Rhyd Erwi (erwau; ford acres cf. 19 & 20 BFE 1776) 350.Cae Crwn (crooked field) 351. Ynis Glandwr (riverside river-meadow) 352. Cae Tyle nos Felin (telynos (metathesised); yellow harp (shaped) field) 353. Waun Pistyll y Llwyn (water-spout meadow near bushes) 354. Gordell ddyesiog (sic) (?tangled churn shaped (field) see E23 BFE) 355. Caer Dwyffordd (two-way field) 356. Wern Newydd (new wetland) 358. Coed Brinhinodd (sic) (brenhinaidd? royal hill wood. See BFE E34 & 35) 359. Cae bach (small field) 360. Pen y Coed (end of the wood) 361. Waun (meadow) 362. Brinhinodd Isha (sic) (brenhinaidd? lower royal see BFE 34 & 35) 363. do Ucha (upper do) 364. Cae Main (narrow field) 365. Coed cae (grazing enclosure) 366. Waun fach (small meadow) 367. Cae (field) 368. Wern (wetland) 369. Waun Ty yr Llwyd (tir; poor land meadow) 371. Wain (meadow)

1776 Schedules:

E1. Farm House Gardens & ye waste about it 2. Worlod (gweirglodd; meadow) 3. Pen twyn bach (top of the small hill) 4. The brake (thicket) in do. 5. Cuvar bach (cyfar; small acre) 6. Cae draw (yonder field) 6½.. Gelly fach House & Garden 7. Y Wern (the wet land) 8. Do isha (lower wet land) 9. Field by Gelly fach House 10. Road from ye house to W. Morgan's Land (William Morgan) 11. Wern Newydd (new wet land) 12. The Coed Cae (the grazing enclosure) 13. Cae Melin (melyn; "yellow" field) 14. Cae Main (narrow field) 15. Wayn Ty-yn-y-Llwyn (house in the bushes meadow) 16. Cae ty-yn-y-llwyn (house in the bushes field) 17. Field by ditto 18. Wood 19. Erw'r Yed (rhyd; the ford acre. cf. 349 re 1841 TAS) 20. Do isha (do lower) 21. Cae'r cude (cude for cudiau/barcudiau; kites' field, cf. Cae Cyd no. 348a re 1841 TAS) 22. Cae Rud-y-dwy Forth (cae ar hyd y dwy ffordd; field along the two lanes) 23. Gardd Duriseog (drysiog; tangled garden) 24. Cae Tyla Noes Velan (telynos, telyn + adj. suffix -os; yellow harp (shaped) field) 25. Wayn Pistyll y Llwyn (meadow by the water-spout bushes) 26. Cae Tyla'r Ynis (river meadow hill field) 27. Wern ishaf (lower wet land) 28. Ynis glan y Dwr (water side river meadow) 29. Cae Crwn (crooked field) 30. The wood by the river 31. Road that leads to Hirwayn 32. Wern goch & wern uchaf (red wetland & upper wetland) 33. Cae bach (small field) 34. Brenhinadd uchaf (?brenhinaidd; upper royal?) 35. Do ishaf (lower Do) 36. The Meadow 37. Quarter of an acre by Do 38. The road by Do.

Tir, y, celli, penuchel; 'land of the proud (conspicuous) grove'

Gelli Dafolog / Dafolws   SN 946094

Farm

Gelli-dafolog 1991 OSPF1108; 1905 OS6″; Gelli Diafolws 1905 HPP; Gellydafolog 1861 & 71 Cens.;

Gelli Davolas 1830 OS; Gelli Dyfolas 1777 PR; Gelly Davolas Farm 1776 BFE; Kelli

Tavolas 1705 BFE; Tyr Kelly Daveloss ycha 1626 Tredegar Estate; Tyr y gelly Daveloss ysha 1626 Tredegar Estate.

Gelli-dafolog farm is in Cwm Cadlan. The second element has been recorded as *dafolog, dafolas, daveloss* and *dafolws*, all containing the Welsh *tafol* 'dock (plant)' plus the adjectival and collective suffixes *og, os, as,* and *ws*. *Gellidafolws* is truncated to *Gellifolws* in the loc. dial. The 1905 form *diafolws* is an example of popular etymology rationalising a locally ambiguous *dafolws,* and unfortunately translating the whole name as 'the Devil's hazel grove' HPP p. 13, (diafol is Welsh for 'devil').

Celli, y gelli (celli, a fem. noun mutates following the def. art.) is Welsh for 'the grove' with *Gelli dafolog/dafolas* giving 'the grove of the dock plants'. The Tredegar Estate (1626) lists two *Gelli Davolos* farms with the distinguishing elements uchaf and isaf. *Gelli Dafolws Isaf* is known today as Ynyswendraeth, (Gelli Dyfolws Issa alias *Yniswendorth* 1759 Tred. Pk. 97/24). It follows therefore that the associated uchaf would be present day *Gelli Dafolog*.

1841 TAS Gelli Davolas (72 acres):
Landowner Morgan Morgan Occupier Morgan Rhys
820. Waunfawr (large meadow) 821. Erw do (Waunfawr acre) 822. Tyle Bach (small incline) 823. Llwyn r Allet (allt; wooded slope bush) 824. Cae dau Llwyn (two bush field) 825. Caer allt Isha (lower wooded slope field) 826. do Ucha (upper wooded slope field) 827. Homestead Groft &c. 828. Cae bach (small field) 829. Gele fach (?gelli fach; small grove) 830. Cae bach (small field) 831. Cae Gwyn (white field) 832. Cae dan ty (field below the house) 833. Cae Ysgubor & Barn

Photo taken on approaching Gelli-dafolog 2014, showing dock plants, the popular name of several species of plants of the genera Rumex, Arctia etc. © DMJ (barn field) 834. Cae Mawr (big field) 835. Cae wrth pen y Tai (field at the end of the houses) 835a. Cottage & Garden 836. Gellu Nyadd Isha (lower Neuadd grove) 837. Clyn Isha (lower meadow) 838. do deri (oak meadow) 839. do cenol (middle meadow) 840. do deri (oak meadow) 841. do bach (small meadow) 842. Gellir Noyadd Ucha (the upper Neuadd grove) 843. Groft (small field) 844. Tir Gwyllt (uncultivated land)

1776 (D/D BF/E 164) Schedules:

S.1. House Garden & waste about it 2. Gelly fach (small grove) 3. ------- 4. The Brake (thicket) in do field 5. Do in Do field 6. Cae bach (small field) 7. Cae Gwyn Uchaf (upper white field) 8. Do ishaf (lower do) 9. Cae Pen twyn (hill end field) 10. Erw fawr (large acre) 11. The Large Meadow 12. Pentwyn 'r allt (hill end wooded slope) 13. The Allt (the wooded slope) 14. Caer Calch (the lime field) 15. Tree Pedwran (three quarter) 16. Gelly'r Nuadd (the hall grove) 17. Field inclosed (sic) out of ditto 18. ---- 19. Gwastod y Coed (the flat land wood) 20. The Meadow in do 21. Clyn y dery bach (small oak meadow)

Celli, tafolog/tafolas/tafolws; "the dock (plant) grove"

Gelli Fach SN 956068

Farm

Gelli fach 1905 OS6"; Gelly Fach 1841 Census D20; Gelly fach House & Garden 1776 BFE; Gelli-vach 1773 PR.

Shown as part of *Gelli Benuchel* with bach as a distinguishing element between the two farmhouses [see Gelli Benuchel & 1776 BFE above]. The former farm is now in ruins.

Celli, bach; the 'small Gelli'

Gelli Ffynhonnau SN 963106

Farm

Gelli-ffynonau-isaf, Gelli-ffynonau-uchaf 1988 OSPF 1084; Gelli-ffynonau-isaf, Gelli-ffynnonau-uchaf 1905 OS6", Gellyffynonau Isaf 1851-71 Census; Gellufynonau & do upper, 1841 Census; Gelliffynone ucha, Gelliffynone isha 1841 TAS; Gelliffynnonnau 1805 Will Jenkin Morgan NLW; Gelly Funnona 1776 BFE Schedules; Gelly Funnona Isha 1776 BFE map; Tire Kell llu y funhonne 1711 Will of Evan Thomas; Tyr Kelly yr ffyn honn 1626 Tredegar Estate.

It appears that the farmstead took its name "from the several springs found on its site" (PNDH 7.55), although the earliest recorded form (1626 above) quotes Tyr Kelly yr ffyn honn (tir celli y ffynnon) using the singular ffynnon rather than the plural ffynhonnau. All the later forms use the plural ffynhonau (with various orthographies) including the loc. dial. ffynnona (1776).

Uchaf and *isaf* are distinguishing elements. 'upper and lower'. The land was divided before 1776, as BFE 1776 shows both *Gelly Funnona* and *Gelly Funnona Isha*.

1841 TAS Gellifynnone Ucha (57 acres):
Landowner Sir Josiah John Guest Occupier William Rees
920. Waste 921. Homested &c. 922. Cae ffynnone (well field) 923. Cae Ysgubor (barn field) 924. Coed cae bach (small grazing enclosure) 925. Byarth Glas Isha (lower green yard) 926. Cae bach 927. Byarth Glas Ycha (upper green yard) 928. Waun y Dryon? (?draen; bramble meadow) 929. Waun wherw (chwerw; bitter meadow) 930. Cae Cenol (middle field) 931. Waun fach (small meadow) 932. Cae Mawr (big field) 933. Wern (alder wet land).
1841 TAS Gellifynnone Isha (22 acres):
Landowner John Thomas Occupier Henry Price
908. Coed cae Ceffyl (horse's grazing enclosure) 909. Narreg Nessa drawr (hanereg; next half-acre) 910. Gelli (grove) 911. Goidd fach (gudd? small concealed field) 912. Lan Bella (furthest up) 913. Do Nessa (next furthest) 914. Cross Llwyd (poor quality field near cross) 915. Homestead Croft road &c 916. Cae bach dan y Ardd (small field below the garden) 917. Narreg Nessa heol (half-acre next to the road) 918. Worlod (meadow) 919. Waste.
1776 (D/D BF/E 164) Schedules Gelly Funnona (Isha?) :
1. House and Garden 2. The Barn 3. The fd by the house 4. Cae bach (small field) 5. Wern (wetland) 6. Cae'r Llan (church's field) 7. Coed cae'r Cefil (horse's grazing enclosure) 8. Nerag (hannereg; half acre) 9. Croft (small field) 10. Do by Do 11. Worlod (gweirglodd; pasture).

The 1776 BFE map records Gelly Funnona Isha. The 1776 BFE Schedules do not name the property; they individually list and name the corresponding fields, land and buildings shown on the BFE map.

Celli, ffynnon, ffynhonnau; 'grove (of the) spring(s)'

Gelli Neuadd   SN 949092
Cottages, Mansion
Gelli-neuadd 1991 OSPF 1108; Gelli Neuadd 1905 HPP 13; Gellynoyadd 1879 ERB; Gelly y Neadd 1841 Census; Gelli Neyadd isaf & Cottage & Gardens 1840 TM; Gelly Nyadd isha 1841 TAS; Gelli'r Noyadd Ucha 1841 TAS; Gelly'r Nuadd 1776 BFE.

Gelli Neyadd isaf (1840 TM) suggests that there was also a *Gelli Neuadd Uchaf*. Both these names occur on the 1841 TAS for *Gelli Davolas* as Field Nos. 836 *Gelly Nyadd isha* (sic) and 842 *Gelli'r Noyadd Ucha*. *Gelly'r Nuadd* (for Gelli'r Neuadd) is also recorded as field no. 16, a part of *Gelli Davolas* (sic) Farm on the 1766 BFE. It is likely that the present day *Gelli Neuadd*

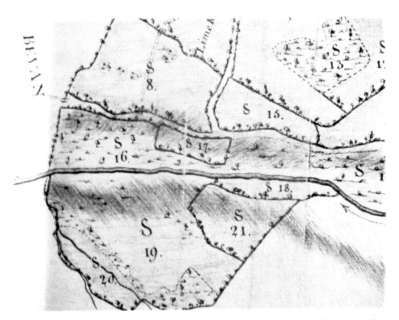

Field no. 16 is Gelly'r Nuadd and no.17 is Field enclosed out of Gelly'r Nuadd,
recorded on the 1776 map above as part of the lands of Gelli Davolas Farm.
Map courtesy of SM and WGAS (D/D BF/E 164)

cottages are located on the site of the earlier fields which were
presumably the site of the earlier *neuadd* or mansion.

   Neuadd is Welsh for a hall, a large residence or mansion. *Gelli'r Neuadd*
means the grove of the mansion or hall. This lost residence, once an
independent dwelling, became part of Gelli Dafolas land. The Gelli'r
Neuadd name has survived as Gelli Neuadd Cottages.

   Celli (y gelli), (y, 'r), Neuadd; 'grove (of the) mansion'

Gelli Tarw   SN 977056

Gellitarw 1911, 1901, 1851 Census; Gelli Tarw 1891 Census, 1840 TM; Gellytarw
1881, 1871 Census; Gelly y Tarw 1841 Census; Tyr Gelli'r Tarw 1790 will of D.T.M.
Jones NLW; Tire kellie y tarw 1697 PRO; Kelly tarw 1550 Penpont; Kelly y Tarrowe
1547 Penpont; Kelly y tarrow 1546 Penpont; tyr gellyr tarow 1515 Penpont.

The earliest forms show the equivalent of *Tir gelli'r tarw* which includes
the def. art. to give a meaning of 'land of the bull's grove', viz. the land
near the small wood where the bull was kept. In time the *tir* element as
well as the def. art. were made redundant, to leave *Gelli Tarw* 'bull's grove'.
The 1515 Penpont document defines the farm's boundaries as 'extending

from stream called Kynan and Wern Vawr to nant melyn & tyr methygyn'. Kynan is the River Cynon, Nant Melyn is prob. Nant Hir and Methygyn is known today as Court Farm.

1841 TAS Gellitarrw (109 acres):
Landowner James Stephens Esq. Occupier Peter Moore
Nos. 477 Waste, 480 Wood, 484 Wood, 495 Homestead &c. 498 Wood and 506 Public House Cottages & Wood (Cross Bychan not named). All the other TAS numbers were without names. This is unfortunate, especially as field numbers 502, 503 and 499 would have been the location of Cwmynysmintan (see above)..

Gelli, y, tarw (the bull's grove).

Gelli Tarw Cottages & Gelli Tarw Junction   SN 098053

Gelly Tarw Cottages 1911 Census; Gelli Tarw Junction 1920 OS6".

Gelli Tarw Junction was on the GWR Vale of Neath railway line. *Gelli Tarw Cottages* were near *Gelli Tarw Farm*. Residents of both cottages in the 1911 Census were railway signalmen.

Both Cottages and Junction take their names from the adjacent *Gelli Tarw* farm.

Glog, Y   SN 956087

Lost Farm
The Glogue 1840 TM; Glogue barn & Plantation 1839 TAS; The Gloge 1790, 77 PR/PNDH 7.73; Glogue Farm 1776 BFE; Glôg 1733 Will of Reynold Davies; Tire y glogg bickae 1692 Will of Morgan Williams;

GLOGUE FARM 1776 (D/D BF/E 164):
B1. House & Gardens B2. Croft by do (small field) B3. Cae'r Fenest (ffenestr would be ffenest in loc. dial.; the window field) B4. Cae'r Fwrn (ffwrn; the oven/furnace field) B5. The Lime Kiln & the rough yard about it B6. Cae discwlva (disgwylfa; discwlva in local parlance; look out field) B7. Cae Lewis fain uchaf (Lewis's upper thin [soil] field) B8. Ditto Ishaf (Ditto lower) B9. Cae bach ishaf (lower small field) B10. Cae dan y ty (field below the house B11. Cae pen twyn (top of the hill field) B12. Cae clyn (clun; meadow field) B13. Coedcae'r Glogue (Glog grazing enclosure) B14. Part of the Great Meadow B15. The two acres on do. [B14 & B15 are not shown on the map]

Glog Farm was in a ruinous state when it was sold to Rev. R. Davies in 1819, (BFE/WGAS). By the time of the 1841 TAS, the land was part of the *Bodwigiad Estate* and the farmhouse was used as a barn.

The correct form is *Y Glog*. Incidentally, the English def. art. is used in the 1840 and 1790s forms. Over the years, the Welsh def. art. became

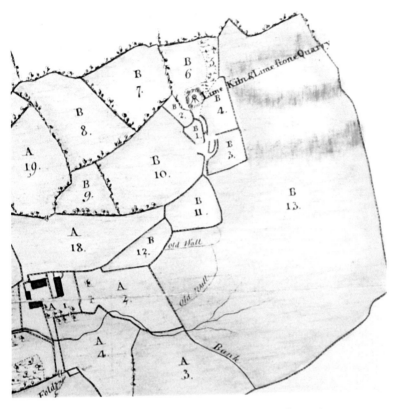

Glogue Farm in yellow marked B1 to B13 on the 1776
Map courtesy of SM and WGAS (D/D BF/E 164)

redundant but the mutated form *Glog* is evidence of its earlier presence. The *glogue* spelling is probably the result of rhyming English word association eg. vogue, rogue, brogue etc.

The place-name element is *clog* 'rock, cliff, precipice' [clog2 GPC] also present in *Mynydd y Glog*, *Twyn y Glog*, *Penyglog Fanddu* etc. The preceding def. art. causes a lenition with clog becoming Y *Glog*. The name suits the local rocky, hilly topography. Lime Kiln and Limestone Quarry of the 1776 BFE map indicates that rock was quarried and burnt to make lime here over two hundred years ago. The earliest form Tire y glogg bickae (tir y glog bica) with Welsh pica as the final descriptive element is 'land of the pointed precipice'.

y, clog; the 'rock, cliff, precipice'

Glyn Celli

Lost

Glyn Celli and Ynys Llwyfog were joined to form Trebannog Fawr (HVHR p. 39). See Clun Celli.

Glyn, celli; 'valley (of the) groves'

Glyn Perfedd

SN 955095

Farm

Glyn-perfedd 1991 OSPF; a'r Glynperfedd 1923 LYH p44; Glyn y porfeydd 1905 HPP 13; Clyn perfedd 1841 Census, 1839 TAS; Clyn Perfedd 1840 TM; Glyn-perfedd 1832 OS1"; Glyn y Perfedd 1778, 74 PR/PNDH 7.58; Tyr Glyn Perveth 1752 Penpont NLW. Tyr Miherer Grm 1626 Cymorth Tred. Est. 124/389 NLW; [Tyr Milherer Grm (Glynperfedd) SEHPP p20)].

Glynperfedd is a farm in Cwm Cadlan located between Nant Cadlan and Garwdyle. It contains two elements, *glyn* and *perfedd*, although the 1841, 1840 and 1839 forms record *Clyn perfedd*, suggesting that the first element is *clun* 'meadow', but these are erroneous as the earlier forms all contain *glyn* 'dingle, dale, dell, wooded valley'. The second element *perfedd* has a number of associated meanings but here it indicates 'middle' or 'remote'. *Glynperfedd* is the 'middle or remote wooded valley'. Cf. *Cefn Perfedd*, Ystradfellte

The farm was previously known as *Tyr Miherer Grm* 1626 above, recorded as *Tyr Milherer Grm* (Glynperfedd) SEHPP p. 20, and I am grateful to AS for identifying the earlier name as Glyn Perfedd. This 1626 name is difficult to explain. *Tyr Miherer Grm* has *tir* 'land' as its first element. The second element *miherer* could possibly relate to the Welsh element *mieri* 'bramble, briers', but that is speculative. The final element *Grm* is also difficult but could be an abbreviation for *gwrm* 'dark', giving 'land of the dark briers'.

1841 TAS Clynperfedd (84 acres):

Landowner Morgan Morgan Occupier William Williams

858. Cae Glas (green field) 859. do 860. Cae Mawr (big field) 861. do 862. Cae bychan (small field) 863. Cae bach (small field) 864. Wern (alder wetland) 865. Cae Garw (uncultivated field) 866. do brith (mottled unculti-vated field) 867. Gwaun y Ton (lay land meadow) 868. Cae Cenol (middle field) 868a. Cae Clover (clover field) 869. do 870. Cae Isha (lower field) 871. do Cefn Isha (lower back (of house) field) 872. Cae pengam (crooked-end field) 873. Homestead &c. 874. Cae yn y Wern (field in the alder wetland) 875. Caer Newydd (new field) 876. Gwaun y do (the do meadow) 877. Waun nest Llwyd (Nest's poor meadow) 878. Cae Glas

(green field) 879. do

Glyn, perfedd; 'middle or remote wooded valley'

Gwaun y Llan

Lost Tenement

Clien gwaien y llan 1547 Penpont.

The above entry in Penpont AD 1547 reads "two tenements in Penderyn called *Clien gwaien y llan* and Kelly y Tarrowe, extending in length from the river Kenon up to a place called pull gwyn, and in breadth from lands called Methygen to nant hire". Methygen is the previous name for the farm known today as Court Farm. See also SEHPP p. 39, as well as HVHR p24.

Clien gwaien y llan would be *clun gwaun y llan* in today's orthography, and translates as 'meadow of the church's pasture', that is, a piece of land that presumably, at one time had been donated to the church. (A similar *Cae'r Llan* appears on Gelly Funnonna Ishaf, BFE 1776 no. 6). Unfortunately, today's precise location is unknown. Its approximate location was close to Court Farm and Gelli'r Tarw.

Gwaun, y, llan; the church's meadow

Gwern Pawl   SN 951101

Former Farm, old school

Gwern-pawl 1988 OS PF; Wern Pawl 1919 LC essay & map. Gwern Pawl 1905 HPP 17, 113; 1779 PR/PNDH; Gwern y Pawl 1840 TM; 1776, 1771 PR/PNDH; 1780, 1775, 1755, 1754 Penpont; 1713 Wills NLW, Evan John; Gwerne y Pawl 1754 Penpont; Gwern y Paul 1780, 1751, 1750 Penpont.

The farm was in use until the middle of the 19th cent. when the land was 'joined with adjacent holdings (TM), with the house abandoned early in the 19th cent. Today the site is evidenced with large piles of rubble.' (PNDH 7.60). There was a school at *Gwern Pawl* between 1780 and 1818 (HPP 113). LC writes of tales his mother heard from his great-grandmother re. *Ysgol Sgubor Gwern Pawl* 'Gwern Pawl Barn School' (LYH p. 7).

1841 TAS Gwern y Pawl (83 acres):

Landowner Morgan Morgan Esq. & Parry Williams Esq. Occupier Rhys Morgan & Richard Evans

845. Cae bach (small field) 846. Waun isaf (lower meadow) 847. Road & Waste 848. Coedcae bach Pwdwr (rotten little grazing enclosure) 849. Homestead Groft & etc. 850. Caer ffynnon (the well field) 851. Pedwaran bach (little quarter) 852. Cae Pedwaran (quarter field) 853. Waun ucha (upper meadow) 854. Waun y cae (the

field meadow) 855. Gwaun y Pawl (the pole meadow) 856. Pedwaran bach (little quarter) 857. Gworlod y Croynant (Croynant meadow; croynant is prob. crau1 GPC 'blood; bloody' & nant 'brook' prob. referring to the water colour, cf. Creunant, Cadoxton-juxta-Neath; the 'bloody' local interpretation may have been linked with Cadlan (erroneously thought to mean battlefield) of which it is a tributary.

Gwern Pawl or *Gwern y Pawl* contains the elements *gwern* and *pawl* with or without the def. art. *Gwern* is Welsh [1]'alder tree(s) (the wood of which resists decay in water)'; [3]'alder-grove, alder marsh, swamp, quagmire, damp meadow'; GPC. The second meaning is the most likely for this location. The second element *pawl* is also Welsh. There are two possible meanings, firstly 'pole, post' GPC or the personal name *Paul*. The personal name *Paul* is improbable due to its scarcity as an old personal name in the area, despite its Biblical connection. *Pawl* meaning 'pole, post', occurs in other Welsh place-names viz. *Bryn pawl*, Llangower, Mer. and *Cefn-pawl*, Abbey Cwmhir, Rads. It is also a field-name element in Gwaun y Pawl 'the pole meadow', TAS number 855 above. As *Gwern Pawl* is near the parish boundary, the use of *pawl* 'pole, post', could refer to a signpost, a boundary marker, a maypole or poss. an ancient totemistic pole. *Y Polyn* 'the pole' also occurs as the name of a public house and restaurant in Capel Dewi, Carms. once occupied *c.* 1970s by Iori Williams, father to Ronnie Williams of Ryan and Ronnie fame.

Gwern, pawl; poss. 'the pole alder swamp'

Heol-Las see Tircoedmeibionrhys   SN 955096
Farm

Heol-lâs 1991 OSPF1108; Heol-Las 1905 HPP 12; 1841 Census D20. Heol Las 1841-71 Census; Heol Lase 1797, 69 PR/PNDH; Tir pant yr Heol 1840 TM & TAS; Rheol 1830 OS map; Tyr Heol 1819 BFE; Yr Heol c1812 HPP 63; Ty Hir 2014.

Heol-las is the generic name for the location of three buildings alongside today's A4059 road that links Penderyn with the town of Brecon. One of the other buildings is called *Ty Hir* 'long house'. The site has also been known as *Tir Pant yr Heol, Rheol, Ty'r Heol* and *Yr Heol*. It was previously known as *Tirplantmeibionrhys* and *Tirmeibionrhys*, see below.

1841 TAS Tir pant yr Heol (94 acres):
Landowner Morgan Morgan Esq. Occupier Rees Price
761. Parsons Mead 762. do 763. Wain dan tir vol (sic for 'foel') (meadow below 'Tir Vole' land) 764. do 766. Cottage Garden &c 766a. Heol (road) 767. do 768. Waun cae Gwailod (bottom field meadow) 769. Cae Gwaelod Mawr (big bottom field) 770. Cae Ysgubor (barn field) 771. Homestead 772. Cae Llewellyn (Llewellyn's

field) 773. Pencae Mawr (big top field) 774. Coedcae (grazing enclosure) 775. Cae Newydd (new field) 776. do 777. Cae bach (small field) 778. Cae Carreg (stone field) 779. do ffynnon Ucha (upper well stone field) 780. Wern (alder wood) 781. Pant ryen (?yr huan; ?sunny hollow) 782. Cae Ffynnon Isha (lower well field) 783. Cae Newydd (new field) 784. Worlod (Meadow) 785. Do; 786. Waun Goch (red meadow)

The *heol* element refers to the main Penderyn to Brecon road which passes alongside these properties. The upkeep of the old road, which ran from Penderyn church was the responsibility of the Parish until the Turnpike Trust became operational from 1813. Tolls were taken at the Turnpike Gate positioned just south of Ynyswenddor and north of the Lamb Inn (see Gate above). The early road would have been a grassy-green, primitive trackway, with parallel brown lines marked by carriage and cart usage. The predominantly green road colour is reflected in the *Heol-las* name, 'green road'. *Glas* is used for 'green' in Welsh when it refers to vegetation, or venues that harbour vegetation, otherwise it translates as 'blue', eg. *brynglas* 'green hill', *erw-las* 'green acre', *glaswellt* 'green grass', but *awyr las* is 'blue sky', *llyfrau gleision* 'blue books', *het las* 'blue hat etc. *Tir pant yr heol* is 'land of the sunken road', while *Ty'r Heol* is 'the roadhouse'. A truncated *Rheol* and a more grammatically correct *Yr Heol* both mean 'the road'. The local dialect pronunciation was *ewl lâs* (RMR).

Heol, glas; 'green road'

Heol y Cyrff   SN 945085
Road
Heol y cyrff 1905 HPP p80;

Dewi Cynon relates in 1905, that this was the name given locally to the road leading to and from the church. "The Main Road. – The old road went from Hirwaun to Brecon, past the church, turning upwards past yr Eithyn at the bottom of Pontbren village. Having passed the church, it proceeded downwards over 'Heol y Cyrff', and upwards as does the present main road." (HPP p. 80 trans.)

That description matches that of today's Church Road. This was the main road until the bottom turnpike road (today's A4059) between Hirwain and Brecon was constructed *c*. 1820. It was probably called *Heol y cyrff* 'the coprses' road' as this was the route that funerals followed to Penderyn church and churchyard.

Heol, y, cyrff; 'the corpses' road'

Heol y Moch

Old Road

Heol-y-moch 1776 BFE (Tir Pen-y-Cae, C43 Pen-y-cae Map);
Heol y Moch is the lost name of an old road that linked Penycae and Nantyderi to Nant Melin, passing by today's Coedymoch and Llwynymoch/Llwyncoch.

The 1776 Briton Ferry Estate Schedules referring to Map no. 43 locate "The Road from Dery House to Heol y Moch". Ruins of Dery House are shown on the map.

Deri 'oak trees' are the same woods that Nant-y-deri stream flowed through and were eponymous with Nant-y-Deri farm. The 1776 map names Heol-y-moch, showing it passing below a lost Escar-y Vedwan (birch tree ridge) in the direction of Nant Melin Uchaf.
Heol-y-moch was probably so called, as it was the road used for driving pigs from their habitat to market or to neighbouring farms.

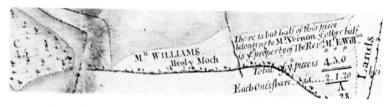

1776 map showing Heol-y-Moch. Courtesy of SM and WGAS (D/D BF/E 164)

Heol, y, moch; 'the pigs' road'/'road (of) the pigs'

Hirwaun Iron Works

SN 962061

Old Furnace, Iron Works

Hirwaun Iron Works 1814   OS Map; Hirwain Iron Works 1813   Maybery Coll.(Sale of); Hirwaun furnace 1802 Maybery Coll.; Hirwayn Furnace Maybery Esqe 1776 Vernon Est. Map.; Herwen Furnace 1775 Maybery Coll.

See Maesyrhydiau (number 132 below) for the BFE Map of 1776 showing Hirwayn Furnace on Maybery's land. The coloured fields are those of the BFE with Maesyrhydia Uchaf (yellow) and Maesyrhydia Ishaf (red). Courtesy of SM and WGAS.

A furnace was built on part of Tir Gwyn Bach farm in 1758 by partners John Wilkins and John Mayberry of Brecon, as well as Thomas Mayberry (John's father) of St. John's in Worcester. In 1760, the iron producing furnace was transferred to the Hirwaun mineral property of the landowning Windsor family, which took its name from the nearby

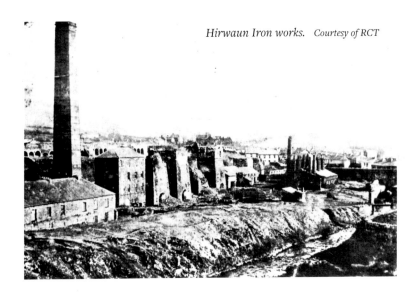

Hirwaun Iron works. Courtesy of RCT

extensive common land known locally as Hirwaun Common and Hirwaun Wrgan (Gwrgan's long moor). The early iron works were known as Hirwaun Furnace (see Herwen Furnace above). For a detailed account see HVHR pp. 48-61 and SEHPP pp. 183-185, by mother and daughter Nansi and Ann Selwood respectively.

Hirwaun, 'long moor'; furnace, ironworks

Hirwaun Village SN 9605

Village

Hirwaun 1991 OSPF; Hirwain Village 1836 GMBGaz.; Hirwain 1762 PPR HVHR 52

Soon after the opening of the ironworks in 1758, cottages were built for workers of the Hirwaun Furnace on the Breconshire banks of the River Cynon and on Coedcae'r felin. Previously the *Hirwaun* name had been associated with the extensive Common also known as *Hirwaun Wrgan*. Before the 1830s, both the industrial and attendant residential districts were called *Hirwaun Iron Works* or simply *Hirwaun Works*, but by 1836 the expanding settlement had acquired *village* status, see above. With the development of the iron works and accompanying growth of the village, the Hirwaun name had spread further afield into the world of business, industry and commerce, as well as religious, educational, political and social circles.

The local Welsh dialect pronunciation in the late 1960s was Hirwan (LME).

Hirwaun Wrgant

Lost Common

Hirwain Wrgan Common 1799 Yates Map; Hirwen Urgan 1536-9 Leland; Hyrweunworgan 1203 Margam 174.

Hirwaun Wrgant was the name of an extensive common located north to south, between part of the southern boundary of the parish of Penderyn and Aberdare village, and east to west, from the River Cynon to the River Neath at the mouth of the Gwrelych stream. Nansi Selwood describes it thus, "The picture we have of Hirwaun Wrgant during the Middle Ages is of a long, sparsely inhabited area of moorland, lying under the precipitous crag of Craig y Llyn and a range of highland curving to the south-east but with dense woods of alder, birch, ash and oak growing along the land bordering the streams which flowed down to the rivers Nedd, Sychryd and Cynon." HVHR 19

A grant of land to Margam Abbey in 1253 (Cartae DLXXIX) included the following bounds (trans. from Latin by RM) " 'from the great pool (Llyn Fawr?) where Wrelech (Gwrelych) rises, proceeding northwards along the river Wrelech into the river Neth (Nedd/Neath), and proceeding eastwards by the river Neth to Redevayn (Rhydfaen), and from Redevayn to the limits/boundaries of Brecon/Brecknock, and thence southwards to the stream Canan (Cynon) and by the stream Canan to Aberdar'

The abbeys of Margam and Llantarnam continually disputed grazing rights on *Hirwaun Wrgant* but a judgement by the Abbot of Citeaux, head of the Cistercian Order, recognised the 1253 grant and gave the rights to Margam.

The elements in *Hirwaun Wrgant* contain Welsh *hir* 'long' and *gwaun* 'high and wet level ground, moorland, heath' GPC, along with personal name *Gwrgant*. *Gwrgant* mutates to *Wrgant* as the personal name follows *gwaun*, a feminine singular noun. The final 't' was dropped through common usage cf. *Hirwain Wrgan* 1799 etc. above. Similarly, early Morcant changed to Morgan and ariant to arian.

Local tradition links the personal name *Gwrgant* to that of *Gwrgant* ab Ithel, father of Iestyn ap *Gwrgant* (fl. 1081-93), the last independent ruler of Glamorgan. However, it must be stated that *Gwrgant* was a popular name in medieval Wales and elsewhere (see G 708, WS 113-14), which included some with links to religious houses. Whether the long moor took its name from a prince's father, Bishop, Abbot, or local notable, will remain unresolved until factual evidence is found.

Gwrgan(t) is also reputedly present in the following place-names:- *Brynwrgan*, Knighton; *Kelli Wrgan*, Llanddarog, Carms; *Cilwrgan*,

Llangurig; *Sarn Wrgan*, near Aberafan. (G 708)
> Hir, gwaun, Gwrgant; 'Gwrgant's long moor'

Jerusalem

Chapel. Private residence

Jerusalem 1857 ds; HPP p108; 1876 YPP; 1905 HPP 108; Capel Jerusalem 1905 OS6".

Capel Jerusalem (Independent) built in 1857 and located on Chapel Road behind the Lamb Hotel is now a private residence. Jerusalem was the Biblical spiritual city of the promised land.

Jerusalem in the early 1900s. Courtesy of SM

Kyffyllos Kynan   Lost
Kyffyllos Kynan 1362 BMW 1043

This lost name is recorded in a document located at the British Museum, dated 1362. *Kynan* is the River Cynon and *Kyffyllos* is Welsh cyffyll 'stock, little stock or trunk of a tree', GPC, with the collective plural suffix *-os* giving *cyffyllos* 'a place abounding in small tree trunks'. The *Kynan* element places it near the river Cynon. GPC does not recognise *cyffylos*, but it does register *cyffyll*, as stated. Today, *boncyff* is used generally for 'tree trunk', rather than the older *cyffyll*.
> Cyffyllos, Cynon; 'small tree trunks (near the river) Cynon'

Lamb Cottages

SN 948089

Lamb Cottages 1867 PR Burials; Lamb Cottage 1866 PR Births.

Lamb Cottages were located on Chapel Road adjacent to the *Lamb Inn*.

Lamb Inn

SN 948089

Public house, district

Lamb Hotel 1972   Vaynor and Penderyn Rural District; Pentref y Lamb 1923 LYH p43; Y Lamb 1923 LYH p35; Ty yr Lamb 1841 Census; Lamb Inn 1841 Census; 1837 GMBG.; 1831 Cambrian; Lamb Inn built 1827 HPP p. 90.

The Lamb is the name of an inn/hotel as well as the name for the upper village of Penderyn. The upper village comprises of *Lamb Road*, Chapel Road, Dôlgynog, Foel Cottages, Beacons Park, Rhoshyfryd, Gelli Neuadd Cottages, as well as the area near the church including the Red Lion, the Rectory, Pantcefnyffordd, Torfoel, Penyreithin and Ysgubor Fawr. At one time, this community included Troedrhiw'rllan, Jeruasalem and Soar chapels plus Y Tafarn Isaf. The old Jerusalem chapel is now a private residence, while Soar chapel is an antiques establishment known as The Penderyn Furniture Co. Penderyn mart used to be located in *the Lamb field* but is now sited opposite the *Lamb Inn* behind Beacons Park. Initially, various local quarries provided employment for many of the inhabitants.

The Lamb Inn with tramroad lines in front c. 1920s
Courtesy of Gareth and Celia Morgan

The Lamb public house built in 1827 by M. Morgans Esq., Bodwigiad (HPP p. 90), made news in 1831 as the holding place for Lewis Lewis, called 'Lewis the Huntsman' in the Cambrian newspaper. He was known as Lewsyn yr Heliwr more accurately translated as 'Lewis the Haulier', related to his work as a haulier between the lime kilns at Penderyn and coal mines at Llwydcoed (DWB). He was captured in Hendrebolon woods and held in the cellar of the *Lamb Inn* for his involvement in the 'Merthyr Riots', which some historians prefer to refer to as the 'Merthyr Uprising'.

The Lamb would be an appropriate name for an inn located in a farming community, especially one close to a sheep mart. The early marts were held in the field behind the inn, before the present site adjacent to Beacons Park was developed. Welsh speakers used to refer to the upper village as *Pentref y Lam*, and the inn as y *Lam* or *Ty'r Lam*. Some of today's Welsh speakers translate the inn name to *Yr Oen*.

1841 TAS Lamb Inn (10 acres):
743. Meadow 744. do 745. do 746. Wood 747. Lamb Inn, Smith's Shop etc. 748. (blank)

Lamb, inn

Lamb Road   SN 947089

Lamb Road 1996 SWVSA.

Lamb Road is the name of the road leading from the Lamb Inn to Dôlgynog.

Llety Rhys   SN 953068

Farm
Lletty-Rhŷs 1991 OSPF1108, 1905 OS6"; Lletty Rhys 1861 Census, 1841 TAS; Lletty Rhys 1851 Census, 1840 TM;

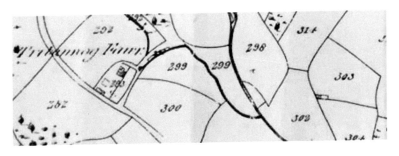

Llety Rhys, field 303, developed with the decline of neighbouring Bwllfa. 1840 TM.

In the 1841 TAS *Lletty Rhys &c.* is recorded under Trebannog Fawr, as an arable field no. 303, of just over two acres. Trebannog Fawr and Melin Trebannog Mill are adjacent to *Llety Rhys*, field no. 303 on the 1840 TM.

The two following lines are part of a verse quoted by Dewi Cynon in HPP.

"Ac yn y Drebanog, a dwedyd i chwi'r gwir,
 Mae Melinydd a morwyn o'r salwa yn y sir."

*(And in the Drebanog to tell you the truth,
the miller and maid are the ugliest in the county).*

'Enw y Melinydd oedd Rhys Hywel Rhys, 1811.' HPP p. 17. He states that Rhys Hywel Rhys was the miller at Trebanog in 1811. Is it possible that the same Rhys Hywel Rhys was the eponymous Rhys of *Llety Rhys*?

Llety, Rhys; 'Rhys's dwelling'

Llwyn Coch   SN 973063
Farm
Llwyncoch 1991 OSPF1108; 1954 OS. Llwncoch (sic) Farm 1939 Vaynor & Penderyn RD;

Llwyncoch was changed from *Llwynymoch* in the 1930s probably for respectability. See Llwyn-y-moch.

Llwyn, coch; 'red bush'. see Llwyn-y-Moch

Llwyn Onn Estate   SN949081
Housing Estate
Llwyn Onn estate 1971-2019 Visited; Llwyn Onn 2002 Map, 1958 Bapt. PR, 1958 (Steve Jones, Deeds).

The early houses of the *Llwyn Onn* estate were opened by the Vaynor and Penderyn District Council in 1958 (Steve Jones deeds). The later houses were built in 1963. The name was taken from that of the former *Llwyn-onn* farm located on Twyn y Glog.

Llwyn, onn; 'ash grove'

Llwyn-onn Reservoir   SO0012
Reservoir
Llwyn-on Reservoir 1991 OSLR, 1952 OS6"; Cronfa Ddŵr Llwyn-onn 1960 AB; Llwyn-on 1905 OS6".

The reservoir commissioned by Cardiff Corporation in 1911 and delayed due to the onset of the first world war, was completed in 1926 and opened in 1927. It took its name from Llwyn-onn farm and cottage located in

Llwyn onn reservoir looking east.   ©*DMJ*

Cwm Taf, parish of Vaynor. The second element *onn* is Welsh 'ash trees' and contains two letter 'ns'. The OS examples only have one 'n'.

Llwyn Onn   SN 958087

Former Farm

Llwyn Onn 1996 SWVSA; Llwynon 1841 Census; Llewynon (sic) 1840 TM; Lwynon house & ffarm 1820 Will of Reynold Davies; Tyr u llwyn onn 1742 Will Thomas Watkin; 1739 Will of Llewelin Meredith; llywn onn (sic) 1700 Will Meredith Llewelin; Tyr llwyn Onne 1626 Tred. Est. (Sr Edw Lewis Kt.).

This former farm and one of the three abodes of local poet Gwilym Harri, was located on a rocky outcrop of thin layered soil on Twyn-y-Glog, between Glyn Perfedd, Garwdyle, The Glogue and Bodwigiad. William Powell opened the *Llwyn Onn* quarry in 1853 HPP 47 resulting in the blasting and crushing of the limestone rock beneath the earlier farmland. The *Llwyn Onn Quarry* is still operational today (2020) but the old farmhouse and most of the farmland has disappeared. See *Cwar Llwyn-onn*.

1841 TAS Llwynnon (66 acres):

Landowner Morgan Morgan Esq. Occupier Catherine Jones

721. Cae Mawr Isha (lower big field) 722. do Cenol (middle big field) 723. Caer freir (breyr? nobleman's field) 724. Cae ffynnon (well field) 725. do Mawr (big field) 726. do Glas (green field) 727. Homestead &c. 728. Co-edcae (grazing enclosure) 729. Gwrlodole (golau mutated and loc. dial; light coloured meadow) 730. Caer As gole (light coloured field near spur asen of land) 731. Plantation 732. Godre r Gwrthgwys (bottom of the Gwrthgwys) 732a. Gwrthgwys (? Gwrth & gwys 'furrow' [difficult ploughing on arable enclosure]) 733. (Blank) 734. Cae bach (small field) 735. do Melyn (small yellow field) 736. Gelligoch (red grove) 737. Wain fawr (large meadow).

Llwyn, onn; 'grove of ash trees'

Llwyn-y-moch

Farm

Llwyn-y-môch 1904 OS25"; Llwin Moch 1841 Census; Llwyn-y-moch 1832 OS1"
Llwynmoch 1813 DTM Jones NLW; Tyr Llhoyn y moch 1691 CL/BRA; Tir Llwyn y
Moch 1656 HVHR 42; Tyr llwyn y moach 1626 Tred. Est. (Sr Ed Lewis Kt).

Llwyn-y-moch farm is now *Llwyncoch* (see above). It is located below
Coed-y-moch and close to the old road known as Heol-y-moch. Coed-y-
moch, Heol-y-moch and *Llwyn-y-moch* suggest that this area was the
historic habitat of pigs, possibly wild pigs. The pigs have vacated their
old habitat, but the names live on, apart of course for the abandoned
Llwyn-y-moch.

1841 TAS Llwyn y Moch (124 acres):
509. Wern Fawr (large alder wetland) 510. Tyle yr Bodin (bodyn; the little man's
hill) 511. Cae Isha (lower field) 512. Morfa Mawr (big wetland) 513. Homestead
&c. 514. Cae Talhon y Ty (field at the upper end of the house) 515. Erw las fawr
(large green acre) 516. Y Cane hir (the long cane fig.) 517. Cae Scybor Isha (lower
barn field) 518. Waun fach (small meadow) 519. Wern ddiris (ddyrys; uncultivated
alder swamp) 520. Cae Scybor Ucha (ysgubor; upper barn field) 521. Caer Wern
Ddiris (Wern Ddiris field) 522. Ban wan y Cae Garrw (banwan is loc. dial
banwaun/panwaun; cotton grass of the uncultivated field) 523. Gotre y Cae Ucha
(bottom of the upper field) 524. Pen y Cae Garrw (top of the uncultivated field)
525. Y Waun (the moorland) 526. do

Llwyn-y-moch was changed to Llwyn-coch in the early 1950s probably
for supposed respectability.

Llwyn, y, moch; 'the pigs' bush'

Llygad Cynon

River source

Llygad Cynon 1991 OSPF1108;1905 OS6"; HPP p76; Llygad Kynon c1700 (1584)
Paroch.

Llygad Cynon is the name for the source of the River Cynon. Llygad is
Welsh for English 'eye' and is often used for the source of a river or
stream cf. Llygad Llwchwr, Llygad Hepste fechan etc. Although Llygad
Cynon is literally 'Cynon's eye', it translates as the 'source' of the Cynon.
   The actual 'source' is a large 45ft. pool probably fed by the
subterranean waters of the upper valley's terminally submerged Cadlan
brook. Dewi Cynon (HPP p76) suggests that the pool is supplied by the
waters of the two Pant y Sychbant streams, as well as the brook that
disappears underground behind Pantycynferth farm. He also offers

explanations for the river Cynon's etymology, preferring Welsh cyn 'chief' and a presumed 'on', 'well or river'. For the meaning of Cynon see Afon Cynon above.

Llygad, Cynon; 'Cynon's source'

Machine House SN 958066

Weighing Machine (Removed)

Machine House 1939 VPRD, 1841, 1871, 1901 Census; Weighing Machine 1859, 1858 PR; W.M. 1915 OS6" Map; Tram Road Machine 1861 census; Penderyyn Machine 1881 census; Machine House (Tramway) 1891 census.

The Machine House on the Penderyn tramline. *Courtesy of SM*

The weighing machine was erected on the Aberdare Canal Company's railroad near the Hirwaun Iron Works *c.* 1794 "so that the Iron Works could pay the toll to the Aberdare Canal Company" SM. The 1841 census has the *Machine House* located between Coke Yard House and the Pandy. In 1850 the weighing machine was moved further along the tramroad to make way for the Vale of Neath railway, HVHR 55. The 1861 census places the Tram Road Machine between Gelly fach and Bryngolwg near to Gelly Benuchel.

Machine, house

Maen Brych, Y SO 003077

Boundary stone

Maen Brych 2015 RCAHMW, 1905 HPP pp 11 & 79; Maen Melin 1905 OS6", 1886 OS25";

"The 'maen' stands at the meeting of Mynydd Hendre Beili, Tynycoedcae and Penmoelallt – a little to the north of the house at the crossroads. The parishes of Merthyr, Aberdare and Penderyn meet at the 'maen'." HPP p. 11. (trans.) . The stone has also been called Maen Melin translated as Millstone (PNDH 7.69). The above photograph was taken in 2015. Access was gained via the Gas Tanks road behind the Residential Care Home, previously The Baverstock's Hotel and the earlier site of the Dynevor Arms. The large speckled stone marks the boundaries of the three parishes of Penderyn, Aberdare and Merthyr Tudful.

Y Maen Brych 2015. © DMJ

Y, maen, brych; 'the speckled stone'

Maescynon
SN 965057

Housing Estate

Maescynon 1991 OSPF1108, 1962 OS6"; Maes Gynon 1951 OS1"

Vaynor and Penderyn Rural District Council started developing the *Maescynon* Housing Estate in 1936, followed by an extension at the end of WW2 (HVHR pp156 & 160). It appears that the estate was built on Cefndon farm fields, numbered and named 411, Cefndon Mawr and 414, Worlod on the 1840 Tithe Map and 1841 TAS. The TAS Cefndon Mawr name would have been too similar to the farm name to have been used as the estate name. The estate was called Maescynon as the field was within a stone's throw of the river Cynon.

Maes, Cynon; 'Cynon field'

Maesrhydiau
SN 965065

Farm(s), Corn Mill, Fulling Mill, Ironworks Houses

Maesyrhydiau 1991 OSPF; Maesyrhydiau Farm 1911 Census; Maes y Rhydia 1840 TM; Maesyrhydie 1819 HPP p118; Maes y rittie ysha 1807 Will Thomas Rees; Maes y Ridia corn mill 1802 Maybery Coll.; New house Rhydiau 1781 PR; Maes-y-Rydia and Tucking Mill 1776 BFE Schedules; Maes-y-Rydia isha 1776 BFE Schedules; Maes-Y-Rhydia Uchaf 1776 BFE map; Maes-Y-Rhydia Ishaf 1776 BFE map;Maes y Rhydia Ucha and the Tucking Mill 1730 CL; Maes y Rudia 1705 BFE; Tur Maes y

Rhidie 1665 HVHR 42; Tyr maes yr hidie 1626 Tred. Est. (Richard Games gent.)

The earliest recorded *Tyr maes yr hidie* 1626, is an attempt at writing *Tir Maes y Rhidiau*, with the final element *rhidiau* represented by the vernacular *rhidie*. The owner was Richard Games Gent., a noted landowner and husband of Mary Games, nee Prichard, of Bodwigiad. In 1665 the Lord of the Manor of Brecon, Thomas Morgan of Tredegar, claimed 7 shillings as Cymhortha (chief rent) for *Tir Maes y Rhidie*. By 1705 *Maes y Rudia* and all the Games' lands had become part of the BFE through the marriage of Elizabeth, Richard and Mary Games's granddaughter, to Thomas, Bussy Mansel's son. The 1776 BFE Map below, shows that the farm had been divided into *Maes-y-rhydia Uchaf* and *Maes-y-rhydia Ishaf* ('higher' and 'lower' respectively).

The establishment of the Hirwaun Ironworks on neighbouring Tir Gwyn Bach lands in 1758 affected *Maes-y-rhydiau*. Parts of *Maes-y-rhydiau Uchaf* and *Isaf* lands were used for stables and cottages for workers at the Ironworks. The depleted Maesyrhydiau Uchaf and Isaf farms were amalgamated *c.* 1813 (SEHPP p. 173);

There were also two mills at *Maes-y-rhydiau*, one corn grist mill or melin, the other a fulling mill or pandy. See *Melin-y-rhidiau* and *Y Pandy* below.

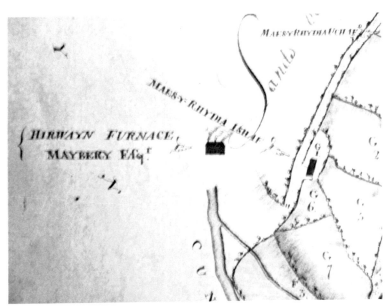

Part of the Briton Ferry Estate Map of 1776   *Courtesy of SM and WGAS (D/D BF/E 164)*

By 1924, *Maes-y-rhidiau* farm became the property of the tenant at that time, and today's comparatively small farm can be seen at the end of Penyard Road, equidistant between Tirgwynbach and Llwyncoch.

1841 TAS Maes y Rhydia (54 acres):
Landowner Morgan Morgan Esq. Occupier William Crawshay Esq.
382. Cottages &c 383. do & Gardens 384. Caer Odyn (kiln field) 385. Cottages & Gardens 386. Cae Tai bach (small houses' field) 387. Waun bant (yonder meadow) 388. do 389. Cae Ton Main Isha (lower narrow leyland field) 390. do Ucha (upper narrow leyland field) 391. Erwr Eiren (plum tree acre) 391a. Old road 392. Erwr Eiren (plum tree acre) 393. Caer Ucha (upper field) 424. Mill Cottage &c. 425. Waste 426. do 427. Groft (small field) 428. Gwaun Pwll hafan Sicca (meadow of ?soap suds pool haven) 429. Ynis Ucha (upper river meadow) 430. Ynis Genol (middle river meadow) 431. Waste 432. do 433. do 434. Ynis Isha (lower river meadow) 435. Wood 436. Cae Pentwyn (hilltop field) 437. Waun Goch (red meadow)

1776 (D/D BF/E 164):
Maes-y-Rhydia & the Tucking Mill:
1. House, Garden and the Tucking Mill 2. Ynis y Pandy (Pandy river meadow) 3. Croft y Pandy (Pandy small field) 4. Cae uchlaw'r ty (field above the house) 5. Cae cenol (middle field) 6. Cae uchaf (upper field) 7. Coedcae ishaf (lower grazing enclosure) 8. Ditto uchaf (upper ditto) 9. The Brake in do 10. Wayn Bant (far away meadow) 11. (blank) 12. The piece inclosed (sic) out of do 13. Acre and half near Cae Pen y Dery 14. The little spot in Mr. Watkins' field.

Maes-y-Rhydia Isha:
1. House & Garden etc. 2. Cae cenol (middle field) 3. Wern in do fd (wet ground in do) 4. Cae uchaf (upper field) 5. Cae'r Berllan (the orchard field) 6. Morva bach (little marshland) 7. Erw'r Eirin (plum tree acre) 8. Tree Quarter (three quarters) 9. The Brake in do 10. The meadow 11. The narrow strip in Mr Mayberry's land 12. Cae Ton Main uchaf (upper narrow leyland field) 13. Do ishaf (lower do).

"Maes y rhidiau means 'the field of the fords'," HVHR p. 40. Nansi Selwood located these fords for animals and humans on the River Cynon "before the coming of industry necessitated the building of bridges". Ibid. It seems logical to agree that these fords once crossed the River Cynon.
Maes, y, rhydiau; 'field (of) the fords

Mays Crone

Lost

Mays Crone 1362 BMW 3 1043

This is probably maes crwn 'round field', but the location is unknown.

Meddygyn

Lost name

Tyr y Methigin 1691 CL/BRA; Tir y Methygen 1665 HVHR 42; Tyr meddigin 1626 Tred. Est. Sir Edward Lewis Knight; Methegen 1547 HVHR 24.

Methygen, *methigin*, *meddigin* and *methegen* above, are all different orthographies or spellings for today's standardised *meddygyn*, a violet plant known as 'self-heal'. *Tir y Meddygyn* translates as 'land of the violet/self-heal'. *Tir y Methygen* became Cwrt y llacca, and later Court Farm. See Court.

Tir, meddygyn, 'land of the violet (self-heal plant)'

Melin Trebannog

Trebannog (corn) mill

Mill (Disused) 1904 OS25"; Mill & Garden 1844 TS 294 Trebannog Fawr; Trebanog Mill 1892 PR; Trebannog Mill 1841 Census [Miller – Robert Clatsworthy], 1831 PR; Vellin Trebannog 1768 Penpont; the water corn grist mill called Velin Trebannog in Penderin. 1748 Penpont.

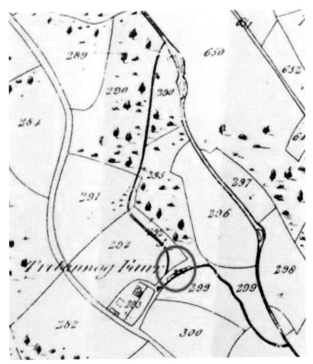

Trebannog Mill (circled) with the mill race (from 290, 291, 292 to 299) TM

This corn mill located on present-day Trebannog Fawr land, was built by William Jones in 1671 (SEHPP p. 55) in competition with the official Pwll Coch mill in Cwm Taf. "It had been built on the banks of the river Cynon, on a tenement called Ynys Llwyfog which was later joined to the farm called Glyn Celli to form Trebannog Fawr and the mill was known as Trebannog Mill." …"The mill was in use until 1899." HVHR 39

See Glyn Celli above and Ynys Llwyfog below.

As stated, the corn mill was called Melin Trebannog (Velin Trebannog in Penderin, 1748 Penpont, see above). It was located adjacent to the later Trebannog Fawr farmhouse shown on the above 1840 Tithe Map. The 1841 census above names Robert Clatsworthy of Somerset as miller. Local rhymester and wit Ifan Bifan from Pontneddfechan, composed a number of verses to him. Here is one to 'yr hen Robyn':

Ni ddylai yr hen Robyn	*That old rascal Robyn*
Gael malu mewn un melin;	*shouldn't grind in any mill;*
Ac aed yn ôl i Wlad yr Hâf,	*Let him return to Somerset*
Mae'n ormod o hen gnafyn.	*Where he can do no ill.*

Gweithiau Barddonol y diweddar Evan Bevan 1899.

Incidentally, miller Robert Clatsworthy did not return to Somerset. He carried on as miller in Trebanog and was buried in Penderyn churchyard on Nov. 18, 1855, aged 65.

Melin Trebannog; Trebannog Mill

Melin y Pwll Coch circa SO 0013
Lost Mill

Pwll Coch Mill in Penyderrin 1799 Mayberry NLW; Lease of Pwllcoch Mill 1701 Mayberry SEHPP; Pooll koch c1700 Penpont (lease by Penry Williams to Jenkin Price); Pwllcocke Mill 1651 Penpont; Pwllcough Mill 1651 HMB Vol 1pp.5-9; Pwllcock Mill 1651 (occupation of Mrs Games) HMB Vol.1 pp 5-9; Pwllcoch Mill 1651 HMB Vol 1; Mellin y Pwll Coch 1597 Exchequer Proceedings Concerning Wales 36.

The earliest recorded form is in the 39th year of the reign of Queen Elizabeth 1 (1597) as *Mellin y Pwll Coch*, where it states that all the mills in the Lordship of Brecon were granted to William Aubrey, Mary Herbert and Edward Herbert. Penderyn is written as Pen---dyrrie and its complainant residents are named William Llewelyn and John David.

By 1651, *Pwll Coch Mill* (in various orthographies) in the parish of Penderyn was named as one of the seven Forest Mills of the County of

Brecknock. Cwm Taf corn mill was the official parish mill, controlled and managed in the mid. 17th cent. by the Games family of Bodwigiad. By 1714 the mill had changed from a corn grist mill to a tucking mill (SEHPP p106), and later, by the 19th cent., to a woollen factory (Vaynor p167). The mill's hamlet was appropriately named Ynysyfelin (see below).

'*Pwll Coch*' (red pool) is probably named after a lost submerged pool on the Taf Fawr river. This part of the river was flooded in 1914 to form the Llwyn-onn Reservoir which was opened in 1926.

Melin, y, pwll, coch; 'the red pool mill'

Melin y Rhydiau   SN 963056

Corn Mill

Melin y Rhydia 1857 Sale HVHR 41; Rhydia Mill (Grist mill)1829 Cambrian; Rhidia Mill c1813 HVHR 40; Maes y Ridia corn mill 1802 Maybery Coll.; Melin Rhydiau 1797 Edward Price Will HVHR p40; Velin Rhydiau 1789 PR; Rydia Mill 1776 BFE; Rhydia Mill 1776 BFE; Rhydiau Mill 1738 Watcyn Prys Lease HVHR p40.

This corn mill was located at Maes-y-Rhydiau,

"in 1677 this mill was bought by Edward Games of Llanelly"; HVHR p. 40. (Llanelly Gwent not Llanelli Carms.; Games was formerly of Bodwigiad). This was the corn grist mill at Maes-y-rhydiau, not to be confused with the fulling mill (Y Pandy). The 1776 BFE map and schedules labelled H1. is 'The ground plot of the mill'; it also states, 'There is no land belonging to this tenement'. This endorses the fact that the corn mill land had already been used to provide cottages and homes for iron workers. The mill was working in 1800, but by 1813, the mill had ceased to operate, for in the ironworks sale catalogue of that year it states that Rhydia Mill was "formerly a mill" (HVHR p41)

The land known as *Coedcae'r felin*, as well as *Heol y felin* (Mill Street) and *Parc Cae'r Felin* (Cae Felin Park) also refer to the old mill at *Melinyrhydiau*. Vaynor and Penderyn Rural District Council bought *Coedcae'r felin* and land south of Merthyr Road in 1934 in order to demolish the old iron works cottages and those 'Under the Arch'. Part of Merthyr Road was formerly called *Heol-y-Felin* (the mill road) and the old millstones now lie at the entrance of Hirwaun Library. HVHR p. 41.

Y *rhydiau* 'the fords', were the old fords that crossed the Cynon at *Maesyrhydiau*. Their locations were probably close to the later bridges of that immediate area.

Melin, y, rhydiau; 'mill of the fords'

Moel Penderyn

Hilltop

Moel Penderyn 1991 OS Landranger 160; 1953 OS6"; Y Foel 1905 HPP p19; The Vole local parlance 1971 – 2020; Foel Penderyn 1918, 1904 OS Maps; Pender-foel 1888 OS; Penderyn foel 1884 OS; The Vole, 50 acres at Pant-y-Cofnerth 1776 BFE.

Moel Penderyn is the name of a bird's head shaped hill (see Penderyn above), some 371 metres above sea level, located west of Penderyn church and south-west of Torfoel farm. The two elements are *Penderyn* and *moel*. Today, *Penderyn* defines the location, but earlier, it could have been a descriptive element. *Moel* is indeed a descriptive element, often used in similar highland places, cf. *Moel yr Wyddfa, Moel Hebog, Moelfre,* etc. Although *moel* can mean 'bald, bald-headed, bare', it is also used for '(bare) mountain, (treeless) hill; top of hill or mountain', and it is these latter meanings that apply here.

 Moel, mutates to *foel* when it is preceded by the definite article viz. Y *Foel*. It is pronounced *fôl* in the Gwentian dialect, exactly like the local Welsh pronunciation of the English word *vole*. In fact, it often used to be written as vole, e.g. *The Vole* and *Wayn dan Tor Vole,* (1776 BFE), also *Tor Vole* (1840 TM & 1841 TAS). Modern standardised Welsh spellings of *moel, y foel* and *torfoel* is the norm these days. Cf. *Twyn y foel,* 'the Foel hill' also known as *Twyn yr Eglwys,* the Penderyn church hill.

   Moel, Penderyn; 'Penderyn's (bare) hill'

Mynydd Penmailard

Lost Mountain name

Mynydd Penmailard, Penmailard 1832 OS, 1814 OS; Penmeulart 1905 HPP p19; Pen Mallard Hills 1729 EB-MapSW;

Mynydd Penmailard was the name of a stretch of moorland between Mynydd y Glog and the River Taf Fawr. For mailard, see *Penmailard* below.

 Welsh *mynydd* does not always translate as English 'mountain'. *Mynydd* is applied to any raised ground, whatever its height. Note that elevated ground of no more than 65 meters near Pengelli/Grovesend, Sir Abertawe/Swansea County, is called Mynydd Lliw in Welsh, and Lliw Common in English on OS maps. However, the highest point of *Mynydd Penmailard* does reach 420 metres above sea level, although the recognised height for a mountain is officially 2,000 feet or 609.6 metres.

 By 1840 the mountain or moorland name had changed from *Mynydd Penmailard* to the older, neighbouring Onllwyn, yet *Penmailard* continues in use for other places in the vicinity (see below).

Mynydd, Penmailard; 'Penmailard mountain'

Mynydd y Glog SN 9709

Mountain, moorland

Mynydd-y-glog 1991 OS Landranger 160; Mynydd y Glôg 1923 LYH p42; Mynydd y Glogue 1840 TM, 1829 Cambrian, HPP 86,87; Gloge 1705 BFE;

Mynydd y Glog is located on high moorland east of Onllwyn and Mynydd Penmoelard. Between 1827 and 1850, the ownership and right of common of one thousand acres of "Mynydd y Glogue" or 'Coed cae glog' was disputed in court cases between Morgan Morgan, Esq., of Bodwigiad and other local landlords. The Bodwigiad estate was successful in all cases. See HPP pp. 86-88.

Mynydd y Glog has three elements, *mynydd*, y and *clog*, the latter sometimes written as glogue, to rhyme with English *vogue, rogue* etc. English *glogue* has a very similar pronunciation to Welsh *glog*, the mutated form of *clog*, 'rock, cliff, precipice' (clog2 GPC). The mountain moorland and coedcae, has numerous rocky outcrops and cairns. The western side of *Mynydd y Glog*, bordering on Twyn y Glog is very rocky and precipitous, with the nearby Llwyn Onn Quarry taking advantage of these topographical features.

Mynydd, y, clog; 'the precipice mountain'

Naint circa SN 9807

Lost

Naint 1923 LYH p42; 1773, 1792, 1795 PR Bapt.; Y Naint 1919 LC essay.

Jenkin Howell locates the *Naint* some two miles from Llygad Cynon towards Merthyr Tydfil at the site of the Aberdare water works (*Y Geninen*, July 1900 p. 214). Lewis Davies (LYH p. 42) also locates y *Naint* near Penmeilart moors. This area is grooved and channelled with small brooklets, and streams.

Naint is the old plural of *nant* 'stream' (modern day *nentydd*). The streams included would be *Nant Hir, Nant Melyn/Nant Moel* along with their feeder springs and streamlets.

Naint; 'streams'

Nant Cadlan SN 9509

Stream

Nant Cadlan 1991 OS Pathfinder 1109;

See Cadlan.

Nant Ceunant Du

SN 9510

Stream

Nant Ceunant Du 1905 OS6"; 1952 OS6"; Pont y Canti Bridge, 2011, PPS;

There is also a *Pont Ceunant Du* (bridge) close to the confluence of *Nant Ceunant du* and Nant Cadlan. This bridge is referred to as "Pont y Canti Bridge on Cadlan road" in PPS p4. It seems that *Ceunant Du* has been truncated to *Canti* in local parlance. The stream takes its name from the *ceunant* (deep dingle) through which it flows. The colour black is symbolically dark. This is Gwern Nant Ddu in PNDH 7.59.

Ceunant, du; 'dark, deep dingle'

Nant Ffrwd

SO 0208

Stream

Nant Ffrwd 1920 OS6", 1905 HPP p79; Nant y Frood 1759 PM map;

"Nantyffrwd rises on the other side of the mountain, above Cwm Waun Newydd, and flows through Cwm y Ffrwd, entering the Taf at Pontycapel. There are beautiful waterfalls on its rough bed. Cwm y Ffrwd is regarded as a very romantic place." HPP 79 trans. See *Ffrwd* etc.

Nant Ffynnon Elin

SN 9812

Streamlet

Nant Ffynnonelin 1988 OSPF1084; Nant Ffynnon-Elin 1905 OS6"; Nant Ffynnon-Ellen 1884 OS6"

Nant Ffynnonelin is the name of a small stream that rises on the lower slopes of Pant y Gadair and flows into Garnant fach before the latter enters Coed Taf Fawr.

The first two elements are nant and ffynnon, but the final element is more problematic. *Nant* is Welsh 'stream' (although originally 'valley, ravine, glen') and *ffynnon* 'well', derived from Latin *fontana*. The final element *Elin* looks very much like the Welsh pers. fem. name *Elin*, but the earlier Ellen (1884) casts doubt on this. It may be the fem. pers. name Ellen, Cymricised as Elin, but earlier forms are needed.

Nant, ffynnon, Elin/Ellen?; 'stream of Elin/Ellen's well'

Nant Gwina

SN 9607

Lost stream name

Cwm Nant Gwine 1841 TAS Pen y Cae 638; Cwm Nant Gwina 1776 BFE Sch. (Tir Pen-y-Cae 36.); Coed cae Cwm Gwina 1776 BFE Sch, (Nant y Dery 19); Nant Cwmin Gwina 1776 BFE Map;

Nant Gwina flowed through *Cwm Gwina* between Tir Pen y Cae, no. 36 and Nant y Dery no, 19 on the BFE 1776 Map. The name was still in use as *Cwm Nant Gwine* in 1841 TAS but is named Nant Bwllfa on the 1991 OSPF 1108 map. (see Pen-y-Cae field names).

The above name contains two elements *nant* 'stream, brook' and *gwina*, probably the local dialect form of *gwinau* as seen in other stream-names in Wales including *Nant Gwinau*, which flows into Llwyn-onn Reservoir on the Vaynor parish side. GPC has *gwinau* the plural of *gwin* 'wine', as 'bay, reddish brown, auburn' (of hair, eyebrows, etc.)', also siwgr *gwinau* "brown sugar". *Gwinau* reflects the bed or water colour of the various *Nant Gwinau* streams of Wales. On the other hand, GC in HEALlE p. 168 notes that two place-name etymologists relate *Gwynai* to Welsh *gwyn* 'white'. That example of *Gwynai* however, has *gwyn* as an element while the above examples of *Gwina* contain *gwin*. IW in Pedair Keinc y Mabinogi p. 335, translates *gwineu* of gwas *gwineu* 'with reddish brown hair'.

Nant, gwinau; 'light brown stream'

Nant Hir   SN 9803

Stream

Nant Hir   1991 OS Landranger 160; 1920 OS25"; Nanthir PM map 1749; y Nant hire 1666 CR; stream called nant hire 1546 Penpont.

Dewi Cynon calls this stream "Nantllechrhaiadr, neu Nant-hir", (HPP p. 79). Nantllechrhaiadr 'stone waterfall stream' is otherwise not evidenced, although BFE 1776 has Llechryd House in ruins on Blaen Nanthir land and records Blaen Nant y Llecha Hills as the source of nearby Nant Melin. *Llech* (stone) or pl. *llechau* is an element in *Llechryd House, Nantllechrhaidr* and *Nant y Llecha Hills*.

Nant Hir forms part of the parish boundary, from its source near Maen Brych to its confluence with the Cynon near Gamlyn farm, separating Penderyn and Aberdare parishes. The stream gives its name to *Nant Hir Reservoir* as well as the residence called *Blaen Nant Hir. Nant Hir* has two elements, *nant* 'stream' and *hir* 'long'.

Nant, hir; 'long stream'

Nant Iorath   SO 0207

Lost stream-name

Cwm Nant Iorath 1840 TM&S no. 1021 Ffrwyd sic Isha;

Small stream rising north-east of Ffrwd Isaf, flowing through *Cwm Nant Iorath* and entering Nant Ffrwd east of Ffrwd Isaf farmhouse, before Nant

Ffrwd's confluence with Taf Fawr. *Iorath* is a form of the personal name *Iorwerth*.

Nant, Iorath; 'Iorwerth's stream'

Nant Maden

SN 9610

Stream, farm

Nant Maden 1991 OS Landranger 160;1905 HPP 18;1879 ERB;1851 Cens.;1750 HPP 67; Nant-maden 1905 OS6; Tirnant y Maden 1840 TM.

It appears that Nant y Spyddaden (see below) changed to *Nant y Maden* during the 1840s. The alteration occurred during the occupation of Charles Meredith. His will written in 1855 has Nant y Spaddadan while the 1841 Census return has Charles Meredith at Nant ysbyddan, yet the 1841 TAS has Charles Meredith at *Tirnant y Maden*. The change from Nant y Sbyddaden to *Nant y Maden* is not a natural philological progression. The literary connection between Welsh Sbyddaden and *Maden* is the rhyme. *Sbyddaden* is an abbreviation of Welsh *Ysbyddaden* 'whitethorn, thorn bush' GPC. *Maden, madyn, madryn* is Welsh for 'fox, reynard'. Coincidentally or perhaps significantly, field 995 on the TAS is Cae Llwynog 'fox field', (rather than llwyn-og bushy). *Madyn* is also a pet form of Madog (WS 157) but it is unlikely that the change is linked to that personal name. *Maden* is the fem. form of *madyn*. Whether this is deliberate to give Eng. 'vixen' or merely accidental in order to rhyme with the earlier *sbyddaden* is difficult to determine.

The local dialect form sbyddaden/spyddaden (for ysbyddaden) may well have been associated with Welsh sbyddadu 'to castrate' making it likely that Tir Nant y sbyddaden was changed to a rhyming *Tir Nant y Maden* for respectability. Cf. Llwyn Coch 'red bush' for the earlier Llwyn (y) Moch '(the) pigs' bush'.

1841 TAS Tirnant y Maden (85 acres):
Landowner Rev. Richard Davies and William Payne. Occupier Charles Meredith 995. Cae Llwynnog (fox field) 996. Tir Quarter Erw (three quarter acre) 997. Trawsdir (cross/diagomal land) 998. Hirdir (long land) 999. do (long land) 1000. Coed cae (grazing enclosure) 1001. Cae Ysgubor (barn field) 1002. Cae dych laing Ty (field above the house) 1003. Homestead & Gardens 1004. Coed cae bach (small grazing enclosure) 1005. Road & Waste 1006. Waun (meadow)

Nant, madyn/maden; 'stream (of the) fox/vixen"

Nant Melyn

SN 9807

Stream, farm names

Nantmelyn 1991 OS Pathfinder 1109; Nant Melyn 1904 OS25"; Nant-melyn-isaf

1904 OS25"; Tir Nant Melyn 1781 Will of Watkyn Phillips NLW; Tir Nant Melyn Ycha 1705 BFE; Tir Nant Melyn Isha 1705 BFE.

Nant Melyn and Nant Moel streams rise on Mynydd y Glog and flow into Nant Moel Reservoir. The 1776 BFE map names the place as Blaen Nant Llecha Hill. *Nant Melyn* alone exits the Aberdare Waterworks dam to flow past Nant-melyn-isaf and *Nant-moel-isaf* farms, before joining Nant Hir at Croesbychan.

Nant-melyn-uchaf was submerged under the waters of Nant Moel Reservoir/Cronfa Nantmoel during its construction between 1893 and 1899 (HPP 50). The elements are *nant* 'stream' and *melyn* 'yellow', with the latter probably referring to the colour of the stream's terrain, rather than the colour of its water. *Uchaf* (upper) and *isaf* (lower) are distinguishing farm-name elements. *Nant Melyn* is also the name of a tributary of the Dare stream in Cwmdare.

1841 TAS Nant Melyn Uchaf (47 acres):
Landowner Morgan Morgan Esq. Occupier Evan Morgan
604. Cae bach (small field) 605. 4 Acres 606. Waun Goch (red meadow) 607. Cae bach (small field) 608. Defetting fach (small pared turf) 609. Waun fawr (big meadow) 610. Coed cae Garw (uncultivated grazing en-closure) 611. Cae do (gazing enclosure field) 612. do Crwm (round field) 613. do Main (narrow field) 614. Coed cae bach (small grazing enclosure) 615. do Pella (furthest grazing enclosure) 616. Croften fach (little small field) 617. Cae draw Nant (stream's yonder field) 618. Cae bach (small field) 619. do Glas (green field) 620. Homestad &c. 621. Croft (small field)

1776 (D/D BF/E 164) Nant Melin Ucha:
I1. Farm House and the Waste Grd abt it 2. Croft (small field) 3. The Brake in Do 4. Cae Draw'r Nant (field beyond the stream) 5. (blank) 6. Cae glace (glas; green field) 7. (blank) 8. (blank) 9. Cae buchan (bychan; small field) 10. (blank) 11. The four acres 12. Cae bach (small field) 13. Wayn fawr (big meadow) 14. Coed Cae garw (uncultivated grazing enclosure) 15. (blank) 16. Cae Crwn (round field) 17. Devetting (difeting; pared turf) 18. (blank) 19. Croftan fach (small little field) 20. Coed cae bach (small grazing enclosure).

Nant-melyn-isaf farm is shown as **Nantmelyn** on the 1991 OSPF 1108 map SN981069.

1841 TAS Nant Melyn Isha (72 acres):
Landowner Earl of Jersey Occupier Lewis Lewis
573a. Wain Isha (lower meadow) 574. Erw ddu (black acre) 575. Wood 576. Bach (small (field)) 577. (blank) 578. Caer Bryn (the hill field) 579. Lodge 580.Cae yr Ysgubor & Building (the barn field) 581. (blank) 82. Byarth (buarth; farmyard) 583. Homestead &c. 584. Cae Pentwyn (hilltop field) 585. Pant Heol (road dingle)

586. (blank) 587. Bach (small) 588. Cae Preseb Mawr (big manger field) 589. Cae Pant Heol (road dingle field) 590. Wain Ucha (upper meadow) 591. Road

1776 (D/D BF/E 164) Nant Melin Isha:

K1. House Garden & the Waste abt it 2. Cae Uchlaw'r ty (field above the house) 3. The Brake in Do. 4. Ynis fach (small river meadow) 5. The Road 6. Cae Pant 'r heol (road dingle field) 7. Cae Pirsilla (persilla; ?parsley field) 8. Do bach (small do) 9. Wayn fach (small meadow) 10. Cae scibor (barn field) 11. Ynis fach in the Coed cae (little river meadow in the grazing enclosure) 12. Coed cae (grazing enclosure) 13. Cae'r Hwch (the sow's field) 14. Do bach (small do) 15. Field by do 16. Wayn uchaf (upper meadow) 17. Wayn ishaf (lower meadow) 18. Erw Dû (black acre).

Nant, melyn; 'yellow stream'

Nant Moel   SN 9807
Stream

Nant Moel 1904 OS25", 1893 AT; Nant Mole 1841 Census D20; Nantymole 1831 Bond David Lewis of, NLW; Tir Nant Moile 1781 Will of Watkyn Phillips NLW; Nant moyll Will of Roger Symond 1662 NA.

Both *Nant Moel* and Nant Melyn rise together on the hill named in Nant Melyn above, before joining together near Nant Melyn Uchaf farm, which was later submerged. *Nant Moel* contains two elements viz. *nant* and *moel*. *Nant* is a 'stream' while *moel* 'bare, bare hill', describes the stream's terrain.

Nant, moel; 'stream (of the) bare hill'

Nant Moel Farm   SN 988066
Farm

Nant Moel Farm 1991 OSPF map; Nant-moel-isaf 1904 OS25"; Nant Meol sic Isha 1841 TAS; Tir y Nant moyll 1662 Will of Roger Symond.

Nant Moel Farm was known earlier as *Tir y Nant moyll* (Tir y Nant Moel), later divided into *Nant Moel Uchaf* and *Nant Moel Isaf*. The *Nant Moel* stream gave its name to *Tir Nant Moel farm*. It is actually located on the banks of present-day Nant Melyn. Both *Nant Moel* and Nant Melyn streams enter *Nant Moel Reservoir*, but the outflowing stream is named Nant Melyn.

1841 TAS Nant-meol(sic)-isha (128 acres):

Landowner Morgan Morgan Esq. Occupier Thomas Rosser
527. Waun fawr (large meadow) 528. Coed Cae (grazing enclosure) 529. Wood 530. Cae bach (small field) 531. do 532. Cae Gwy (?egg shaped field. Cf. map) (533. do du (black field) 534. do pant (dingle field) 535. Barn Road & Waste 536. Wood 537. Cae Ysgubor (barn field) 538. do Melyn (yellow field) 539. Waun (meadow)

540. do fach (small meadow) 541. Homestead &c. 542. Caer Garreg (the stone field) 543. Caer Coed (the wood field) 544. Cae bach (small field) 545. do Mawr (big field) 546. do Coed Isha (lower wood field) 547. Wood

Nant, moel; 'stream (on the) bare hill'

Nant Moel Reservoir

SN 9807

Reservoir

Nant Moel Resr 1991 OS Pathfinder 1109; 1974 OS First Series; Nant Moel Reservoir 1904 OS25"; (Aberdare & District Council Water Works);
The following line from the Aberdare Times newspaper names both of the feeder streams for this reservoir. The OS maps of the time only name Nant Melyn.

Nant Moel Reservoir 2017. © *DMJ*

"a new storage reservoir be provided near the junction of Nant Moel and Nant Melyn streams". Aberdare Times, 30/9/1893. The Aberdare Water Works chose *Nant y Moel* as the reservoir's name, as it is the name of one of the feeder streams, as well as the name of nearby *Nant Moel Uchaf* farm. As previously stated, the reservoir's waters covered *Nant Melin Uchaf* farm and land. The reservoir's capacity was estimated at 40 million gallons.

Nant Moel Uchaf
SN 9807
Farm

Nant-moel Uchaf 1991 OSPF 1108; Nant Mole Uchaf 1841 Census D20; Nant Moel Ucha 1841 TAS:

Much of this farm's land was submerged under the reservoir, along with most of Nant Melyn Uchaf. This accounted for the demise of both farms leaving nothing but the ruins of Nant Moel Uchaf farm.

1841 TAS Nant Moel Ucha(87 acres):
Landowner Morgan Morgan Esq. Occupier Evan Jones
622. Cae Erwdyr (acreland field) 623. Cae Lloi (calves' field) 624. Homestead Road &c. 625. Cae Carreg (stone field) 626. Coed Cae (grazing enclosure) 627. Cae Shany (Shani's field) 628. Waun fawr (big meadow) 629. Cae Bryn (hill field) 630. Coedcae fry (high grazing enclosure).
Nantmoel, uchaf; 'upper Nantmoel'

Nant Sychbant
SO 0110
Stream

Nant Sychbant 1952 OS6"; 1919 OS25"; 1904 OS25"; Sych-pant 1830 OS First Series; Nant y Sychbant 1749 PMoel. map;

Nant Sychbant rises on the eastern slopes of Pant Sychbant flowing into Taf Fawr just north of Coed Penmailard. The elements are nant 'stream', sych 'dry' and pant 'dingle, hollow', giving 'stream (of the) dry hollow' or 'Sychbant stream'. The porous nature of the rocky terrain would account for the dry stream. Cf. Afon Hebste, Sychryd. The 1749 form has the def. article, 'the Sychbant stream'.
Nant, sychbant; 'Sychbant stream'

Nant y Bwllfa
Stream

Nant y Bwllfa 1991 OSPF 1108; 1904 OS25"; 1884 6";

Nant y Bwllfa rises below Nant-y-deri farm and flows past Bwllfa farm into the River Cynon. The early name for this stream before it joined Nant-y-Deri was Nant Gwina (see above). It takes its name from Bwllfa farm through which it flows (see Bwllfa above). Dewi Cynon wrote (trans.) :

Nant y Bwllfa.-
This is made up of three small streams with their sources at Waunderi and Penderi. It is a strong stream with heavy floods, and it flows into the River Cynon near the Gelli. HPP 79.

Nant, y, Bwllfa' 'the Bwllfa stream'

Nant y Deri

Stream, lost farm

Nant y Deri 1991 OSPF 1108 (stream); Nant-y-Deri 1904 OS25" (stream); Nant-y-deri 1904 OS25" (small-holding); Nant-y-deri (Ruins) 1884 OS6"; Nantyderi 1905 AL; 1869 Birm.Post; Nant y Dery 1841 Census D20; 1776 BFE; 1738 CL/BRA; Nant y Deri 1705 BFE.

Nant y Deri is the name of a stream and former smallholding. The farm took its name from the stream that flowed past the farmhouse. The stream rises in Waunderi (oak meadow), joining Nant y Bwllfa below the farmhouse ruins. It is called *Nant y Deri* as there was once an abundance of oak trees (deri) on its banks.

1841 TAS Nant y dery (49 acres):
Landowner Morgan Morgan Esq. Occupier John Jones
669. Cae bach (small field) 670. Coed cae Isha (lower grazing meadow) 671. Worlod (gweirglodd; meadow) 672. Homestead &c 673. Cae Lloi Isha (calves' lower field) 674. Cae bach (small field) 675. Cae Lloi Ucha (calves' upper field) 676. Waun (meadow) 677. Cae bach (small field) 678. Cae Ucha (upper field) 679. do 680. (blank) 681. Waun fach (small meadow) 682. 3 Erw Nant y deri (Nant y deri 3 acres) 683. Do (Nant y deri 3 acres) 684. Cae bach (small field) 685. Coed cae (grazing enclosure) 686. Cae Cerrig (stone field) 687. Cenol (middle) 688. Cae bach (small field) 689. Coed cae Isha (lower grazing enclosure)

1776 (D/D BF/E 164) Nant-y-Dery:
D1. The Farm House, Garden & the waste abt it. 2. The Croft (small field) 3,4,5. Crofts inclosed and the Coed cae 6. The Road from the House to the hill 7. Croft west side of do road 8. Coed cae isha (lower coed cae) 9. Do cenol (do middle) 10. Furthest coed cae 11. Wech Erw Nant y Dery (Nant y Dery's six acres. Wech is loc. dial. chwech) 12. Cae pella (furthest field) 13. Cae uchaf (highest field) 14. (blank) 15. The Brake north side of do fd. 16. Cae'r Lloy ishaf (calves' lower field) 17. Ditto uchaf (do upper) 18. Wayn fach (small meadow) 19. Coed cae Cwm Gwina (Cwm Gwina's grazing enclosure) 20. Cae Draw'r Nant (field beyond the

stream) 21. Wood between do and the Brook 22. Five acres on the Great Meadow 23. The piece in Do ie. near Heol y Moch.

Nant, y, deri; 'stream (of) the oak trees'

Nant y Geugarn SN 9915

Stream, former Farm

Nant y geugarn 1988 OSPF 1084; Nant y Gougarn 1905 OS6"; Nantygugarn 1905 HPP 11; Nant y Gygar 1840 TM; Nant y Geygar 1649 Penpont.; Tyr nant y guigar 1626 Tred. Est.; Tir Nant y Geygarr (poss, scribal error for geygarn) 1615 Penpont.

Nant y Geugarn is the name of a stream that rises on *Cefn Nant-y-gougarn* and used to enter Taf Fawr just below the old Blaen Taf, Crew Isaf and *Nant y Gygar* farms. Today, it flows through Coed Taf Fawr into Cantref Reservoir. Most of Blaen Taf, Crew Isaf and *Nant y Gygar* farms are submerged below the reservoir's waters.

Nant-y-geugarn has three elements, *nant* 'stream;, y 'the' and *geugarn* 'hollow cairn'. *Gougarn* (1905) is the loc. dial. pronunciation, while the early forms have omitted the final consonant. The whole means 'stream of the hollow cairn'. One cannot identify the exact cairn, but it is either near the stream's source, on its banks or under its waters. *Nant y Geugarn* is also the name of the stream that flows from the Werfa, past the river hole in Aberdare Golf Club and Ynyscynon House to enter the old Aberdare Canal near Cwmbach. *Nant y Geugarn* to Pant y Gadair is the northern boundary of Penderyn parish.

1841 TAS Nant y Gygar (79 acres):
Landowner Penry Williams Esq. Occupier Himself
1461. Plantation 1462. Cae pen y Coed (field at the end of the wood) 1463. do 1464. yr pen Waun (the mead-ow's end) 1465. Cae Coed (wood field) 1466. Worlodd hwnt (gweirglod; yonder meadow) 1467. do fach (small do) 1468. Cae Garw and Cae Pwdwr (uncultivated field & rotten field) 1469. Old house Cae bach &c. (old house, small field) 1470. Waun Newydd (new meadow)

Nant, y, ceugarn; 'stream (of) the hollow cairn'

Nant Ysbyddaden SN 9610

Lost stream, farm

Nant y Spaddadan 1855 Will of Charles Meredith NLW; Nant ysbyddan 1841 Census; Charles Meredith; Cwm Nant y Spithaden alias Wain y Spithaden 1789 Maybery; Tir Nant y Spithadarn 1758 Maybery Coll.; Cwmb Nant y Spithaden 1758 Maybery coll.; Tyr Nant Spithaden 1713 Will of Evan John NLW;

Nant Ysbyddaden was the name of a stream and smallholding in Cwm

Cadlan. The 1840 TM for Nant Maden shows an unnamed stream flowing through the fields entering the Cadlan stream at Beili Helyg. This is probably *Nant Ysbyddaden*, as it is the only stream present on the farmland. *Ysbyddaden* is Welsh for English 'hawthorn' and was taken as the stream-name because of the presence of hawthorn bushes on its banks. It is unlikely that the stream took its name from *Ysbaddaden* the giant in 'Culhwch and Olwen' of the *Mabinogion*. The farm took its name from the stream. The name changed to Nant Maden *c*. 1840s. See Nant Maden.

Nant, ysbyddaden; 'hawthorn stream'.

Ogof Fawr SN 986097

Cave

Ogof Fawr 1991 OS Pathfinder 1108;1937 Tred. Est.; 1905 OS6"; 1840 TM; Cave 1991 OS Landranger 160; Ogof fawr, Ogof vawr 1749 PMoel. map;

Ogof Fawr is the name of a cave on Pant Sychbant into which Nant Cadlan flows.

Entrance to Ogof Fawr. Courtesy of Jonathan Williams and Rocca

The elements are Welsh *ogof* 'cave' and *mawr* 'large'. The 1991 OS Landranger map marks it only as 'Cave'. Most of the above sources name it as *Ogof Fawr*. In 1937, the Tredegar Estate gave "a grant to Vaynor and Penderyn RDC of water rights in a stream on *Ogof Fawr* in the parish of Penderyn". That stream is named Nant Cadlan on various OS Maps.

Ogof, mawr; 'large cave'

Onllwyn

Mountain area

Onllwyn 1991 OSPF 1109;1903 OS6"; 1840 TM; 1749 PM map; 1839, 1803, 1737, 1726, 1593-94 SEHPP. Onlloyn c1700 (1584) Parochialia.

Onllwyn is a 200 acres expanse of mountain located between Maen Melin, Ogof Fawr, Penamailard Farm and Ffrwd Uchaf Farm on the 1952 OS 1:25,000 map. The 1593-94 document describes *Onllwyn* as consisting of 200 acres of waste ground with "all lyme kyllnes and lyme stones there upon", (SEHPP p. 57). The name's etymology does not reflect this early industrial activity but represents a more rural aspect of the environs. *Onllwyn* contains two elements, *onn* 'ash trees' and llwyn 'bush, brake, copse, grove, woods', indicating a piece of land containing ash trees. *Llwyn onn* has the same elements in reverse order. The 1832 OS1" has Mynydd Penmailard at this location.

Onn, llwyn; 'ash grove/woods'

Pandy, Y

Lost fulling mill

The Pandy 1996 SWVSA; Pandy Cottages 1911 Census; Pandy Road 1911 Census; Maes-y-Rhydia and the Tucking Mill 1776 BFE Schedules; Ynis y Pandy 1776 BFE Schedules F2; Croft y Pandy 1776 BFE Schedules F3; Pandy 1735 Will Reynold Davies; 1796, 1799, 1802 PR Bapt.; Tucking Mill at Maesyrhydiau 1681 SEHPP p173 (Will of Hugh Thomas);

The Pandy or Tucking Mill on the banks of the River Cynon, would have served the needs of weavers of the Parish of Penderyn and of those on Hirwaun Common. Weavers would take their home-woven cloth to the tucking or fulling mill to be treated before being hung out on tenterhooks to dry in large tenter frames (HVHR 38). The field that housed these frames was known in Welsh as Cae d(d)eintur 'tenter field'.

The Pandy or Tucking Mill of Hugh Thomas's will of 1681 became part of the BFE. It was converted into cottages at the end of the 18th century (SEHPP p173), and therefore does not appear on the 1841 TAS. The water from the mill races was needed for the iron works, hence its demise.

The name survives as *The Pandy*, *Pandy Road* and *Pandy Cottages* (see above).

Pandy, Y Pandy; 'the fulling mill'

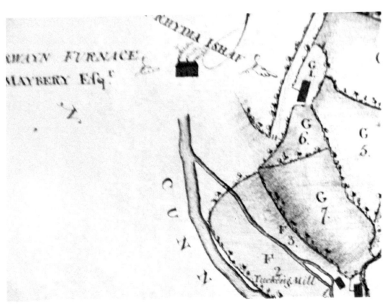

1776 BFE map showing the Tucking Mill on Maes-y-Rhydia Uchaf land (coloured yellow). Maes-y-Rhydia Ishaf lands are coloured red).
F2 is Ynis y Pandy (Pandy river meadow); F3 is Croft y Pandy (Pandy small field);
Map courtesy of SM and WGAS (D/D BF/E 164).

Pant-cefn-ffordd (Pant Cyfnerth)   SN 945085

Pantcefnffordd 2014 Streetmap; Pantcynfurth 1914 Kelly; Pant-cefn-y-ffordd 1905 OS6"; Pantycynferth 1905 HPP Dewi Cynon; Pantycynfarth 1871 Census; Pantcefnyffordd 1851; 1861 Census; Pant y Cyn-farth 1857 Will Catherine Rees; Bant y Cunfarth 1841 Census D20; Pantycynferth 1840 TM; Pant Cyfnerth Ffarm 1796 Will of Mary Powell (Penycae); NLW; Pant y Cyfnerth 1785 Will of John Powell NLW; Pant y Cyfnorth 1778 PR; Pant y Cynfar 1762 WP 42 pupils; Pant Cofnerth 1705 BFE; Tyr Pant Cyvnerth 1626;Tyr Pant kyffnerth 1609 RISW GGF 1/84; Tire pwll Cyfnerth 1553 RISW/GGF1/99; Poill Kyvynerth 1526 Tredegar Est. Rec.

Pantcefnffordd is the present name of the farm on the back road between Penderyn and Rugos (Rhigos, Ricos), partly bordering Penderyn churchyard. The name seems to suit the location as it lies in a hollow (pant) on the back road (cefn ffordd). The 1840 Tithe map however names the farm *Pantycynferth*, with a difficult final *cynferth* element. Fortunately, earlier forms of *Pantcyfnerth* 1796, *Pant Kevenerth* 1567, and *Tir Pwll Kyfnerth* 1553 confirm that the final element is *cyfnerth*, rather than the difficult *cynferth*.

Over the years, the early *cyfnerth* changed to *cynferth* through metathesis viz. the letters f and n changeing places. The same process happened to Dynfant (Dunvant) earlier Dyfnant (dwfn 'steep' and nant 'valley') as well as Llynfi, earlier Llyfni (llyfn 'smoothe' for a smoothe flowing river). But what of *cyfnerth*?

The word *cyfnerth* 'help, aid, strength, support' appears as a noun in GPC, as well as an adjective 'strong, firm, resolute; assisting supporting'. The early *Tir Pant Cyfnerth* 1609 (in today's orthography) and *Tire Pwll Cyfnerth* 1553, would then translate as 'land of the supporting hollow' and 'land of the supporting pool' respectively. These names suggest a fertile hollow and a well stocked pool of fish perhaps.

The late Melville Richards however, shows examples from the middle ages of *Cyfnerth* as a personal name, eg. *Tir Ievan ap Cyfnerth, Tyddyn Cyfnerth* etc. as well as *Llyfr Cyfnerth* 'Cyfnerth's Book', the name of one of Hywel Dda's books of law, named after *Cyfnerth* ap Morgeneu. It is possible then that *Pant Cyfnerth* means 'Cyfnerth's hollow' and *Pwll Cyfnerth* 'Cyfnerth's pool', ie. belonging to *Cyfnerth*.

In short, the early final element *Cyfnerth* changed to *Cynferth*. Over the years, when the personal name *Cyfnerth* was forgotten and changed to *cynferth*, it became meaningless. The name was eventually changed from its medieval obscurity to a clearly understood *Pantcefnffordd*.

1841 TAS Pantycynferth (173 acres):
Landowner Thomas Williams Esq. Occupier Howell Rees
114. (blank) 114a. Waste 115. (blank) 116. (blank) 117. Quarry &c. 118. Tyler Fenwent

Pantcefnffordd with Moel Penderyn in the background   2020 DMJ

Pwll Pantcefnyffordd, Pwll Cyfnerth. 2015 DMJ

(lenited, loc.dial. for mynwent < Lat. mon(un)menta; the chuchyard hill) 119. Caer Benllan (pen, llan; the field at the church end) 120. Homestead Croft &c. 121. Erwr Gwenyn (the bees' acre) 122. Cae Pant (dingle field) 123. do 124. (blank) 125. Cae Pwdwr (rotten/poor field) 126. (blank) 127. Tyle bach (small hill) 128. (blank) 129. Pant bryn y Gof (Bryn the blacksmith's dingle or dingle of the blacksmith's hill) 130. (blank) 131. (blank) 132. Y Feol (sic) (the Foel) 133. Waun fawr (big mesadow) 134. (blank) 135. (blank) 138. Cae bach (small field); 173 acres.

Pwll, cyfnerth; 'Cyfnerth's pool'

Pant, cyfnerth; 'Cyfnerth's hollow'.

Pant Sychbant

SN 985102

Moorland

Pant Sychbant 1991 OSPF 1108; Pant y Sychbant 1905 HPP p76; Pant Sychpant 1884 OS6";

The name of moorland near Onllwyn mountain and the *Sychbant* farms. *Pant Sychbant* is the source of the stream called *Nant Sychbant*, probably so called because its source is at *Pant Sychbant*. Ogof Fawr and Nant Cadlan are also located here. The initial *pant* of *Pant Sychbant* is superfluous, as it already contains *pant* as its final element. The elements are Welsh *sych* 'dry' and *pant* 'hollow' which adequately describes the dry nature of the dingle's rocky terrain.

Pant, Sychbant; 'Sychbant hollow'

Pant y Gadair

SN9913

Moorland

Pant y Gadair 1988 OSPF 1084; Pant y Gatar 1919 LC essay & map; Pant y Gader 1905 OS6";

This moorland is located on the bottom slopes north east of Cadair Fawr to which its name is linked. *Pant y Gatar* 1919 has a final element which reflects the Gwentian dialect, while the 1905 example Pant y Gader hints at a dialectic form of *cadair*. *Pant y Gadair* is the 'hollow' below *Cadair Fawr* hill, from which it takes its name. For *cadair*, see *Cadair Fawr*.

Pant, y cadair; 'the Cadair's hollow'

Pantgarw

SN 945099

Smallholding

Pant-garw 1991 OSPF 1108; Bantgarw 1923 LYH; Bant Garw 1841 Census D20; Pant y garw 1841 Census D20; Ty yn y Pant Garw 1821 BFE; 1793, 1791 PR; Pant Garw 1814 OS Map;

Pant-garw is the name of a smallholding on the A4059 just opposite the entrance to Cae Hywel Isaf. The road dips in the hollow near the house. *Ty yn y Pant Garw* 1821, aptly describes the house's location as 'house in the rough hollow', with rough indicating the uncultivated and difficult nature of the location.

Pant, garw; 'uncultivated/rough hollow'

Penderyn Church   St. Cynog's

SN 945086

Church

Eglwys y Plwyf 1905 HPP pp95-102: St Cynog's Church 1904 OS25"; Penderyn Church Restoration Fund Dec 24, 1891 WM; Penderyn (St. Cynog) 1855 Arch.Camb. 1886 p274; St. Cynog 1833 Top. Dic.; Penderyn Church, churchyard 1776 BFE Map; Tir Eglws Penderin 1691 Court Leet; Tyr Eglwys Penderin 1626 Tred. Est. (John Herbert gent.). Penyderyn – Rectoria 1557 Harleian; Sancti Canoci Pennederyen 1484 Lateran Register 838; Eccl'ia de Pennederyne 1410 ERSD; Ecclesiam que vocatur Pennyderyn 1291 CCRV 338;

The earliest recorded mention of the church of Penderyn is in the Calendar of Chancery Rolls Various p338 which tells of a dispute between Humphrey de Bohun, Earl of Hereford and Gilbert de Clare, Earl of Gloucester. De Bohun, Lord of Brecknock, accused De Clare, Lord of Glamorgan and holder of Morlais Castle, of raiding his lands in Breconshire. Memorandum 5, Edward 20 (1291) states that de Clare's men "broke into a certain church which is called Pennyderyn and took

St Cynog's church Penderyn courtesy of Penderyn Past and Present.

and carried off both chalice and the ornaments and all other property which they found there." (Latin).

The 1410 document from the Episcopal Registers of St David, records the earliest named clerks (priests) of the church. "...in Haverford the aforesaid Vicar General admitted David ap Henry Clerk to the church of Pennederyne in the Diocese of St David vacant by the late John Coydour late rector of the same." The earliest, before 1410 was the named John Coydour (possibly Welsh coedwr 'woodman'), followed in 1410 by David ap Henry. [Haverford is today's Haverfordwest]. In 1484 (above) the rector is named Geoffrey ap Thomas (Galfrido Thome).

The church, in the diocese of Swansea and Brecon, is dedicated to St. Cynog. An early connection between church and saint is recorded in 1484 "To Geoffrey ap Thomas (Galfrido Thome) rector of the parish church of St Cynog (Sancti Canoci) Pennederyen..." Latin. The noted historian Sir John Lloyd wrote:

"Cynog was, according to legend, the son 'of Brychan, founder of the kingdom of Brycheiniog, and Banadlwedd, daughter of a king of Powys. He is chiefly commemorated in Brycheiniog, where churches at Defynnog, Ystrad Gynlais, Penderyn, Battle, Llangynog, and Merthyr Cynog, are all named after him, the last being reputed his place of burial. These churches, with their chapels, account for a large part of the modern county of Brecknock. Other churches bearing his name are Boughrood in Rads. and Llangynog in Montgomeryshire; two extinct churches of this saint stood also at Llangunnock on the Garren in south-west Herefordshire and Llangunnock on the Pill Brook in central Monmouthshire. Cwrt Brychan is close to the latter. No account of Cynog would be complete which did not refer to the torque which, it was averred, had been given him by his father and which became a most precious relic in the estimation of the whole countryside. It has not survived, but Giraldus Cambrensis had seen it and gives a detailed description, which, though not easy to interpret, points, in the opinion

H. Holiday east window at Penderyn Church, donated by the Morgan family of Bodwigiad. (*Courtesy of S. Morgan*)

of Sir T. D. Kendrick, to its probably being Welsh or Irish work of the Viking period, ie. the 10th or the 11th century." Sir J. E. Lloyd, DWB.

Gŵyl Cynog (Cynog's Feast) occurred on October 7th (LC essay). The oldest part of today's church is the Norman Tower. The main body of the church was rebuilt in 1894 and reopened in 1895.

The church held land in other parts of the parish as can be seen in Tir Eglwys Penderyn 1691 and 1626. The church was closed in 2016.

Penderyn Community Centre   SN 949081

Community Centre
2020 Canolfan Cymunedol Penderyn Community Centre;

The Penderyn Community Centre was built *c.* 1984 on derelict land known as Yr Eithyn, which had previously been the location of 19th century cottages. They were demolished in the late 1950s. The centre was extended to its present size in 2007 and is known today as Canolfan Cymunedol Penderyn Community Centre.

Penderyn Distillery   SN 948082

Distillery
The company was formed in 1999 as The Welsh Whisky Company. The first bottle of *Penderyn* Whisky was sold in 2004. See *Penderyn* above.

Distyllfa Penderyn Distillery.   2020 DMJ

Penderyn Reservoir

SN 938072

Penderyn Resr 1991 OSPF 1109; Penderyn Reservoir (Montain Ash U.D.C.W.W.) 1953 OS6" Map; Penderyn Reservoir Under Construction 1919 OS6" map;

In 1911 Mountain Ash UDC undertook work on this reservoir located between Tai Cwplau and Trebanog Uchaf. The contractors were Messrs Underwood & Bros.. The reservoir was opened in 1920.

Penmailard / Penmoelallt

SO 015094

Estate, Farm, wood, moorland/mountain, rock

Penmailard 1991 OSPF 1109; 1841 Census UP;1841 TAS; 1840 TM; 1832 OS AMR; 1814 OS; 1791 PR/PNDH; Coed Penmailard 1991 OSPF 1109; Craig Penmailard 1991 OSPF 1109; Penmeilart 1923 LYH p42; Penmeulart HPP p16; Penmailard Farm 1879 ERB; Penmaillard Farm 1818 Cambrian; Mynydd Penmailard 1814 OS Map; Penmaylard 18th cent.Tredegar (10) NLW; Penmallard 1790 PR; Pen Mallard Hills 1787 J. Carey Map; 1729 E. Bowen Map; Pen maylert 1689 GRO DVL/319/3/ RM; Penmoelallt 1991 OSPF 1109; Penmoelallt Farm 1991 OSPF1109; Pen-moel-allt 1974 OS First Series; 1879 ERB/PNDH; Penmoelallt (Penmeulart) 1905 HPP p16; Penmaelallt 1785 Will of William David NLW.

There is discrepancy and some confusion between *Penmailard* and *Penmoelallt*. They are the same place with *Penmoelallt* occasionally displacing the earlier *Penmailard*. *Penmeulart* (HPP p. 16) is the local Welsh dialect form, also recorded as *Penmeilart* in LYH p. 42.

'The Penmailard Estate belonging to the Williams family and others' is noted on Hilary M. Thomas's *A Catalogue of Glamorgan Estates* p. 121. Thomas Williams of Neath bought the estate from John Herbert of Holwell, Somerset in 1734. His son Dr Thomas Williams succeeded him as owner. By 1840 the property had been handed down to Vaughan Nash Edwards. The following names were linked to the 1749 estate: Frood Isha, Frood Genol, Frood Ucha, Frood Ycha Vach, Penmailard, Sychbant Isha, Sychbant Ucha and Onllwyn. The name *Penmailard* was taken from the largest farm in the group.

Penmallard/Pen Mallard seems to contain English mallard (wild duck) as a second element. The earliest form, Welsh Pen maylert 1689, contains a Cymricised maylert (see GPC) for mallard. The shape of a mallard's head is seen in the shading (representing land elevation) on the 1840 Tithe Map opposite. It is possible that the contour of the elevated ground, was visibly similar to the mallard shaped head of the map. Richard Morgan mentions a possible mallard etymology in SBrecsPN p123. Cf. Penderyn 'bird's head'.

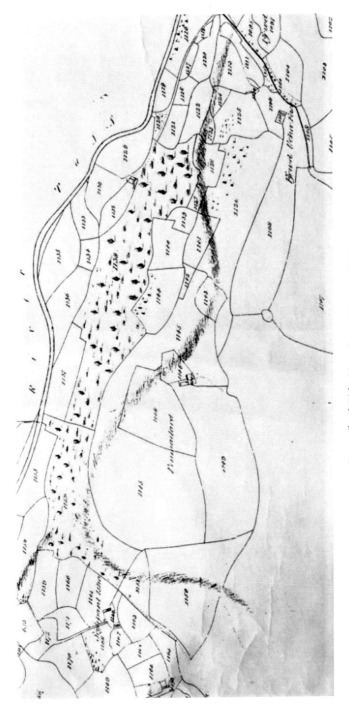

Pennailard Tithe Map 1840. Courtesy of NLW

Craig Penmailard is 'Penmailard rock', and Coed Penamailard, 'Penmailard woods'. Mynydd Penamailard replaced Onllwyn on maps, with the mountain taking the estate and farm name because Penmailard farm contained nearly 1,000 acres of Onllwyn as sheep-walk.

1841 TAS Penmailard (1188 acres (including 966 acres on Onllwyn)): Landowner, Vaughan Nash Edwards. Occupier, David Thomas.
1126. Coed cae (grazing enclosure) 1127. Cae bach (small field) 1128. Cae Gwar dan Goed (field of the mound under trees; gwar is lit. 'nape of the neck'.) 1129. Ynis Wen (white river meadow) 1130. do Grigog (grugog cf. y rugos; do heath) 1131. Barn & Garden 1132. Pydeuen (?piden ?penis (shape)) (1133. Ynis Grigog (grugog; heath river meadow)1134. Cae bach (small field) 1135. Cae coed draw (yonder grazing enclosure) 1136. Ynis Ucha (upper river meadow) 1137. Graig (the rock) 1138. do 1139. Cae bach (small field) 1140. Coed cae ffynnon Goch (red well grazing enclosure) 1141. Cae Newydd (new field) 1142. Cae bach (small field) 1143. do 1144. Cae heol Ucha (upper road field) 1145. Cae penmailard (Penmaailard's field) 1146. Croft (small field) 1147. Homestead &c. 1148. Cae penmailard (Penmailard's field) 1149. Pant Gwyn (white hollow) 1150. Coed cae Newydd (new grazing enclosure) 1010. Onllwyn (moorland of 966 acres, see above).
Pen, mallard; ?'mallard's head'?

Penmoelallt
SO 009094
Moorland, farm
Penmoelallt 1991 OSPF 1109; Penmoelallt Farm 1991 OSPF1109; Pen-moel-allt 1974 OS First Series; 1879 ERB/PNDH; Penmoelallt Farm 1911 Census; Old Penmoelallt Farm 1911 Census; Penmoelallt Cottage 1911 Census; Penmoelallt (Penmeulart) 1905 HPP p16; Penmaelallt 1785 Will of William David NLW.

Penmoelallt and *Penmailard* are related place-names. Dewi Cynon recognises the link as he records both as *Penmoelallt (Penmeulart)* in HPP p16. For *Penmailard*, see above.

In 1901 Ffrwd Fach Uchaf and *Penmoelallt* were neighbouring farms on the *Penmailard* Estate. By 1911 Ffrwd Fach Uchaf had changed its name to *Penmoelallt*, and the first *Penmoelallt* had become *Old Penmoelallt* and *Penmoelallt Cottage*, both *old* and *cottage* used as distinguishing features for the property of Robert Shelton, Gamekeeper. The 1952 OS6" map lists two farms as *Penmailard*. The 1989 OSPF 1109 has *Penmailard* and *Penmoelallt*.

The earliest recorded form with *allt* as a final element is *Penmaelallt* 1785. William David's will, states that he desires William Watkins of *Penmaelallt* to be one of the guardians of his children.

It seems that *Penmaelallt* is an attempt at rationalising the final element of the earlier *Penmailard* name (*Penmaylard* 18th cent.Tred.; *Pen maylert* 1689,

GRO), with an easily understood *allt* 'wooded hill' replacing an ambiguous *ard*. *Penmaelallt* eventually changed to *Penmoelallt* 'top of the bare wooded slope' which contained recognisable, if incongruous, Welsh elements.

Pen, moel, allt; 'top (of the) bare wooded slope'

Penpont   SO 004126

Lost farm

Pen-pont 1922 OS6"; Penpont 1914 Kelly; 1905 HPP16; 1871-1841 Census;1840 TM; 1837 Will of Herbert Jones; Pen-y-bont 1830 OS map; Pen Pont ar Daf 1780 PR; Penpont ar Dave 1699 Penpont; (Tir) pen y bon tar dave 1683 Penpont;

Penpont was the name of a farm situated on a hillside (see TAS names) in Cwm Taf just south of Pont ar Daf bridge. The *pont* element in the name refers to this bridge, while *pen* indicates that it was at the top end of the bridge, on rising ground, rather than the bottom end.

1841 TAS Penpont (113 acres):
Landowner Rev. Richard Davies & Wm. Payne. Occupier Hugh Jenkins
1351. Bryn banal (broom hill) 1352. Ynis y Gorof (river meadow by the precipice) 1353. do Isha (lower river meadow precipice) 1354. Homestead &c. 1355. Gelli fach (small grove) 1356. Erw Las (green acre) 1357. Twyn (hill) 1358. Caer Mynydd (the mountain field) 1359. do 1360. Caer Groft Ucha (the upper Groft field) 1361. Caer Groft (the Groft field) 1362. Dwy Erw (two acres) 1363. Cae bach (small field) 1364. Ynis Ucha (upper river meadow) 1365. Road and Waste 1366. Cae Mar (sic) y coed (?it's not mawr. -field (on the edge of) the wood 1367. Coed y Garnant (the Garnant wood) 1368. Caer yn y Coed (field in the wood) 1369. Waun (meadow).

Penpont farmhouse and buildings plus many of the fields were submerged when the Llwyn-onn reservoir was built. Pontar-ar-Daf bridge was also submerged in 1927 but remains can be seen in dry summers when the water is at its lowest. The higher *Penpont* fields are now part of Coed Taf Fawr.

Pen, pont; 'top end (of the) bridge'

Pentre Celliau   SN 993117

Former Farm

Pentre-cae-lleia 1952, 1905, 1884 OS6"; Gellia Farm 1926 Kelly; Pentre Celliau 1905 HPP 16; Pentrecellia 1841 Census UP; Pentre Cellie 1841 TAS, TM; Gelliau 1830 OSM; Gelleea 1780 Tred. Est., 1772-97 Ed. Thos. Map; Kelliau 1729 PR; Cellie 1690/91 SEHPP;

The early name for this Cwm Taf farm was *Celliau*, shown as *Kelliau* 1729 PR, the dialectic *Cellie* in 1690/91 and written as *Gelliau* on the 1830 OS map, with a presumed missing definite article. By 1840, *pentre* (*pentref*) was added to the name eg, *Pentre Cellie* 1840 TM, presumably to avoid confusion with *Gellibenuchel* which was often known by its abbreviated form of *Gelli*. Today, *pentref* means 'village' but earlier, it referred to the end (pen) of the *tref* 'farm', usually where the villeins or the lord's dependents lived. The 1884 OS6" mappers chose to write a fanciful *Pentre-cae-lleia* 'smallest field (of the) village/small farm', possibly to try and elucidate *Pentre Cellia*, although that name ought to have been understood by local Welsh speakers. *Pentre-cae-lleia* was still in use on the 1952 OS map, although "the farmstead is no longer evidenced, as a forestry road has obliterated any remains and all the land has been afforested as part of Coed Taf Fawr since *c.*1950." PNDH 7.100.

Celliau is the plural of *celli* 'grove, copse', very often written in its mutated form *gelli* without the definite article *y*, which causes soft mutation following a singular, feminine noun ie. *y gelli*. The plural *celliau* should not normally mutate after the definite article, but it does in this case, as *Gelliau* 1830 shows.

1841 TAS Pentre Cellie (116 acres):
Landowner Sir Charles Morgan Occupier John Jenkins (as Penyglogfanddu)
1311. Cefn y Waun (the meadow ridge) 1312. Coedcae dan y Llwyd (sic) (?ty llwyd; grazing enclosure beneath the grey or Lloyd's house? The TM shows a rectangular building in the field near the homestead) 1313. Gelli fach (small grove) 1314. do ucha (upper do) 1315. Homestead &c. 1316. Cae Mawr (big field) 1317. Drain bach (small bramble) 1318. Cae do (do field) 1319. Coed cae (grazing enclosure) 1320. Cae bach (small field) 1321. Coed cae (grazing enclosure) 1322. Cae Mawr (big field) 1323. Llwyn llafir (llafur; labour intensive bush field) 1324. do Cae Mawr (do big field) 1325. Cae Mawr (big field) 1326. do 1327. Cae Newydd (new field) 1328. Caer Llwyn (the bush field) 1329. Cae Mawr (big field) 1330. Cae bach (small field) 1331. Barn &c.
Pentre, celliau; 'village, small farm (of the) groves'

Pentwyn (1)   SN 956069
Former Farm
Pen-tŵyn 1954 OS^"; Pen-twyn 1904 OS25"; Pentwyn 1841-71 Census;

A former smallholding on the top of a slope near Llety Rhys, now in ruins and probably abandoned early in the 20th century.
Pen, twyn; 'top (of the) hill'

Pentwyn (2)   SN 924078
Former Farm
Pentwyn (ruins) 1841 TAS; Pentwyn Farm 1781 Tred. Est.;

A former small farm on a hilltop neighbouring Tyle'r Morgrug in 1781, and part of Tyle'r Morgrug field no. 27. Pentwyn Ruins & Cae bach on the 1841 TAS. For the meaning see above.

Pentwyn Isaf SO 008108

Farm

Pen-twyn-isaf 1991 OSLR 160; 1905 OS6"; 1884 OS6"; Pentwyn-isaf 1905 HPP 16;
1851-71 census; Pentwyn 1841 Census; TAS; 1840 TM; 1830 OS;

Pen-twyn-isaf is a smallholding just below Llwyn-onn Reservoir in Cwm Taf.
It is named *Pentwyn* on the 1840 TM. *Isaf* was added to Pentwyn between
1841 and 1849, to differentiate between it and the other Pentwyn farm in
Cwmtaf which became *Pen-twyn-uchaf*. *Pentwyn Isaf* (93 acres) was a much
larger farm than Pentwyn Uchaf (46 acres) as shown on the 1841 TAS.

1841 TAS Pentwyn (93 acres):

Landowner – Rees Price. Occupier – John Jones.

1204. Waun cae (meadow field)	Pasture	13	2	3
1205. Coed cae Ucha (upper enclosure)	do	10	1	13
1206. Homestead &c.		0	2	33
1207. Cae bychan (small field)	Meadow	3	0	8
1208. do Isha (lower do)	Arable	2	0	25
1209. Cwch (beehive or boat-(shaped))	Pasture	0	2	33
1210. Coed cae bach (small enclosure)	do	3	2	0
1211. Erw Grin (dry acre)	Arable	2	1	4
1212.	Pasture	0	1	37
1213. Groft (small field)	do	0	1	7
1214. Tir Newydd (new land)	do	1	2	38
1215. Ynis y Gwenith (wheat river meadow)	Meadow	2	3	14
1216. do	Arable & Wood	3	2	27
1217. Cae dderwen (oak tree field)	Meadow	2	1	9
1218. Grinig fach (?small dry field)	Arable	1	3	26
1219. do Goedog (do wooded)	Pasture & Wood	4	0	21
1220. Cae Carnydd (cairns' field)	Pasture	1	1	9
1221. Erw'r flech (?aflach 'arrow' acre)	Arable	1	2	23
1222. do Draig *for Graig*?(do dragon/rock)	do	1	2	15
1223. Graig felin (yellow rock)	Woods & Pasture	8	1	29
1224. Ynis fach (small river meadow)	Arable	1	3	18
1225. Cae Graig (Graig 'rock' field)	Pasture	1	2	27
1226. do bach (small do)	Arable	0	1	18
1227. Prisk (prysg? copse)	Wood & Pasture	4	0	15
1228. Caer do (Prysg field)	Pasture	1	2	29
1229. Cae Mawr Isha (lower big field)	Meadow	6	2	15
1330. (sic) do Ucha (upper do)	Pasture	9	3	31
		93	0	7

Pentwyn, isaf; 'lower Pentwyn'

Pentwyn Uchaf
Former Farm

Pen-twyn-uchaf 1905 OS6"; 1886 OS6"; Pen-twyn-uchaf Plantation 1905 OS6"; Pentwyn Uchaf 1905 HPP 16; 1861 Census; 1849 Will Evan Watkins NLW; 1844 gs; Pentwyn 1841 Census.

Pentwyn was also the name of a smallholding and plantation located in Cwm Taf between Berth-Llwyd and Bryn Prydydd. The 1841 TAS has Evan Watkin as Landowner and Occupier. He was also registered at *Pentwyn* on the 1841 Census. By 1849, *Pentwyn Farm* had changed to *Pen-twyn-uchaf*. Baptisit minister John James was at *Pentwynicha* (sic) in 1851. The former smallholding is now afforested and has been part of Coed Taf Fawr since 1950. This farm was half the size of *Pentwyn Uchaf* and was known earlier as *Tir bach* 'small land'.

1841 TAS Pentwyn (46 acres):
Landowner – Evan Watkins. Occupier – himself.

1419. Ynis (river meadow)	Arable	4	3	10
1420. Waun y Gorof (precipice meadow)	Meadow & Wood	1	2	35
1421. Wern fach (small alder wood)	Pasture	1	3	25
1422. Cae Glas (green field)	Arable	3	0	24
1423. Cae Ysgubor (barn field)	Meadow	2	0	12
1424. Homestead Road &c.		0	1	32
1425. Caer Pele (balls' ?games field)	Pasture	2	2	22
1426. Cae Ucha (upper field)	Arable	5	0	27
1427. Coed cae (grazing enclosure)	Pasture	4	1	37
1428. Waun (meadow)	Meadow	19	2	21
		46	0	5	2

Pentwyn, uchaf; 'upper Pentwyn'

Pen y Cae
Farm

Pen-y-cae 1991 OSPF 1108; 1905 OS6"; 1830 OS; Pencae 1905 HPP 14; Pen y cac 1841 Census D20; Penycae 1835 Will Thomas Howell (Howell Davies of) NLW; 1844 Will John Powel; Tir Pen y Cae 1776 BFE; Pen y Kae 1705 BFE; Tyr Pen y Kae 1691 CL/BRA; Tyr Pen y kaie 1626 Tred. Est. (Wm. ap Rs gent.); tyre pen y cay 1566 Penpont; tyr pen kay 1537 Penpont.

This farm is located on rising ground from the River Cynon to Nant y Deri and Nant Gwine (gwinau) and was until recently, the home of the noted Selwood family (see Bibliography and Introduction). The 1841 TAS records its size as just over 177 acres. Dewi Cynon (HPP p. 14) states that the meaning of *Pen y Cae* is clear ie. 'top of the field'. That may be the case today, but *cae* had an earlier meaning of a hedge (of bushes or thorns), that closed off a piece of ground. William Salesbury defines *cae* in his dictionary dated 1547 as 'hedge'. This is contemporaneous with the farm-name's earliest recorded forms of 1537 and 1566. Today *cae* means the field within the hedge. The early names contain *tir* 'land, ground, territory etc.', giving 'land at the end of the hedge'. It is also possible that the early farm may have had a defensive hedge around its land. *Tir Pen y Cae* would then refer to the land within this hedge rather than to a particular field.

Cae is sometimes written as *ca*, denoting the local Welsh dialect and as *kaie*, *kay*, *caie* etc. by non-Welsh speaking scribes.

1841 TAS Tir pen y Cae (177 acres):

Landowner Morgan Morgan Esq. Occupier Mary Harry

632. Waun deri (meadow of the oak trees) 633. Cae pen do (field at the top/end of Waun deri) 634. Do 635. Llwyn y Deri (the oak copse) 636. Road 637. Heol Erw (acre alongside the road) 638. Cwm Nant Gwine (Nant Gwine's wooded valley) 639. Coed cae do (do grazing enclosure) 640. Cae draw Nant (field beyond the Nant) 641. Cae Garw (uncultivated field) 642. Coed cae Pella (furthest grazing enclosure) 643. Cae Llewellyn Thomas (Llewellyn Thomas's field) 644. Cae Cenol (middle field) 645. do Isha (lower do) 646. Erw Llwyd (Lloyd's or poor-quality acre) 647. Waun y Gwaun (meadow of the (great) meadow) 648. Clyn Llwyd (clun; Lloyd's or poor-quality meadow) 649. do 650. Coed cae Llygad (grazing enclosure of Llygad (Cynon)) 652. Cae bach (small field) 653. Erwi Cernydd (cairns' acres) 654. Cae Lloi (calves' field) 655. Homestead &c. 656. Pentwyn y Scybor (top of the barn hill) 657. Erwi Mynydd (mountain acres) 658. Cae bach (small field) 659. Pant do (do hollow/dingle) 660. do 661. Coed cae (grazing enclosure) 662. Groft (small field) 663. Garden 664. Cae Glas (green field) 665. Groft (small field) 666. Road & Waste 667. Cae bach (small field) 668. Cae Glas Ucha (upper green field)

1776 (D/D BF/E 164) Tir Pen-y-Cae:

C 1. Cot and Garden by Cae Glace (glas; green field) 2. The Waste ground abt the Road 3. Pen twyn y scibor (top of the barn hill) 4. Erw'r munydd (the mountain acre) 5. Tir Newydd (new land) 6. Coed cae (grazing enclosure) 7. Pant bach (small dingle) 8. Rough ground in Do 9. The little Spot by the Mill Stream (Melin Trebannog) 10. Llwyn Vallan (apple tree) 11. Ynis glan'r Avon (riverbank river meadow) 12. The Coed cae (grazing enclosure) 13. Clyn Llwyd (grey or Lloyd's meadow) 14. Wain y Gwair (grass/hay meadow) 15. Erw Llwyd (grey or Lloyd's acre) 16. The Brake in Do 17. Erw'r Cernidd (acre of the cairns) 18. The Farm Yard & House 19. Cae'r Lloy (the calves' field) 20. Cae isha (lower field) 21. Wayn y Gwair (grass/hay meadow) 22. The Brake between Do & Wayn pella (waun pella 'furthest meadow') 23. Do between Do & the Road 24. The road 25. The fld by Do

26. The Lane north side of Do fld 27. The 2 little flds North side of Do Lane (now in one) 28. (blank) 29. Cae Llewelyn Thomas (Llewelyn Thomas's field) 30. Coed cae pella (furthest grazing en-closure) 31. (blank) 32. Cae Glace (glas; green field) 33. (blank) 34. The Garden by Do fd 35. (blank) 36. Cwm Nant Gwina (Nant Gwina's wooded valley) 37. (blank) 38. The piece near Dery House 39. Rough Ground in Do 40. (blank) 41. pt of the Great Meadow 42. The Wood in Ditto 43. The road from Dery House to Heol y Moch 44. Pen y Cae Dery (top of the field of oak trees) 45. Llwyn y Dery Buchan (copse of the small oaks)

Tir, pen, y, cae; 'land at the end of the hedge',
later pen, y, cae; 'top of the field'

Pen y Coed SO 0011
Former Farm

Pen-y-coed 1905 OS6"; 1880, 1789 Tred. Est.; 1830 OS; Pencoed 1905 HPP 16, 1879 ERB, 1841-71 Cens. Pen y Coed 1840 TM; 1781 Tred. Est.; 1780 PR;

This former farmstead was located above the woods in Cwmtaf. In 1840 *Pen y coed* was listed together with Berthllwyd under the occupancy of Thomas Jenkins and ownership of Sir Charles Morgan Bart. Since 1950 it had been part of Coed Taf Fawr where the ruins of house and barn remain.

For 1841 TAS see Berthllwyd and Penycoed in Berthllwyd (Cwm Taf) above.

Pen, y, coed; 'top of the wood'

Penyglog Fan-ddu SN 993118
Former Farm

Penyglogfanddu 1905 HPP 17; 1871 Cens.; Pen-y-glog-fan-ddu Ruin 1884 OS6"; Pen y Glog van ddu 1851 Cens.; Clogfandu 1841 Cens.; Pen-y-Glog-Fan-Du 1780 Tred. Est.; Tyr Pen y Glog van thy 1691 CL/BRA;

Tir Pen y Glog Fan Ddu was a farm located in Cwm Taf neighbouring Pentre Cellie and Pen yr Heol on the 1840 TM. The property was not listed on the 1881 census but there are no ruins visible today on the former location near the picnic site, called Sycamore Grove on the 1988 OSPF 1084 map. The remainder of the old farm has been part of Coed Taf Fawr since *c.* 1950.

Dewi Cynon (HPP 17) explains the meaning as 'top of the black high rock', which is a fair translation of the place-name.

1841 TAS Penyglogfanddu (c.47 acres; with Pentre Cellie 116 acres):
Landownwers – Sir Charles Morgan Bart. Occupier – Jenkin Jones (as Pentre Cellie).

1300. Peny cae ucha (top of the upper field) 1301. Wain (waun; meadow) 1302. Caer Glog (the Glog field) 1303. do Isha (lower Glog field) 1304. Tir Newydd (new land) 1305. Coed cae Glog fanddu (grazing enclosure near Glogfanddu) 1306. Penrheol (top of the road) 1307. Gelli (grove) 1308. Byrdir (short land) 1308a. Home-stead &c. 1309. Y Wain (the meadow) 1310. Waste

Pen, y, clog, ban, du; 'top of the black high rock'

Pen-y-pound   SO 005125

Former farm

Pen-y-pound 1929 PR, 1865 gs. PNDH 7.108; Pen-pound 1905, 1884 OS6", 1832 OS; Penpownd 1905 HPP p16; Penpound 1871, 1841 Census, 1841 TAS, TM; Pen y Pound 1853 Will of Rev. David Davies, Baptist Minister NA; Pen-Pound 1808 Will Howell David NLW.

Located in the old hamlet of Ynysyfelin this small *Pen-y-pound* farm was active until the construction of the Llwyn Onn Reservoir. The remaining land is afforested as part of Coed Taf Fawr. The name has been recorded with and without the definite article. *Pen* implies 'end'.

There is some controversy regarding the final element. Dewi Cynon favours Welsh *pownd* 'a pond' (HPP p. 16) while R. F. Peter Powell prefers English *pound* 'a pound, pen' for animals (PNDH 7.108). Of the two, I am inclined to favour Dewi Cynon's *pownd*, as GPC defines it 'pond, leat, ditch'. *Pen-pound's* two neighbouring ponds and leat ditch supports that etymology. On the other hand, English pound 'a pound, pen' for animals cannot be discarded.

1841 TAS Penpound (58 acres):

Landowner - David Lewis. Occupier – Meredith Jenkins

1332. Escyr (esgair; ridge) 1333. Waun (Meadow) 1334. Coed caer Wain (meadow grazing enclosure) 1335. Cae bryn ucha (upper hill field) 1336. Coed cae bach (small grazing enclosure) 1337. Homestead &c. 1338. Cae Newynydd (hunger field) 1339. Erw Llewellyn (Llewelyn's acre) 1340. Cae dan ty (field below the house) 1341. Cae ty Cwrdd (meeting house field) 1342. Tir Hir (long land) 1343. Cae bryn Isha (lower hill field) 1344. Gurcws ?crocus 1345. Brake 1346. Ynis dan y felin (river meadow below the mill) 1347. Erw (acre) 1348. Chapel (Bethel) 1349. Cae bach Tafarn (pub's small field (Red Lion))

Pen, pound/pownd; 'end of the pound' or 'end of the pond, leat'

Pen-yr-eithin   SN 948082

Residence, farm

Penyrithin 1996 SWVSM, 1852 Will of John Jones; Penyreithin 1991 OS Pathfinder 1108, 1905 HPP p14; Penyreithyn Farm 1939 VPRD; Pen yr Eithyn 1852 Will John

Jones NLW; Pener Hithin, Pen y Ethin 1841 Census; Ty yr Heol 1841 Census;

Pen-yr-eithyn is the name of a residence and farm on Church Road opposite Ysgubor Fawr. Dewi Cynon informs us that an old name for the place was *Ty ar yr Heol* 'house on the road', because it was on the side of the road (HPP p. 14). There are two cottages shown on the 1840 TM, numbered 142 as part of Ysgubor Fawr. These are *Pen yr Eithyn* and *Tyn yr Heol* of the 1841 census. He also states that *Penyreithin* is a recent name (1905), emanating from the uncultivated grazing enclosure below the house, known as *Yr Eithyn* 'the gorse/furze'.

Penyreithyn takes its name from its location at the top of the *Eithyn*.

Pen, yr, eithyn; 'top of Yr Eithyn'

Pen-yr-heol   SN 991112
Former Smallholding

Pen-yr-heol 1905, 1884 OS", 1880 Tred. Est., 1830 OS.; Penyrheol 1926, 1914 Kelly, 1905 HPP pp18,17; Pen yr heol 1841 Census UP; Pen r Heol 1841 TAS, 1840 TM; Pen yr hewl 1781 Tred. Est.; Tyr Pen yr hewl 1691 BRA; Tyr Pen yr heoll 1626 Tred. Est. (Sr Edw Lewis Kt.

The former smallholding took its name from its position on top of the road between CwmTaf and Penderyn. *Pen yr hewl* 1781 and 1691 has the local Welsh dialect form *hewl* for the final element *heol*. There is nothing remaining of this small farm, which today is a picnic site in Coed Taf Fawr.

1841 TAS Pen r Heol (80 acres):
Landowner Sir Charles Morgan Bart. Occupier Thomas Jenkins
1290. Coed bach (small wood) 1291. Worlod ddu (black meadow) 1292. Cae dan y Ty (field below the house) 1293. do 1294. Homestead &c. 1294a. Gardd Gerrigog (stony garden) 1295. Croft (small field) 1296. Cae Llest (lluest; field with a tent/temporary dwelling) 1297. Ton Mawr (big lay land) 1298. Cae dan y Glwydd (clwyd; field below the gate) 1299. Coed cae (grazing enclosure)

Pen, yr, heol; 'top of the road'

Pont Hepste   SN 945112
Bridge

i Bont Hepsta 1923 LYH p20

Pont Hepsta is the local Welsh dialect form for *Pont Hepste* ie. Hepste Bridge on the Ystradfellte Road alongside Tai Hirion, some two hundred yards after turning off the A4059.

Pont, Hepste; 'Hepste bridge'

Pontbren-llwyd

Footbridge, Hamlet

Pontprenllwyd 2018 Estyn report, 1905 HPP p42, 89, 1847 Will of Mary Jenkins
NA,1748 WP (50 pupils); Pontbren Llwyd 1991 OSPF 1109, 1905 OS25", 1923 LYH
p38, o'r Pompran 1923 LYH p10; Pontprenllwyd Pontbrenllwyd 1923 LYH p43;
Pompren 1914 Y Darian; Pompren Llwid 1841 Census D20; Pontbrenllwyd 1835
Will Thomas Howell NLW; Pont-pren-llwyd 1832 OS; Pompren Llwyd 1778 PR;
1748 WP; Pont-Bren-Llwyd a Foot Bridge 1776 BFE; Pont Bren Lwyd 1744/5 BFE;
Pont Bren Llwyd 1705 Jersey;

Pontbren-llwyd is the name of a footbridge and hamlet located at the lower
end of Penderyn village. The BFE map of 1776 below, shows the exact
location of the footbridge crossing Nant Cadlan, opposite Bodwigiad's old
smith's shop. The 1841 Census named *Pompren Llwid* as having 67
inhabitants while the 1840 TM showed 12 buildings grouped around a

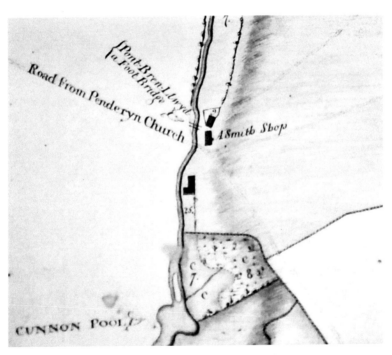

The footbridge known as Pont-Bren-Llwyd in 1776.
Courtesy of SM and the WGAS (D/D BF/E 164)
Numbers 7 and 9 belong to 'Bodwiggiad Farm' - 9 is 'Home and Garden by the
Smith Shop; 7 is 'Ynis Cwrt y Gwtar'; C7 & C8 are 'Pant bach' and are part of
'Tir Pen-y-Cae'. 'Cunnon Pool' is Llygad Cynon.

Chapel (Siloa) near the footbridge. By 1905 the hamlet had grown to 28 dwellings, 2 Public Houses, a shop, as well as a school. The local quarries provided employment for many inhabitants. Today's community incudes three housing estates (Llwyn Onn, Bryn Onnen and Woodland Park), Trebannog Terrace, houses along Pontpren Road and Church Road as well as Ysgol Gynradd Gymuned Penderyn Community Primary School and Penderyn Distillery. *Glan-yr-afon* ('the river bank') is believed to be the location of the earlier home of poet and weaver Gwilym Harri. An 18th cent weaver's cottage was located in the garden, just below the old *pompren*.

Weaver's cottage in Glan-yr-afon garden, believed to be the onetime home of poet and weaver Gwilym Harri. Photo courtesy of Penderyn Historical Society

The name contains two elements, Welsh *pontbren* '(wooden) foot-bridge' (GPC), plus *llwyd*, which can either be a colour 'grey, russet, brown', or 'faint, pale', or possibly a personal name. The element probably describes the colour of the early wooden footbridge. Some of the above forms include the local Welsh dialect pompren/pompran. It may be pertinent to note here that there are two field-names on nearby *Pen-y-cae* farm (see above Pen-y-cae 1841 TAS & 1776 BFE) that contain *Llwyd* as an element, which may be linked to the *Llwyd* of Pontbrenllwyd, possibly indicating an earlier owner or occupier named *Llwyd*.

Incidentally, some places lower down the Cynon Valley used cwmwr for a footbridge eg. Cwmmwr ycha, yssa, Cwmwrddy, Cwmmwr dyon etc.

For more details on the early hamlet see HPP p89.

The footbridge. *c.1920 courtesy of Penderyn Historical Society*

Pontbren, llwyd; 'Llwyd's or grey/brown (coloured) wooden foot-bridge'

Pontplanca   SN 952085

Bridge

Pontplanca 1877 gs. Dd. Davies, Siloa; Y Bontplanca 1905 AL; Pontyplanka 1871 Census; Bontplanca 1905 (19th cent.) HPP p. 47.

Quarry locomotive heading for Pontplanca. *Courtesy of SM*

Pontplanca originally was the name of a footbridge, which was strengthened to take the weight of quarry locomotives and trucks. It was the location for four families in the 1871 Census, including David Davies, whose gravestone at Siloa bears his name and dwelling place.

The name contains two elements, *pont* and *planca*. *Pont* is 'bridge' and *planca* is the local dialect form of *planciau* 'planks', which probably describes the floor of the bridge.

Pont, planciau; 'bridge (of) planks'

Pontycapel Mill

SO 029077

Pont y capel 1841 Census; Pont-y-cappel Mill 1818 Cambrian; Pont Capel 1729 E Bowen map; Pontycappel 1714 Vaynor PR; Pontycapel mill on Ffrwd Isaf 1689 GRO/ VL 319/1.

This former mill was located on the Penderyn Parish side of the *Pontycapel* Bridge spanning the River Taf Fawr near Cefncoedycymer village. The earliest recorded form is from a GRO document dated 1689. Its location is shown on Ffrwd Isaf on a 1749 Penmailard Estate Map (GRO/D/D La 58). It worked as a cornmill until *c.* 1840 when it was demolished and replaced by the *Pontycapel* Brewery. A water colour of *Pontycapel* mill and bridge, painted by Penry Williams *c.* 1830 may be seen at the Cyfarthfa Museum. The bridge in the painting is a two-arched bridge, but a later photograph of *Pontycapel* Brewery shows a one-arched bridge. 'The two-arched stone bridge was built about 1775 and rebuilt again as a single-arch bridge in 1855 after the floods of 1854.' (Griffiths, MT).

Pontycapel Brewery and bridge. *Courtesy of Elwyn Bowen*

The single arched Pontycapel bridge Nov. 2020. © DMJ

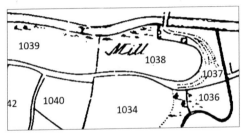

The Mill (recorded on field no. 1038 'Cae Poth' and 1037 'Mill Cottage Road &c.' as part of Ffrwd Isha, on this sanitized Parish of Penderyn Tithe Map), is Pontycapel Mill.

Pontycapel contains two main elements plus the definite article. The first element *pont* refers to the 'bridge' spanning the Taf Fawr river. The final element Welsh *capel* is English 'chapel', The chapel is pre 1689 and is claimed to be a chapel of ease under Vaynor church (Vaynor p. 243). That may be the case as the 1689 date is too early for any of the local 18th century chapels.

Pontycapel, mill; 'mill near Pontycapel'

Pont-yr-efail-fach   SN 954097

Bridge

Pont-yr-Efail-fach 1991 OSPF 1108; Cwm-yr-Efail-Fach 1905 HPP p76.

Yr Efail Fach appears to be the name of one of three streams that feed Nant Cadlan, along with Nant-ddu and Nantmaden.(HPP p. 76) The stream flows through *Cwm-yr-efail-fach* and under *Pont-yr-efail-fach*. The name contains three elements and the definite article. *Pont* 'bridge', *efail* 'smithy' and *fach* 'small' giving the bridge, under which the stream called *Yr Efail Fach* flows. The stream was probably given its name from the 'small smithy' on its banks, but there are no visible signs or remains of such a smithy.

Pont, yr, gefail, bach; 'bridge of the (stream) of the small smithy'

Pwll-y-dylluan

ST 9409

Farmstead

Pwll-dylluan 1981 OSM; Pwll huan 1919 LC essay & map; Pwll Huan 1905 HPP p12; Pwllyan 1871 Census; Pwllian 1851 Census; Bwll y Caerlluan 1841 Census D20; Tyr Pwll y ddullyan 1727 Will Howell John Jenkin; (tir) Pwll y Dhylluan 1619 Penpont; Ryde poll y ddyllyan 1468 MWBM 1039.

This farmstead is located on the Penderyn Parish banks of the river Hepste north-east of Bryn-cul of Ystradfellte parish. The 1949 OS map has two fords marked across the river, one linking *Pwll y Dylluan* to Bryn-Cul, with the other c100 yards to the north. A ford is listed on the earliest recorded form of this place-name as *Ryde poll y ddyllyan*, 1468 above (*rhyd* is Welsh 'ford').

The recorded names have several variations to the final element viz. *huan, Caerlluan, ddullyan, Dhylluan* and *ddyllyan. Huan, yan,* and *ian* of census returns are probable contractions of *dylluan.* Unfortunately, Dewi Cynon (HPP p12), interprets *huan* as Welsh for 'sun, sunlight,' although earlier and later forms of the place-name confirms *tylluan,* Welsh 'owl' as the final element. *Caerlluan* of the 1841 census is an actual dialect form for *tylluan,* as are *Calluan* GPC, and *Cyllian* TYR. *Dylluan* is the mutated form, following the definite article - *y dylluan,* while *ddylluan* has a superfluous extra mutation. *Dhylluan* is a 17th century spelling of *ddylluan.*

The first element *pwll* Welsh 'pool, pit' refers to a pool in the river alongside one of the fords mentioned above. This pool near the ford, would at one time, in all probability, have been frequented by an owl. The Welsh speaking residents appropriately named the spot *Rhyd pwll y dylluan* 'ford (of) the owl's pool', with the farmstead adopting the descriptive *Pwll y Dylluan* name.

1841 TAS Pwll y Llyan (56 acres):

Landowner – Thomas Walter Powell Esq. Occupier – William Thomas Esq.

806. Coed cae (grazing enclosure) 807. Ynis Isha (lower river-meadow) 808. do Ucha (higher river-meadow) 809. Graig (rock) 810. Cae Mawr (big field) 811. Waun y Cwrlid (meadow with a covering growth) 812. Homestead &c. 813. Cae bach (small field) 814. do & Road 815. Cae Main (narrow field) 816. Cae bach

(small field) 817. Coed cae (grazing enclosure)
> Pwll, y, tylluan; 'the owl's pool', from earlier **Rhyd, pwll, y,**
> **tylluan 'ford (near) the owl's pool'**

Red Lion, The / Y Llew Coch   SN 947085

Public House

Red Lion Inn 1904 OS25", 1858 MT&GA, 1843 Cambrian, 1834 GMBG; Red Lion 1849, 1863 PR, 1841 Census,

The Red Lion Inn, also known locally as *Y Llew Coch*, is located directly opposite Penderyn Church. It was known as the *Red Lion Inn* as far back as 1834, but it was also called *Y Tafarn Uchaf* (the upper tavern), in contrast to *Y Tafarn Isaf* (the lower tavern) which used to be located near the site of the present Old Rectory.

Inquests were held in the public house in the early 19th century, as well as public auctions of properties. People attending church weddings and funerals would also frequent the tavern. When poet Edward Thomas visited the church in 1914, a funeral had taken place and he noted that *"The rest of the male mourners were drinking and talking up above at the Red Lion opposite the church."* (Berg dept. New York Public Library.) A newspaper report dated 1858, tells of a dinner held at the Red Lion Inn following a pigeon shoot at neighbouring Ysgubor Fawr "where they were most bounteously supplied with an excellent dinner and cwrw da." (MT&GA).

The Red Lion is the most popular name of British public houses. It is a heraldic symbol linked to many historical figures including Welshmen Llywelyn the Great and Owain Glyndwr.

There was also a *Red Lion* public house (1840 TM) in the hamlet of Ynysyfelin, now submerged under Llwyn-onn Reservoir.

> **Red, lion, inn**

Rhos Hyfryd   SN 946089

Housing estate

Rhoshyfryd 1996 SWVVA; 1991 OSPF; 1957 PR; 1948 TL;

Rhoshyfryd housing estate is located opposite the Lamb Inn below the junction of Chapel Road and Cwm Cadlan Road. It was built after the second world war by the Vaynor and Penderyn Urban District Council. Welsh *rhos* 'moor' should not be confused with English rose, which is Welsh rhosyn. *Hyfryd* is Welsh 'pleasant'.

> **Rhos, hyfryd; 'pleasant moor'**

Sgwd yr Eira

SN 930099

Waterfall

Sgwd yr Eira 1991 OS Pathfinder 1108; Scwd-yr-Eira 1972 V&P Official Guide p10; 1908 TCT; Ysgwd yr Eirw 1919 LC map; Sgwd Eirwy 1905 HPP p78; Scŵd yr Eira 1904 OS6"; Sgwd yr Ia 1902 TCT; Ysgwd yr Eira 1888 OS6"; Culhepste Cascade 1810 HB Vol. iv p67; Eirw Hepste 1810 ibid; Hepste cascade 1810 ibid;

Sgwd yr Eira is the name of a waterfall on the River Hepste.

There is a pathway behind and below the waterfall. This pathway is accessible with care. *Cilhepste* (as in Culhepste Cascade 1810) was an element in the names of nearby farmsteads. See above. This *Cilhepste* Waterfall has also been known as *Eirw Hepste*, *Ysgwd yr Eirw* and *Sgwd yr Eira*.

Several attempts have been made to explain the meaning of *Sgwd yr Eira* including imaginative interpretations of the final element, eg. Sgwd, eirwy; 'waterfall of cold water' (Eir 'cold' and wy 'water'), HPP 78; this meaning is contrived. In TCT 1902 an article by Cadrawd has '*Ysgwd yr Eira* or as some call it *Sgwd yr Ia*'. *Sgwd yr Ia* 'the ice cascade' is fanciful.

GPC has *eirwy* as 'cataract, waterfall', and this is found in TJ's "Eirw Hepste or Hepste cascade", 1810. It appears, as suggested by FJN in RSHVN p. 50, that the OS map compilers assumed that *Eirw* cascade would be Welsh *Sgwd yr Eirw*. Unfortunately, *Sgwd yr Eirw* is tautologous with both elements meaning 'a cascade'. Furthermore, FJN implies that the mapmakers confused *eirw* with *eira* resulting, by 1886 in *Ysgwd yr Eira* 'waterfall of snow'. Whether by accident or otherwise, *Sgwd yr Eira* is

Sgwd yr Eira. *Courtesy of Steve Jones*

well established and has long been accepted as the picturesque name for this popular waterfall.

> Sgwd, yr, eira; 'waterfall (of) snow'; from earlier 'Ysgwd yr Eirwy, Eirw Hepste, Hepste Cas-cade and Cilhepste Waterfall'

Siloam

SN 950081

Chapel

Siloam 2017 Visited; Built 1823 Rebuilt 1857 ds; Siloa, Pontprenllwyd 1905 (1823) HPP p104; Capel Siloa (Baptist) 1904 OS25".

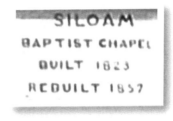

Siloam is the name of a Baptist chapel built in Pontbrenllwyd in 1823 and rebuilt in 1857, see datestone above. There is some discrepancy with the name. Some sources record *Siloam*, while others use *Siloa*. The plaque on the chapel wall reads "Siloam Baptist Chapel Built 1823 Rebuilt 1857". For further details see HPP p107. The Chapel was closed in 2015.

Siloam was the name of a spring and pool of water outside Jeruasalem. Jesus cured a blind man after telling him "Go, wash in the pool of Siloam." (John 9:7.) "Dos ac ymolch yn llyn Siloam." (Ioan 9:7). At one time, Siloam members were baptised in the waters of the nearby river Cynon.

> Siloam; Biblical lake-name

Soar

SN 949089

Chapel

Pulpit and Big Seat at Soar Chapel. *Courtesy of SM*

Eisteddfod Penderyn

[Undeb Cymru Fydd]

Dydd Sadwrn, Mawrth 5, 1949

Yn dechrau am 5 o'r gloch gydag Adran y Plant

Yng NGHAPEL SOAR

SYLWER.—Os bydd angen cynhelir Rhagbrofion (Prelims) i'r plant yn yr Ysgoldy am ddau o'r gloch.

Arweinyddion
Y Parch. GLYN JONES, B.A., Hirwaun
Y Parch. E. J. HUGHES, B.A., Hirwaun

Beirniaid
Cerdd ... ... LUTHER JAMES, Ysw., B.Sc., Aberdar
Adrodd a Llen ... Y Parch. JACOB DAVIES, B.A., Trecynon
Gwaith Llaw ... Mrs. HILDA M. JONES, Vicarage, Ystradfellte

MYNEDIAD - 1/6. PLANT, 6ch.

Y Cyfansoddiadau i fod yn llaw yr Ysgrifennydd erbyn Dydd Sadwrn, Chwefror 26, 1949.

Enwau'r Ymgeiswyr i fod yn llaw yr Ysgrifennydd erbyn Dydd Mercher, Mawrth 2, 1949.

Ysgrifennydd :
Miss GWYNETH ROBERTS, 8 Heol y Capel, Penderyn, ger Aberdâr

Pris y Rhaglen - 3c. Trwy'r post, 4c.

Stephens a George Cyf., Y Wasg Drydan, Aberdar. 3027

A poster for Penderyn Eisteddfod to be held at Soar Chapel in 1949.
Courtesy of SM

Capel Soar (Independent) 1904 OS25"; Independent Chapel 1884 OS6"; Capel Soar 1905 (1860) HPP p11.

Soar Independent Chapel is located on Chapel Road in the upper village. The chapel was built in 1859, opened in 1860 and extended in 1874. It was rebuilt in 1912. It closed *c.* 1993. For further details see HPP p110. As well as religious services, the chapel was used for cultural activities such as eisteddfodau.

Today the chapel building is home to The Penderyn Furniture Co.

Soar was a Biblical place of refuge for Lot. Soar chapel was a place of refuge.

Soar; 'place of refuge'

134

Sychbant Isaf SO 008101

Former Farm

Sychbant-isha 1981 OSM, 1955 OSM, 1905 OS6"; Sychbant 1926, 1914, 1891 Kelly, 1905 HPP p18, 1871 Cens. Sychbant isaf 1879 ERB, 1861, 1851 Cens.; Sych-pant-isaf 1832 OS; Sychbant Issa 1749 PMoel. map GRO.

Sychbant Isaf is located close to Pant Sychbant and Cefn Sychbant with fields bordering Nant Sychbant. The stream rises in Pant Sychbant and flows east into Taf Fawr. The farm takes its name from the stream and its source. In 1749 it was listed as one of the farms of the Penmailard Estate. *Isaf* and *Uchaf* are distinguishing elements for the two *Sychbant* farms. *Sychbant Isaf* is the larger of the two farms at 137 acres on the TAS, with *Sychbant Uchaf* a mere 37 acres. Both farms are now part of Coed Taf Fawr.

1841 TAS Sychbant Isha (137 acres):
Landowner – Vaughan Nash Edwards Esq. Occupier – John Jones.
1151. Ffynnon (well) 1152. Graig (rock) 1153. Creigudd Isha (lower rocks) 1155. Wood 1156. Graig Daniel (Daniel's rock) 1157. do 1158. do 1159. Tirhir (long land) 1160. do Ucha (upper do) 1161. Stang (stake, pole?) 1162. Homestead &c. 1163. Cau ffynnon (well field) 1164. Pen y ddwy Erw (top of the two acres) 1165. Ddwey Erw (two acres) 1166. do 1167. Cae Lloi (calves' field) 1168. Wern (alder wood) 1169. Pen y whech Erw (top of the six acres) 1170. Wern Isha (lower wet ground) 1171. Wynddol (white meadow) 1172. Godre Wynddol (bottom of the white meadow) 1173. Erw Grwer? (Grewr; herdsman's acre?) 1174. Graig Daniel (Daniel's rock) 1175. do 1176. Ynis fach (small river meadow) 1178. Barn Road &c. 1179. Cae Mawr (big field) 1180. Wood 1181. Cae bach (small field) 1182. Cae NewRhin? (Newryn?stout fellow's field?) 1184. Nerer (hanerer; half acre) 1185. Cae Llwyn (bush field) 1186. Waun las (green meadow) 1187. do fawr (big do)
Sych, pant, isaf; 'lower dry hollow'

Sychbant Uchaf SO 008101

Former Smallholding

Sychbant-uchaf 1981 OSM, 1955 OSM, 1905 OS6"; Sychbant uchaf 1879 ERB; Sychpant Ucha 1840 TM; Sychbant Ucha 1785 Will of William David NLW; Sychbant Ycha 1749 PM map GRO.

As *Sychbant Isaf*, but with *uchaf* as the distinguishing element. There are prehistoric cairns etc. on nearby Onllwyn which may have influenced one of the field-names below.

1841 TAS Sychpant Ucha (37 acres):
Landowner – Vaughan Nash Edwards Esq. Occupier – John Jones (continued).

1188. Cae Ifan (Ifan's field) 1189. Cae bach (small field) 1190. Homestead &c. 1191. Cae bach (small field) 1192. do 1193. Pedinen? dan y ddun (? below the ?) 1194. Cau hoffer? (offer? harness? Field) 1195. Coed cae (grazing enclosure) 1196. Cae dyndin? Ucha (upper hill-fort? field) 1197. do 1198. Cae bach (small field) 1199. do 1200. Cae Genol (middle field) 1201. Waun Isha (lower meadow) 1202. do Ucha (upper do) 1203. do Isha (lower do)

Sychbant, uchaf; 'upper Sychbant'

Sychryd
SN9207

Stream

Sychryd 1991 OSPF 1108. 1953 OS6", 1905 OS6", 1878 OSM;1905 HPP p10; Sych-ryd 1893 LL p367; Sy-chrydd River 1880 Tred. Est.; Sychryd brook 1784 Bute Est.; Sych-Rhyd River 1780 Tred. Est; Nant Hepstwr 14th cent. SWB; Hepstur c1150 LL p134.

Sychryd is the name of a stream that is fed by the Camnant, Nant Llechau and Nant Wyrfa near Trebanog Isaf, before flowing to Pwll y Crochan, (the cauldron's pool) on to Pwll y Berw (the boiling pool) and entering the River Mellte just below Dinas Rock. The name contains two elements Welsh *sych* and *rhyd* meaning 'dry ford', with many such crossings linked to this stream.

The early name for the river was *Hepstwr* (Hepstur LL) which is etymologically *hesb* and *dŵr* 'dry river'. The name appears in the text of the Book of Llan Dâv as part of the boundary "of the episcopate of Llann Dâv in the time of Oudoceus". The footnote on p367 states that "Hepstwr, i.e. Hesp-δwr, is not the Hepste" but is in fact the *Sychryd*.

Sych, rhyd; 'dry ford' from earlier hesb, dwr; 'dry water/river'

Tafarn Isaf, Y
SN 944085

Lost tavern

Tafarn Isaf 1919 LC map; 1923 LYH p25; Ty-Isaf; Tuy isha 1852 PR;Ty Isaf 1851 Census; Ty Ishaf (Rees Rees publican) 1841 Census; Publick House 1776 Map BFE; 1703 Stone?

Y *Tafarn Isaf* 'the lower tavern' was lower down the hill, and Y *Tafarn Uchaf* 'the upper tavern' was higher up the hill opposite Penderyn Church. Y *Tafarn Isaf* was demolished and the site remains empty on the bend below the Old Rectory. The public house was also known as y *ty isha* 'the lower house'. Y *Tafarn Uchaf* is now known as the Red Lion Inn or Y Llew Coch. The BFE map opposite shows the positions of the two taverns in 1776.

Y, tafarn, isaf; 'the lower tavern'

The above stone in Pantcefnffordd dated 1703 is said to have belonged to Tafarn Isha.   Courtesy of Mr B Shelton

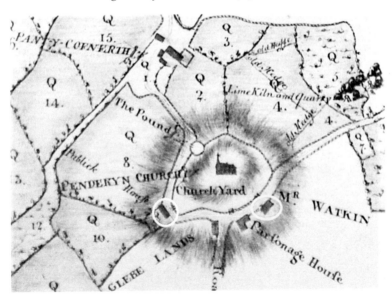

The white circled building is Y Tafarn Isaf and the yellow circle surrounds Y Tafarn Uchaf.   1776 BFE Map, courtesy of SM and WGAS (D/D BF/E 164)

Tafarn Uchaf, Y

SN 947085

Tavern also known as the Red Lion inn
Y Tafarn Ucha 1919 LC map; Tafarn Uchaf 1905 HPP p46;
See the Red Lion Inn.

Y, tafarn, uchaf: 'the upper tavern'

Tai Cwplau

SN 936071

Farm
Tai-cwplau 1991 OSPF 1108, 1905 OS6"; Tai Cwpla Farm 1914 Y Darian; Tai Cuple
1851 Cenusus; Tay Cwpla 1841 Census D20; Tay cupla 1841 Census D20; Taicyplau
1830 Will Morgan Jenkins NLW, 1812 PR; Ty Cwpla 1830 OS; part of Trebannog
Ucha 1841 TAS No. 215 House &c.; Ty Cupla 1802 PR Brths;

Tai Cwplau is the name recorded on the 1991 OSPF map for a small farm
to the west of Penderyn Reservoir. It is named Trebannog Uchaf on the
1840 TM and Part of Trebannog Ucha on the 1841 TAS. There are three
Trebannog Ucha farms named on the 1841 TM and TAS.

Confusion between the Trebannog Ucha farm names resulted in the
southernmost Trebannog Uchaf becoming *Tŷ Cwpla* or *Taicyplau* in the
early 1800s.

1841 TAS part of Trebannog Ucha:

Landowner – Morgan Morgan Esq. Occupier – Morgan Daniel.

201. Upper Piece 202. Coed cae (grazing enclosure) 203. Cae draw (yonder field)
204. Gilwern fach (small wet-land nook) (205. Do Fawr (big do) 206. (blank) 207.
Fawr Erw (big acre) 208. Tyle Melyn Isha (lower yellow hill) 209. do Ucha (do
upper) 210. Wood 211. Cefn y cae (the field ridge) 212. Cae Ysgubor (barn field)
213. Tyle ddu (black hill) 214. Clwtyn (a clout, patch) 215. House &c. 216.
Homestead 217. Cae Mawr (big field) 219. Road & Waste

1776 (D/D BF/E 164) Trebannog - Thos. John Lewelyn for the Moiety of,
O 1. Two Cots and Gardens 2. Cae draw (yonder field) 3. The wood in do 4.
Gilwern fach (small wetland nook) 5. Ditto fawr (big ditto) 6. (blank) 7. Coed cae
(grazing enclosure) 8. The upper piece 9. Part of Trebannog uchaf house 10. The
Barn 11. Beast House & Rick Yard 12½. The Brake in do 12. Cae'r Scibor (ysgubor;
barn field) 13. Cae mawr (big field) 14. Cefn y cae (the field ridge) 15. The Wood
16. Tyla melin uchaf (upper yellow hill) 17. Do isha (lower do) 18. Tair Erw (three
acres) 19. Tyla Du (black hill) 20. Clwtin (patch)

1776 (D/D BF/E 164) Trebannog Uchaf:

P 1. The Farm House 2. The Barn 3. The Beast House. 4. Field behind the house
5. The lane from ye house to Hirwain 6. Cae bach (small field) 7. Banwen (cotton
grass) 8. Wern pwll y cefil (wetland of the horse's pool) 9. Croft (small field) 10.
Clyn clun y Dery (meadow of the oak trees) 11. Cae yn y coed (field in the woods)

12. Cae'r engling (the englyn field. See Trebanog Uchaf) 13. Gwayn dola (field of the meadows)

The name contains two elements. The first is *tŷ* 'house', occasionally as the plural *tai* 'houses', while the second *cwplau* or *cyplau* is not so straightforward. The *Tai-cyplau* or *Tŷ cwpla* name was adopted in the early 1800s and refers to the rectangular building marked P3 on the 1776 BFE map. The building was marked as 'house' in 1840 but has since been demolished. Prior to being a family home, it was described as a '*Beast House*' i.e. a byre, a place to house cows etc. Many of these early buildings were constructed with pairs of large beams called Welsh *cyplau*. Having been converted from animal quarters to houses, *Tai-cyplau* would have been a suitable name for houses with large visible beams or *cyplau*. *Cyplau* is also Welsh for 'a couple', 'a pair' GPC. The 1776 row of buildings may have been converted to a pair of houses. C.f. Murycyplau, Llanystumdwy,

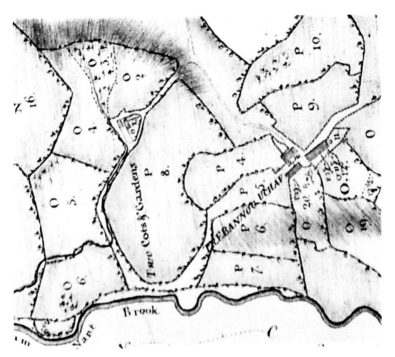

The BFE 1776 map showing Trebannog Uchaf with three blocks of buildings.
P1 (the farm house) is at the end of field P4 (field behind the house);
P2 (The Barn) is at the end of field O20 (clwtin 'patch') and P3 (The Beast
House) is the rectangle shaped block on O11 (Beast House & Rick Yard).
Courtesy of SM and WGAS (D/D BF/E 164)

Caerns.; Tyddyn y Cyplau, Penmynydd, Anglesey and Cyplau, Meorionydd (HEF p. 108). *Cwpla* has two possible derivations. Firstly as the local dialect form of *cwplau*, and secondly as the local dialect form of *cwblhau* 'to complete'. In the first instance, *Tŷ cwpla* could mean the 'couple's house' or the 'house with coupled beams', while if it represents *cwblhau*, *Tŷ Cwpla* would mean the 'finished house', which would suit the converted beast house. The usual explanation for *cyplau* is 'coupled beams'.

**Tai, cyplau; 'houses (with) pairs of beams' or Ty, cwpla;
'finished house'**

Tai'r Lamb   SN 947088

Houses

Tai'r Lamb 1861 PR;

   Tai'r Lamb are 'houses' (near) 'the Lamb' Inn.

Three Oaks   SN 956068

Lost Tavern

Three Oaks 1939 V&PRD; Three Oaks (B.H.) 1904 OS25"; Three Oaks Inn 1871 Census; Three Oaks 1865 PR, 1851 Census;

The *Three Oaks* Inn was located on the side of the old tramroad between Penderyn and Hirwaun. Today there are oak trees near the site which probably accounts for the old tavern's name.

Tir Argoed Blith

Lost name

Tur Argoed Blith (David John Llewellin) 1644 Tred. Est.
        Possibly 'land of the productive woodland'.

Tir Coed Meibion Rhys   See Heol Las

Lost Farm-name

Tircoedplantmeibionrhys 1850 gs; Koed Plant Meibion Rees 1705 BFE; Tyr Coad Mybon Rees 1667 Will of Evan Morgan; Tire Koed Meibion Rice 1578 Will of Griffithe David ap Rees

Tircoedplantmeibionrhys used to be the name of a farm on the main road leading from Penderyn to Ystradfellte. It is known today as *Heol Las*. Over the years the farm had a number of names including *Rheol, Tyr Heol, Pant yr Heol*, and finally *Heol-las*, which is named as Rees Price's home in the 1841 Census, although he much preferred the old name, as recorded on his gravestone (opposite) in 1850.

The impression given was, that this Rees, was the eponymous Rhys of *Tircoedplantmeibionrhys*. This is false. Rees Price inherited the holding's lease from his uncle Edward Price of "Ewysharold", Herefordshire. Rees Price died in 1850, aged 78. The Tircoedplantmeibionrhys name had been in use, many years before the days of Rees Price and his children.

Archived records show earlier examples of *Koed Plant Meibion Rees* in 1705, *Tyr Coed Mybon Rees* in 1667 as well as Tier koed meibon Rice in the will of Griffith David ap Rees of Aberdaer in 1578.

"called Tire koed meibon Rice" from the will of Griffith David ap Rees, Aberdaer, 1578.

Whoever the eponymous Rhys was, he and his sons were alive before 1578, and his son's children (plant meibion Rhys) were probably treading this earth in the early 1600s. Unfortunately, one is unable to identify Rhys with certainty. It is tempting to accept the Rhys present in the names of Griffith David ap Rhys and his brother Llewelyn David ap Rhys, holders and inheritors of *Tire koed meibon Rice* in 1578, as the Rhys of the place-name.

Other named inheritors are David ap Morgan and Evan ap Lewes. It is likely that Griffith David ap Rees, along with his brother Llewelyn David ap Rees, were cousins to David ap Morgan and Evan ap Lewes, and that their fathers (David, Morgan and Lewes) were brothers, and the sons of Rhys. Whoever Rhys was, we can say with certainty that he was not Rees Price, nephew of Edward Price of Ewysharold.

The elements in the name are *tir* 'land', *coed* 'trees', *plant* 'children', *meibion* 'sons' and the personal name *Rhys*, giving 'the woodland of the children of the sons of Rhys', from an earlier 'woodland of Rhys's sons'.

Tir, coed, plant, meibion, Rhys; 'land of the woods of Rhys's sons' children'

Tir Fadog Llwyd

Lost name

Tyr kaie Vadocke llwyd 1626 Tred. Est.

Tir Gwyn bach   SN 959064

Residence, previous farm and industrial site

Tir Gwyn Bach 1997 HVHR; 1905 HPP p15; 1840 TMS; Tirgwynbach 1991 OSPF1108; Ty and Tyr Gwyn bach 1758 Maybery 1 NLW; Tire y tu gwinbâch 1711 Will of Evan Thomas NLW.

Today *Tirgwynbach* is the name of a property at the end of "the Dark Lane" on the outskirts of the village of Hirwaun. The land of present-day Tirgwynbach is much reduced from the pre 1758 farmhouse and land. It was in 1758, that part of *Tirgwynbach* was sold by John Jenkin to John Wilkins, Thomas Mayberry and his son John Mayberry. This was the site of Herwen Furnace, later extended to become known as Hirwaun Iron Works. Note William Crawshay's name below.

The 1711 form shows that the meaning of *tir y ty gwyn bach* 'land of the small white house' is preferable to 'land of little Gwyn's house'. A 19th cent. photo of the house shows it as a 'white house'.

1841 TAS Tir Gwyn Bach (64 acres):
Landowner William Crawshay Esq.   Occupiers – Himself
372. Upper Meadow 373. Middle do 374. Lower do 375. Caer Redyn (fern field) 376. Cae Bach (small field) 377. Pasture 378. Pond 379. Cae Mawr (big field) 380. Cottage and Gardens 381. Herwain (sic) Iron Works Coke Yard etc.

Tir, y, ty, gwyn, bach; 'land of the small white house'

Name on the gate of the property. 2020 *courtesy of Steve Jones*

Tir Hywel Hir

Lost name

Tir Howell Hir 1644/5 Tred. Est.;Tyr Howell hire y John Games 1626 Tred. Est. (John llen ddy gent); Tyr Howell hire y Richard Powell Walter 1626 Tred. Est. (John llenw); Tir Howell hir 1617 Will of John Llewellin David, NA;

For *Hywel Hir* of Penderyn, *c.* 1370, grandson of Hywel Fwya ap Trahaearn of Dyffryn Tav, see Bleddyn ap Maenyrch 39 (Bartrum). The *Hywel Hir* properties may be in Cwm Taf, as they appear either side of Abernant on the 1626 list.

Tir Jenkin Gwyn Fawr

Tyr Jenkin Gwin vawr 1626 Tred. Est. (Jenkin Morgan)

Tir Jenkin Llwyd Gruffydd

Tyr Jennu llowyd Griff 1626 Tred. Est. (John Herbert gent.)

Tir Jenkin Thomas David

Tir Jenkin Thomas David 1781 Will of Watkin Phillips NLW

Tir John Dafydd Fach y Rhys ap John Ychan

Tyr John dd vach y R sap John ychan 1626 Tred. Est. (Rs wiij ap Rs)

This property was probably located in Cwm Taf Fawr, possibly Wern Fawr, as it was listed next to Tyr nant y guigar (Tir Nant y Geugarn).

Tir Llewelyn Thomas Powell

Tir Llewelyn Thomas Powell alias Troed y Rhwe 1644 Tred. Est.

See *Troedyrhiw*

Tir Llwyn Celyn

Tir Lloyn Kelin 1657 Tred. Est.

Tir Maes Rhys

Tyr Maes Rs 1626 Tred. Est. (Sr Hen wiym Kt)

Tir Main

Tir Mane 1555 RISW GGF 1/100

Possibly linked to Tremaen?

Tir Mawr

Lost name

Tir Mawr 1705 BFE; Tyr mawr nup David ap dd 1626 Tred. Est. (Richard Games gent.); Tir Mawr yn y dre 1560 RISW GGF 1/101

Tir Mawr is probably a truncated form of the earlier *Tyr mawr nup David ap dd*, as well as *Tir Mawr yn y dre*. *Tir mawr nup David ap dd* means that the land of *Tir Mawr* was lately (Latin nuper) in the hands of David ap dd, while *Tir mawr yn y dre* translates as the 'big land in the estate', with *tref* meaning 'residence, farm, estate' etc. (see GPC) rather than today's meaning of *tref* as 'town'.

Tir Meherer GRM

Tyr Miherer Grm 1626 Tred. Est. (Sr Edw Lewis Kt.)

See *Glyn Perfedd*

Tir Pen y Cae y John Gwyn

Lost name

Tyr Pen y kaie y John Gwin 1626 Tred. Est. (Thomas griff. gent)
This property is listed next to Tyr y Byllva and may well represent today's Penycae.

For John Gwyn of Penderyn, *c.* 1400, see Morgannwg 5 (Bartrum).

Tir Pwll Cynferth   Lost name

see Pant Cynferth/Pant Cefn y Ffordd

Tir Rhys ap John Ychan

Tyr Rs ap John ychan 1626 Tred. Est. (R sap Jenu)

Tir Thomas Ddu ?Cest

Tyr Thomas ddy Kest 1626 Tred. Est. (Sr Edw Lewis Kt.)

Tir y Cae Du

Tyr y kae Dy 1626 Tred. Est. (Watkin Pheb gent.)

Possibly Ysgubor Fawr (if Watkin Pheb gent is the same person as Phelip Watkin of Tyr Pant Cyvnerth.

Tir y Cefnty   Lost

Tir y keventie 1468 MWBM

Tir y Dyled

tire y dylad 1553 RISW/GGF1/99

dylad is is the dialectic form of *dyled* 'debt'.

Tir y Gelli Ddwll   Lost name

Tyr y gelly ddwll 1626 Tred. Est.(Richard Games gent.)
See Y Glog

Tir y Gorwydd   Lost name

Tir y gorwydd 1739 HPP 52.; Tyr y Gorwidd 1626 Tred. Est. (Sr Edw Lewis Kt.)
Tir y Gorwydd is Cae'r Arlwydd (SEHPP p. 41)

Tir y Rhiw   Lost name

tyr y Riwe 1526 Tred. Est. Rec.

Tor y Foel   SN 943085
Farm

Tor-y-foel 1991 OS Pathfinder 1108; Torvol 1851 Census; Tor fole 1841 Census; The
Vole 1841 TAS; Tor-y-foel 1832 OS; Tor-y-Fole (farm) 1829 Cambrian; Tor y voell
1635 Tredegar;

Tor-y-foel farm located on the eastern slopes of Moel Penderyn, was the
birthplace of local printer, writer, musician and philanthropist Jenkin
Howell (1836-1902). His gravestone in Penderyn churchyard contains the
following elegy by Watcyn Wyn:

> Gwron yn mysc dyngarwyr – a'r llenor
> Llawnaf o bob synwyr;
> Nawdd i leng o farddol wyr
> Ac enwog yn mysc canwyr.

> A hero among philanthropists – and a writer
> Most gifted with wisdom.
> A protector to legions of poets
> And supreme among singers.   (trans.DMJ)

Known locally as Y Foel or the Vole, Moel Penderyn (see above) is a high
hill with a conspicuous bird's head shape. It sits on a geological fault line
that extends from Swansea Bay to Herefordshire, known as the 'Neath
disturbance'. This fault is a visible feature on Moel Penderyn. *Tor-y-foel*
farm is the nearest habitat to this geological feature.

Tor-y-foel has two elements plus the definite article. The first element is Welsh *tor* which has a number of meanings, two of which may apply here. The first defined in GPC under *tor*[1] is 'a breaking; gap, breach, interruption' etc. that could describe *the Foel's* visible fault line. The second meaning which may also be applicable is *tor*[2c] 'breast, slope, flank or side of (mountain, hill)' etc. Both meanings are suitable for *Tor-y-foel*.

The final element *moel*, lenited to *y foel*, is taken from *Moel Penderyn*, indicating the farm's close location to it. The whole, *Tor-y-foel*, has a meaning of either 'the Foel fault' or 'side of the Foel hill'.

The local dialect pronunciation is *Torfôl*, as heard in a 1974 recording (RMR); cf. *Y Fôl* for *Y Foel* and the anglicised *Vole*. *Tor-y-foel* is the accepted standardised spelling.

Cf. Torpantau, Brecs.; Torfaen, Monm.; Llanfihangel Torymynydd, Monm.; Torbant, Pembs.

Tor, y, moel; 'the Foel fault' or 'side of the Foel hill'

Trebanog   SN 9407

Estate, Farm

Trebanog 1905 HPP p17; 1621 HB 11 p156; Trebannog 1831, 1811, 1810, 1793 PR; 1776 BFE;1768 Penpont; 1705 BFE; Dre Bannog 1689 Will of William Morgan; Trebainnocke 1626 Will of William Prees NA; House at Bainocke 1626 ibid; Trebannog 1555 RISW/GGF1/100; y tir mawr yn y Dre Bannog 1560 RISW/GGF1/101;

Trebanog is currently the name of a number of farms in the parish eg. *Trebanog Fawr*, *Trebanog Fach*, *Trebanog Uchaf* and *Trebnog Isaf*, while *Trebanog Genol* used to be the name of one of the *Trebannog* farms. (see below). The *Trebanog* name dates back to the 1500s, with some toponymists linking the name to the much earlier *Gavannog* (see above). The 15th and 16th cent. *Trebanog* estate was classed as one of the Gentry houses of Breconshire (AB) with the estate at one time, including Cefndon, probably Pantycynferth, Ysgubor Fawr, and early lands such as Tyr Mawr David ap David, Tyr Klin y Menneth, Glyn Celli, Ynys Llwyfog, Cae Iorwerth and Tremayne etc. (see RISW docs. & HVHR. p. 39).

Trebanog contains two elements, *tref* and *panog*. *Tref* is a Welsh sing. fem. noun originally, 'house, dwelling place, homestead', including the land held with the homestead. Much later it developed into the modern meaning of 'town'. The loss of the final syllable is common in Welsh place-names. *Tre(f)* mutates to *dre(f)* following the def. art. eg. y tir mawr yn y Dre Bannog 1560.

The second element may be a contraction of the earlier *gavannog* (see

Gavannog above). However, if *Trebanog* is the original name for the farm and estate, then *panog*, Welsh *pân* 'cotton grass' plus the adjectival suffix *-og* giving a place abounding in cotton grass, is likely. Cf. *Banwen* (panwaun; 'bog-cotton moor') field no. 7, *Trebannog Uchaf*, 1776. Dewi Cynon suggests *banog* 'prominent, conspicuous' (HPP p12), but this would give *Trefanog* cf. *Y Fan, Pen-y-fan*.

For the 1841 TAS see individual *Trebanog* farm names. For 1776 BFE Thomas John Lewelyn for the Moiety of *Trebannog*: see *Tai Cyplau*.

At its height, the *Trebanog* estate could have extended from *Penderyn* Church in the north to the *Camnant* brook in the south, *Afon Cynon* in the east to *Rhydfaen* in the west.

Tref, panog; 'cotton-grass farm'

Trebanog Cottages SN 949072

Lost name

Trebanog Cottages 1926, 1925, 1915 PR; 1916 BCT; 1901 Census; Ynysfawr Cottage 1911 Census; Ynysfawr 1891 Census; Trebanog Fawr Cottage 1892 PR; Trebanog Gate 1857, 1855, 1852, 1848, 1827 PR. Ynys Fawr 1841 TAS.

Trebanog Cottage was the name of one of two cottages that used to be located on *Trebanog Fawr* farmland. The cottages were also called Ynysfawr Cottages. In 1892 the Worthing family cottage was called *Trebanog Fawr Cottage*. In 1901 it was *Trebanog Cottage* while in 1911 the Worthing home had become *Ynysfawr Cottage* (see Census returns). *Trebanog Turnpike Gatehouse* was located near the roadside on *Ynys fawr* field (no. 301 on the 1841 TAS and 1840 TM). *Trebanog Cottage* and *Ynysfawr Cottage* are later names for the redundant *Trebanog Turnpike Gatehouse* recorded as *Turnpike Cottages* in 1821 (PR).

In 1914 the Finch family's address was *Trebanog Terrace*, but in 1926 their address was *Trebanog Cottages*. It seems that some of the later *Trebanog* terraced houses also adopted the *cottages* suffix, but they should not be confused with the earlier *Trebanog Cottages* that once stood opposite the entrance to today's Ty Newydd Hotel. The present bungalow, property of Mr and Mrs Oliver, situated close to the location of the old *Trebanog Gatehouse*, preserves the Ynysfawr name.

Trebanog, cottages; 'cottages on Trebanog land'; ynys, mawr;
'large river-meadow'

Trebanog Fach SN 945074

Residence, old farm

Tre-banog-fach 1991 OSPF 1108; Trebanog Fach 1911, 1861 Census; 1905 HPP p17;

1892, 1888, 1800, 1792 PR; Trebannog Fach 1847 Will Edward William NLW; Trebannog Vach 1807 Will Thomas Rees NLW, 1783 PR; Trebanog, Will of Rees William Prees 1621.

The old 17th cent. farmhouse is now an outhouse, and a modern residence has been erected in its place. The farm was listed as having 200 acres on the 1851 Census returns. The farmhouse is recorded as a 17th cent. longhouse in The Houses of Breconshire, Brycheiniog Vol. 16, 1972 p. 39. It is a much older building than *Trebanog Fawr* which is regarded as a 19th cent. farmhouse. This farm was the likely home of Rees Williams of *Trebanog*, who died in 1621 op. cit. p. 8 (see 1621 above).

Over the years, this farm was known as *Trebanog, Trebanog Ganol* and *Trebanog Fach*. On the 1841 TAS, *Trebanog Genol* (aka *Fach*), *Trebanog Fawr* and one of the three *Trebanog Ucha* farms were all owned by the Rev. Richard Davies and William Payne. *Trebannog Genol* and *Trebannog Fawr* were occupied by Thomas Edwards. *Trebannog Ucha* was occupied by Edward Williams. The 1841 Census returns have Thomas Edwards at *Trebannog Farm* and Edward William at *Trebannog ganol*. The PR Burials have Edward William placed at *Trebannog Fach* in 1846 aged 90. Dewi Davies, writing in 1905 names *Trebanog, Trebanog Isaf* and *Trebanog Fach* in his farm list HPP p. 17. He does not list *Trebanog Uchaf* or *Trebanog Ganol*. One must assume that his *Trebanog* is *Trebanog Fawr* as the farmer or occupier is named as Mr. John Harries who is also the named occupier of *Trebanog Fawr* on the 1901 Census. It seems that the distinguishing elements of the *Trebanog* farms have caused confusion locally as well as with maps, census returns and other printed documents.

Trebanog, bach; 'small Trebanog'

Trebanog Fawr

SN 949073

Farm

Tre-banog-fawr 1991 OSPF 1108; Trebanog Fawr 1911, 1861 Census; 1896,1847, 1844,1843, 1841, 1839 PR; Trebanog-fawr 1830 OS; Trebanog 1802, 1800 PR; Trebannog Fawr 1841 Census, 1840 TM, 1798, 1795 PR ;

Trebanog Fawr is the name of the farm that was located adjacent to *Melin Trebanog* or *Trebanog Mill*. *Trebanog Fawr* is not an old name. The mill is reputed to have been built in the 17th cent. but *Trebanog Fawr* farmhouse is said to be a 19th cent. building (Brycheiniog, Vol. 16 p. 8). Although named *Trebanog Fawr* 'large Trebanog', the 1851 Census returns record it at 110 acres with nearby *Trebanog Fach* 'small Trebanog' at 200 acres and *Trebanog Isaf* 'lower Trebanog' at 160 acres. It may be that the term Fawr referred to the size of the 'new' 19th cent. farmhouse, coupled with the 1841 TAS showing that the two adjacent farms (*Fawr* and *Genol/Fach*) were jointly owned and occupied, giving a combined large unit of over 300 acres. *Trebanog Fawr* does not appear anywhere earlier than 1795 and was reputedly formed from joining the tenements named Glyn Celli and Ynys Llwyfog (HVHR p. 39). The earlier farms are named *Trebanog* or *Trebannog* with different distinguishing elements viz. *uchaf, isaf, fach* and *ganol*.

1841 TAS Trebannog Fawr (130 acres):
Landowners – Rev. Richard Davies & William Payne. Occupier – Thomas Edwards 280. Wern y Gan (?gân; ?white spotted alder swamp) 281. Caer Odyn (the kiln field) 282. Y Gelli (the grove) 283. Fedw bach (small birch) 284. Cae Clyn Isha (lower meadow field) 285. Cae Clyn Ucha (upper meadow field) 286. Cae wil Howell (Will Howell's field) 287. (blank) 288. Coed cae Llwyd (grey or Lloyd's grazing enclosure) 289. Caer Garreg (field of the stone) 290. Wern y bedw Mawr (large birch trees wet land) 291. Wern y Lloi (calves' wet land) 292. Croft and Croft fach (small field and little small field) 293. Homestead & 294. Mill and Garden 295. Wern Cwm y dwr (alder swamp of the valley near the water) 296. Ynis ddy (ddu; black river meadow) 297. Ynis fach (small river meadow) 298. do Wern (alder swamp do) 299. Morfa coch & Island (red marsh) 300. Cae Cefin heol (field at back of road) 301. Ynis fawr (large river meadow) 302. do Draw (yonder do) 303. Lletty Rhys &c (Rhys's abode) 304. Wern (alder swamp) 305. Coed cae bach (small grazing enclosure) 306. do 254. Waun y Gwayr uyrs (?ysgâr; shared grass meadow. nos. 254 & 255 are near Trebannog Uchaf) 255. do 370. Peder Erw (four acres)

Trebanog, mawr; 'large Trebanog'

Trebanog Ganol
Lost name
Trebannog ganol 1841 Census; Trebanog-ganol 1830 OS; Trebannog Ganol 1798 PR; Trebannog Genol 1705 BFE;

Trebanog Ganol was also known as *Trebanog Fach*, but the former name has not been used since the 1840s. It probably had the canol 'middle' suffix as it was roughly equidistant between *Trebanog Mill* and *Trebanog Uchaf*. Note the local dialect genol of 1705. The 1841 TAS had a total 248 acres which is large for this district.

1841 TAS Trebannog Genol (248):
Landowners – Revd. Richard Davies, William Payne (Contnd (from Trebannog Ucha)) Occupier – Thomas Edwards
256. Bryncoch (red hill) 257. Waun hir (long meadow) 258. Ishin Bach (eisin; small husk (place)) 259. Waun hir (long meadow) 260. Bryn y Gwys (the pig hill) 261. Waun Gron (cron2 GPC; cow parsnip meadow; the field is not round, therefore

it is unlikely to be cron1 GPC ') 262. Caer Odyn (the kiln field) 263. Tir Gwilt (gwyllt; uncultivated land) 264. Caer Coed (the wood field) 265. Ton (lay land) 266. Digoed (cleared of wood) 267. Wern Tile Cae Mawr (alder tree swamp of Cae Mawr hill) 268. Cae Mawr (big field) 269. do 270. Tile (tyle; hill) 271. Homested & y lon (& the lane) 272. Croft (small field) 273. Coed Cae (grazing enclosure) 274. (blank) 275. Cae Lloi (calves' field) 276. Tir Newydd (new ground) 277. Cae (field) 278. do 279. Y Wern (alder tree swamp)

Trebanog, canol; 'middle Trebanog'

Trebanog Isaf

SN 929071

Farm

Tre-banog-isaf 1991 OSPF 1108; Trebanog Isaf, Rhigos 1911 Census; Trebanog Isaf, 1905 HPP p17; 1864 PR; Trebannog Ishaf 1841 Census D20; Trebannog Isha 1840 TM; 1834 GMBG; 1705 BFE; Tyr klin y menneth 1626 SEHPP;

Trebanog Isaf is the most westerly of the *Trebanog* farms bordering Camnant brook. The *isaf* (local dialect *ishaf*) distinguishing element describes its lower elevation at *c.* 650 ft above sea level, compared to the other slightly more elevated *Trebanog* farms. AS has this farm as *Tyr klin y menneth* in 1626 (SEHPP p. 19). *Tyr kiln y menneth* would be *Tir clun y mynydd* in today's orthography and could be translated as 'land of the mountain meadow', although this does not conform with the *isaf* distinguishing element. It may be that *clun y mynydd* is used here for a meadow in 'unenclosed land' (see GPC), rather than a 'mountain' meadow. NS has *Trebanog Isaf* as *Clyn y mynygh*.

1841 TAS Trebannog Isha (144 acres):
Landowner – Morgan Morgan Esq. Occupier – John Morgan
177. Cwm car Ton (valley of the lay land field) 178. Coed cae fenlan? (upper end? grazing enclosure) 179. Wyther (eight acres) 180. Road 181. (blank) 182. Coed cae (grazing enclosure) 183. Wern (alder swamp) 184. Hen Waun (old meadow) 185. Cae dderwen (oak tree field) 186. Cae Clyn (meadow field) 187. Wood 188. Gardd felin (yellow garden) 189. Cae Mawr (big field) 190. Erw (an acre) 191. Cefn y coed (back of the woods) 192. Ynis fach (small river meadow) 193. Cottage &c. 194. Cae dan ty (field below the house) 195. Homestead &c. 196. Gilwen (gilwern; alder swamp nook) 197. Cae bach (small field) 198. Clyn Afon (river meadow (Clyn Evan in BFE 16, which accounts for its distance from the river)) 200. Wain Newydd (new meadow)

Trebanog, isaf; 'lower Trebanog'

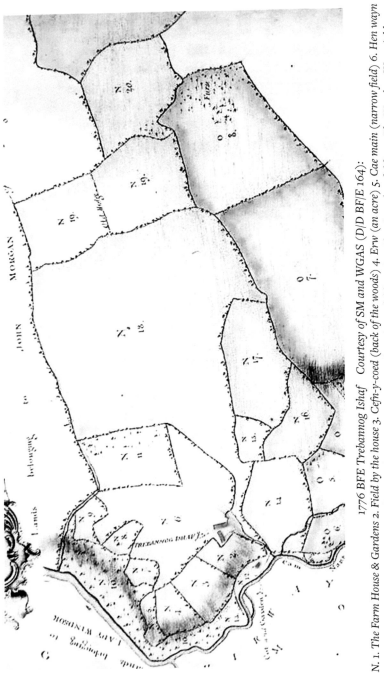

1776 BFE Trebannog Ishaf   Courtesy of SM and WGAS (D/D BF/E 164):

N. 1. The Farm House & Gardens 2. Field by the house 3. Cefn-y-coed (back of the woods) 4. Erw (an acre) 5. Cae main (narrow field) 6. Hen wayn (old meadow) 7. Gardd Velan (yellow garden) 8. Cae'r Derwan (the oak tree field) 9. Cae Clyn (meadow field) 10. The Wood 11. Wern (alder swamp) 12. Cot. Garden & the croft 13. Ynis fach (small river meadow) 14. Gilwern (nook by the alder swamp) 15. Cae bach (small field) 16. Clyn Evan (Evan's meadow) 17. Wayn Newydd (new mwdow) 18. Coed cae (grazing enclosure) 19. Blank 20. blank

Trebanog Terrace

SN 950075

Row of houses

Trebanog Ter. 1996 SWVSA; Tre banog Terrace 1919 OS6"; Trebanog Terrace 1931, 1916, 1914 PR;

Trebanog Terrace is the name for a row of six houses built in Pontbrenllwyd *c.* 1914 by Messrs Underwood and Bros as water board cottages, linked with the Penderyn Reservoir. It was named *Trebanog Terrace* as the row of houses were constructed on land that had previously belonged to *Trebanog Fawr*, (see 1841 TAS & 1840 TM). In 1917 Conscientious Objectors placed in Penderyn were accommodated in these houses. Some residents used to refer to the terraced homes as 'Conshy houses'.

Trebanog Uchaf

SN 941074

Farms

Tre-banog uchaf 1991 OSPF 1108; Trebannog Ucha 1841 TAS; part of Trebannog Ucha (2) 1841 TAS; Treba-nog-uchaf 1830 OS; Trebanog uchaf 1798 PR; Tir Mawr David ap David 1560 RISW;GGF/101;

The 1841 TAS shows three separate entries for *Trebanog Uchaf*, two of which are owned by Morgan Morgan and occupied by Morgan Daniel and William Jenkins, while the third is owned by the Rev. Richard Davies and William Payne in the occupation of Edward Williams.

The fields named in both 1776 BFE and the 1841 Daniel Morgan property show that *Trebannog Moiety* of Thos. John Lewellyn of 1776 is the same property as Morgan Morgan owns and Morgan Daniel holds, in the 1841 TAS. The farm size is 62 acres in the 1841 TAS. The 1841 Census has Daniel Morgan, Farmer aged 70, at Tay Cupla. The 1905 OS6" Map has Tai-Cwplau at that location. This particular *Trebannog Ucha* property is known today as *Tai-cwplau*.

The 1841 TAS property of 79 acres also called *Trebannog Ucha*, again owned by Morgan Morgan, but occupied by William Jenkins, stands alongside the 62-acre property. The third *Trebannog Ucha* farm of 130 acres of the 1841 TAS, fields numbered 232 to 253, is owned by the Rev. Richard Davies and William Payne and occupied by Edward Williams. This is also adjacent to the other two *Trebannog Ucha* farms owned by Morgan Morgan.

Trebannog Uchaf was known as Tir Mawr David ap David in 1626 (SEHPP p19). A document dated 1560 states that David ap David of Penderyn and his son Morgan ap David, sold *Y Tir mawr yn y Dre Bannog* to Gwilym Ieuan Fychan of Ystradfellte (RISW/GGF/101). It is reasonable to assume that this land later became known as *Trebanog Uchaf*. It is also likely that *Cae Yorwerth* became part of *Trebanog Uchaf*.

1841 TAS part of Trebannog Ucha (62 acres):
Landowner – Morgan Morgan Esq. Occupier – Morgan Daniel.
201. Upper Piece 202. Coed cae (grazing enclosure) 203. Cae draw (yonder field) 204. Gilinen fach (celynen; small holly tree) 205. Fawr (big) 206. (blank) 207. Tair Erw (three acres) 208. Tyle Melyn Isha (lower yellow hill) 209. do Ucha (upper) 210. Wood 211. Cefn y cae (back of the field) 212. Cae Ysgubor (barn field) 213. Tyle ddu (black hill) 214. Clwtyn (a patch (of ground)) 215. House &c. 216. Homestead 217. Cae Mawr (big field) 219. Road & Waste

1841 TAS part of Trebannog Ucha (79 acres):
Landowner – Morgan Morgan Esq. Occupier – William Jenkins.
202a. Coed cae (grazing enclosure) 218. Homestead 219a. Road & Waste 220. Cae bach (small field) 221. (blank) 222. Wern pwll y Ceffyl (wet ground of the horse's pool) 223. Building &c. 224. (blank) 225. Croft (small field) 226. Clyn (clun) deri (oak trees meadow) 227. Cae yn y coed (field in the wood) 228. Coed cae (grazing enclosure) 229. (blank) 230. Gwain Dole (dolau; the meadows' meadow) 231. Caer Engling (the englyn field, poss. englyn crwca 'crooked, bent, curved'.)

1776 BFE Trebannog Uchaf (64 acres):
P. 1. The Farm House 2. The Barn 3. The Beast House 4. Field behind the house 5. The lane from ye house to Hirwayne 6. Cae bach (small field) 7. Banwen (panwaun; cotton grass) 8. Wern pwll y cefil (ceffyl; alder swamp of the horse's pool) 9. Croft 10. Clyn y Dery (oak trees meadow) 11. Cae yn y coed (field in the woods) 12. Cae'r Engling (Engling's field); this is an unusual field-name, but Richard Morgan compares it to Penyrenglyn, Ystradyfodwg, where the final element is not related to englyn, a stanza in Welsh poetry, but possibly consists of the intensifying prefix an- (en-) and glyn 'a valley' giving 'a deep dingle/valley'. Today unfortunately, Cae'r Engling lies beneath the waters of Penderyn Reservoir which makes it difficult to confirm the presence of such a deep dingle/valley). 13. Gwayn Dola (dolau; meadows' meadow)

1841 TAS Trebannog Ucha (130 acres):
Landowner – Revd. Richard Davies, William Payne. Occupier – Edward Williams
232. Cae dan y ty (field below the house) 233. Cae bach (small field) 234. Cae Nath Howell (Nath(aniel) How-ell's field) 235. do 236. do 237. Waun Fawr (big meadow) 238. Coed Cae (grazing enclosure) 239. Waun Erw (meadow acre) 240. Cwech (sic) (chwech; six (acres)) 241. Caer Marchog (the horseman or knight's field) 242. do 243. Wern Bwdwr (unproductive alder swamp) 244. Gurlodd (sic) (gweirglodd; meadow) 245. Cae dan y ty (field below the house) 246. do 247. Wern fach (small alder swmp) 248. Y Clyn (the meadow) 249. Homestead & 250. Cae

dych lawr y Ty (field below the house) 251. Caer Marchog (the horseman or knight's field) 252. Y Derri (the oaks) 253. Saith Erw (seven acres)

Trebanog, uchaf; 'Upper Trebanog'

Tremaen

Lost name

Tremane 1553 HPP 52

"confirmed to Gwilym ap Phylip a tenement of land called Tremane situate in Penderin: extending in length from Trebanog as far as land called Cae Yorwerth; and in width from Nant Camnant to Carn Lloyn Hytholl,"

From this description *Tremaen* is adjacent to, or possibly part of Gilfach Rhydfaen. Both place-names have the same final element. *Tremaen* contains two elements, *tref* 'farm' and *maen* 'stone', cf. Cilhepste Cerrig.

Tref, maen; 'stone farm'

Troedyrhiw

Lost

Troed-y-rhiw 1905 OS6", 1830 OS; Troedrhiw 1905 HPP 18; Troed rhyw 1841 Census; Tir Llewelyn Thomas Powell alias Troed y Rhwe 1644 Tred. Est.

This farm located in Cwm Taf is now submerged under Llwyn-onn reservoir. The farmhouse is under the western end of the dam wall. *Troed* is 'foot' and *rhiw* is 'hill' giving 'the foot of the hill'. It would have been at the foot of Nant Sychbant hill. In the 17th cent. this property was known as *Tir Llewelyn Thomas Powell*.

1841 TAS Troed y rhiw (50 acres):
Landowner – Morgan Williams Esqre. Occupier – Edward Lewis.
1231. Gwaun (meadow) 1232. Coed cae (grazing enclosure) 1233. Cae bach (small field) 1234. Hendre Wen (white old farm) 1235. Caer Pistill (the spring/spout field) 1236. Homestead &c. 1237. Hendre Wen (white old farm) 1238. Coed bach (small trees) 1239. Fedw fach (small birch tree) 1240. Cae dan domen (field below dung-heap) 1241. Plantation &c. 1242. Ynis (river meadow) 1243. do Ucha (upper do) 1244. The Close 1245. do 1246. Waste

Troed, y, rhiw; 'foot of the hill'

Troedrhiw'r Llan   SN 945088

District, lost tavern

Troedrhiwllan 1942 PR; Troed Rhiw'r Llan 1855 PR; Troedrhiwllan 1773 PR Bapt.

Troedrhiw 'rllan is the name of the district, <u>at the foot of the hill</u>, descending from St Cynog's church towards the Lamb Inn. It was also at

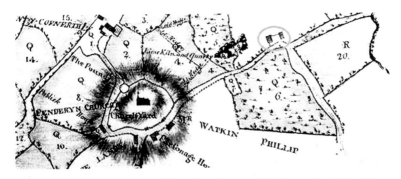

Two circled buildings in Troedrhiw'rllan in 1776. Q6 is Cae'r Rue (rhiw) 'the hill field' & R20 is Parson's mead, both linked to the Troedrhiw'rllan place-name.
Photo courtesy of SM & WGAS (D/D BF/E 164)

one time, the name of a public house which stood in front of Abernant Quarry (HPP p. 44). Before 1827 and the building of the Lamb Inn, the only two buildings in *Toedrhiw 'rllan* were Hywel Williams, Wernlas's cottage and the *Toedrhiw 'rllan* tavern. The stones from the old tavern were used to build Mr Herbert Williams's house (living there in 1905, HPP p90). The renowned local historian, poet, philanthropist and businessman Mr Jenkin Howell remembered the walls of the old tavern still standing but the roof had collapsed; there was an orchard of plum and apple trees behind it, (recorded in 1905. ibid).

Troed, rhiw'r, llan; 'foot of the church hill'

Tŷ Isaf

Ty Ishaf 1841 Census D20; Ty Isaf 1851 Census; Ty-Isaf; Tuy isha 1852 PR;

See Y Tafarn Isaf

Ty'n-y-ton
SN 931070

Lost Tavern, cottage
Ty'n-y-ton (B.H) 1918 OS6"; Ty'n-y-ton 1953 OS6", 1878 OS25"; Tynton Cottage 1939 VPRD; Tin Ton (Public House), & Cottage 1891 Census;Tyn ton 1871 Census, 1864, 1856 PR; Railway Cottage 1911, 1901 Census; Railway Inn 1911, 1901, 1881, 1871, 1861 Census; Tinton Huts 1851 Census; Tyn y ton 1841 Census D20; Ty'n y Ton 1810 PR; Tŷ yn y ton 1775 PR; Tyn yr Ton 1772 PR; Tŷ y Tonn 1771 PR.

Tynyton or *Ty yn y ton* was the name of an early cottage and later the name of a beer house adjacent to the Rhigos* (Rugos) Halt on the Neath to Aberdare railway line. The cottage was recorded on the 18th cent.

Rugos Halt with the Ty'n-y-ton/Railway Inn in the background prob. c. 1930s
Courtesy of Aberdare Library

parish registers, but the Beer or Public House was built later, alongside the railway line and opened in 1851. The tavern was recorded as the *Tin Ton* (*Public House*) in 1891. It was also called the Railway Inn, due to its proximity to the Vale of Neath railway line.

Ty'n-y-ton has two elements as well as the definite article. The first element is either *ty'n* an abbreviation of *tyddyn* 'smallhoding' or *tŷ* 'house'. The second element is *ton* 'lay-land', viz. a green, or land left unbroken, not ploughed or turned over. The whole place-name would give 'the house in the lay-land'.

* *Rugos, y rugos,* is Welsh *grugos* (*grug* 'heather', plus the adjectival suffix *-os*), mutated to y *rugos*, following the def. art., giving 'the heath', 'the (place of) heather'. *Ricos* represents the pronunciation of the local Gwentian dialect. *Rhigos* is a misspelling of *Rugos*. (see CVPN pp. 85-86).

Tyddyn or tŷ, yn, y, ton; 'smallholding or house in the lay-land'

Tyle-morgrug

SN 925075

Residence

Tyle-morgrug 1991 OSPF 1108; Tyla yr Morgrig 1841 Census D20; Tyler Morgreg 1841 TAS; Tyle'r Morgrig 1840 TM; Tyla morgrûg 1834 Will Rachel Watkins NLW; Tyle morgrug 1830 OS; Tyle'r morgrug 1794 PR; Tylau-Morgrig 1781 Tred. Est.Map.

Tyle-morgrug is the name of a former smallholding located just north of Trebanog Isaf, bordering the Sychryd stream. The tenement is shown on the 1781 Tred. Est. map, along with Pentwyn. Both properties were part

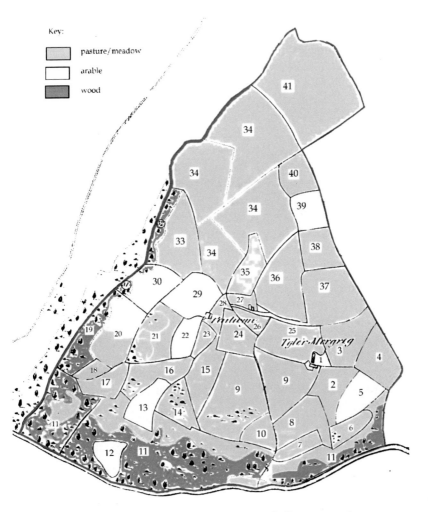

Sanitised 1840 Tithe Map of Tyle'r Morgrug (including Pentwyn) ©DMJ

of Clyn Rhydfaen until the mid. 18th cent.. The farmhouse was rebuilt in the mid. 19th cent. with the farm operational until 1966. Since 1984, the property has been owned and renovated by the Chichester Youth Adventure Trust and is described and used today as a cottage and bunkhouse.

1841 TAS Tyler Morgreg (sic) (192 acres):
Landowner – Sir Charles Morgan Bart. Occupier – William Jenkins.
1. Homestead 2. Wern (alder swamp) 3. Coedcae (grazing enclosure) 4. Worlod

(gweirglodd; meadow) 5. Gelli (grove) 6. Penycwm (top of the wooded dale) 7. Cae bach (small field) 8. Pen y cwm (top of the wooded dale) 9. Coedcae (grazing enclosure) 10. Cae Newydd (new field) 11. Graig (rock) 12. Cae bach (small field) 13. Caer coed (the wood field) 14. Cae Cwm (wooded dingle field) 15. Cae Mawr (big field) 16. Wern Las (green alder swamp) 17. Caer Gwenith (the wheat field) 18. Digoed bach (small wood clearing) 19. Coed (wood) 20. Gelli ddu (black grove) 21. Gwernydd bach (small alder swamps) 22. Cae dan ty (field below the house) 23. Morfa bach (small marsh) 24. Cae Pwdwr (unproductive field) 5. Worlod (meadow) 26. Morfa bach (small marsh) 27. Pentwyn Ruins & Cae bach (Pentwyn ruins & small field) 28. Groft ty fry barn &c. (high house small field, barn etc.) 29. Worlod fawr (big meadow) 30. Cae John (John's field) 31. Wood 32. Coed (wood) 33. Caer Waun (meadow field) 34. Waun (meadow) 35. Caer Waun (meadow field) 36. Caer Sayce (Saes; the Englishman's field) 37. Cae cae Isha (lower field field) 38. do Ucha (upper do) 39. do 40. Pump Quarter (five quarters) 41. Nawer (nine acres)

From time to time, the definite article has been included and omitted from this place-name. *Tyla* is the local dialect pronunciation of Welsh *tyle* 'hill'. There is also a *Tyle Morgrug* in Cwm Nedd. The final element *morgrug* 'ants' is not uncommon in Welsh place-names cf. *Bryn Morgrug*, Alltwen, Pontardawe, *Pant y Morgrug*, Cilybebyll, *Twmpath y Morgrug*, Crucadarn., Brecs. etc. and describes a hill or ground frequented by ants, or possibly figuratively in *Tyle-morgrug* for a small hill.

Tyle, y, morgrug; 'the ants' hill'

Tyn y Cwm SO 022091

Residence

Tynycwm 2010 AZSA; 1952 OS6", 1920 OS6"; Ysgubor 1901, 1884 OS6";

This residence was previously evidenced as Ysgubor on the 1901 and 1884 OS6" maps, and as TS1131 Barn & Garden under Penmailard on the 1840 TM & TAS.

The name contains two elements and the definite article. The first element is either Welsh *tŷ* 'house' or *tyn*, the abbreviated form of *tyddyn* 'small-holding'. The second element *cwm* 'valley, dale, bowl-shaped depression' is more likely to refer to a 'small wooded valley' in south Wales place-names, cf. Cwm Taf, Cwmbach, Cwmdâr, Cwmaman etc. In this instance, *Tyn y Cwm* would refer to a 'dwelling in the wooded dingle'. The woods in that part of Cwm Taf is known as Coed Penmailard.

Tyn, y, cwm; 'dwelling in the wooded valley'

Wern Fawr

Lost Farm

Wern-fawr 1952 OS6"; Wern Farm 1954 PR; Y Wern 1905 HPP p16; Wern Fawr 1871, 1861 Census, 1840 TM; Wern 1851, 1841 Census, 1813 OS Map; Y Wern vawr 1729 E. Bowen map; Tyr Rees Jon. Ychan 1691 CFL/BRA; Rs ap Jenu~ Tyr Rs ap John ychan 1626 Tred. Est.;

Wern Fawr was the name of a farm with a large farmhouse, in ruins since the 1950s, in a part of Coed Taf Fawr. In 1841, it was a farm, of *c.* 110 acres. It was known as *Y Wern* or *Wern Fawr* from 1729, with a possible earlier name of *Tir Rhys ap John Ychan*.

The name has two elements as well as the definite article which is often assumed. The first element *gwern* 'alder trees', 'alder swamp' mutates to *wern* after the definite article, assumed or otherwise. The second element *mawr* 'big, large' describes the first element, giving a large alder swamp or large alder trees. The former is probably the more acceptable. The terrain has been afforested since the 1950s and is unlikely to show its earlier characteristics.

1841 TAS Wern Fawr (110 acres):

Landowner – Mrs Eliza Ann Maddox. Occupier – Morgan Morgan.

1387. Waun Isha (lower meadow) 1388. Ynis y Mayr (maer? the steward's? river meadow) 1389. Tyle Mawr (big hill) 1390. Worlod (gweirglodd; meadow) 1391. Gorof (wooded precipice by a river) 1392. Cae Crwm (crooked field) 1393. Wern fach (small alder swamp) 1394. Homestead &c. 1395. Coedcae du (black grazing enclosure) 1396. Cae Glas (green field) 1397. do Mawr (big green field) 1398. do Main (stone' green field) 1399. do fallan (apple green field) 1400. do Ysgubor (barn do) 1401. Coed cae Garw (coarse grazing enclosure) 1402. Gwaun y Wern (the alder swamp meadow)

(y), gwern, mawr; '(the) large alder swamp'

Wern Isaf

Lost smallholding

Wern Isaf 1920, 1905, 1884 OS6";

Wern Isaf was the name of a smallholding on the lower slopes of Cefn Sychbant between Abernant and Troedyrhiw. The site has been afforested as Cwm Taf since the 1950s. The first element is the same as in *Wern Fawr* with *isaf* 'lower' as a distinguishing second element.

Gwern, isaf; 'lower alder swamp'

Wernlas

Farm

Wern Lâs 1923 LYH p25; Wernlas 1841 Census UP; 1843 Will William Morgan; Gwern las 1789 John Lloyd; 1739 HPP p52; Tyr y werne laes 1626 Tred. Est. (Sr Edw Lewis Kt.)

Wernlas is the name of a farm in Cwm Cadlan, It is recorded at 97 acres in the 1841 TAS. The 1789 form omits the definite article while the earliest example has *Tir y wern las* in modern orthography giving 'land of the green alder wetland'.

1841 TAS Wernlas (97 acres):

Landowner – Morgan Morgan. Occupier – Richard Howell

961. Coed cae (grazing enclosure) 962. Cae draw (yonder field) 963. Weirglodd (meadow) 964. Cae Cenol (middle field) 965. Croft Garn (cairn small field) 966. Waun cil y Coed (meadow of the nook in the woods) 967. Croft 968. Erw fain (narrow acre) 969. Caer Garreg (the stone field) 970. Ysgyryd (rugged, rocky) 971. Cae Crwn (curved field) 972. Cae Mawr Isha (lower big field) 973. do Ucha

Sanitised 1841 TM of Wernlas with Nant Cadlan flowing through the fields.
©DMJ

(upper big field) 974. Cae bach (small field) 975. Wern (alder trees) 976. Cae bach (small field) 977. do 978. Homestead &c. 979. Wern draw y ty (alder trees beyond the house) 979a. Road &c. 980. Caer Prydydd (the poet's field) 981. Waun Goch (red meadow) 982. Wern (alder trees) 983. Coed cae (grazing enclosure)

Wernlas has two elements *gwern* 'alder trees; wet land', mutated to *wern* after an assumed or lost definite article, and *glas* 'green', mutated to las following a feminine noun, giving green wet ground, with alder trees. Nant Cadlan may contribute to some fields being wetter than others, with fields numbered 975. *Wern*, 979. *Wern draw y ty* and 982. *Wern*, all containing *gwern* 'alder marsh' etc. as an element and bordering the stream.

Gwern, glas; 'green wet, alder trees land'

Woodland Park
SN 947077
Housing estate
Woodland Park 1996 SWVSA; 1981 OS map; 1975, 1968 PR;

Woodland Park estate was opened in 1964 on land previously known as Fedw Fach 'small birch', (no. 283 Fedw fach), on the 1841 TAS. *Park* was added to *Woodland* probably due to its past association with land surrounding a mansion and the estate's present proximity to the Brecon Beacons National Park.

Ynys Fawr
See Trebanog Cottages

Ynys Llwyfog
Lost tenement
Ynys Llwyfog 1703 Maybery NLW.

Clyn Celli and *Ynys Llwyfog* became Trebannog Fawr (HVHR p. 39). See Trebannog Fawr and Melin Trebannog/Trebannog Mill. *Ynys* is 'river meadow' and *llwyfog* means 'abounding in elms' GPC.

Ynys, llwyfog; 'river meadow of elms'

Ynys-daf
Lost Smallholding
Ynys-Dâf 1922 O6"; Ynys-Daf 1905 OS6": Daniel Bevan Shoemaker of Ynisdaf 1853 Will of Rev. Dd. Davies, Pen y Pound; Inistaf 1841 Census UP; Ynys-dâf 1830 OS1"; Ynys Taf 1794 PR; Ynystaf 1822, 1791 PR.

Ynys-daf was the name of a small-holding located between Abernant and Troed-y-rhiw in Cwm Taf Fawr. In the 1841 TAS, David Davies occupied both Abernant and *Ynis Daf*, while the 1841 Census has the Rev. David Owen at *Inistaf*. The two farms are now submerged under the waters of Llwyn-onn Reservoir.

The place-name contains two elements, *ynys* 'river meadow' and *Taf* a shortened form of the River *Taf Fawr* that used to flow close to *Ynys-daf* and Abernant farms. *Taf* mutates to *Daf* following a singular feminine noun as shown in some of the above examples.

1841 TAS Ynis Daf (44 acres)

Landowner – Morgan Williams Esqre. Occupier – David Davies

1247. Worlod & Homestead (meadow & Homestead) 1248. blank 1249. blank 1250. Close bach (small yard) 1251. Close (farmyard) 1252. do 1253. do dan y Wern (below the alder marsh) 1254. Coed cae (grazing enclo-sure) 1255. Gwaun (meadow).

Ynys, Taf; 'Taf river-meadow'

Ynyswendraeth

SN 946094

Farm

Ynyswendraeth 1989 OS P1108; Yniswendrath 1854 SRB, PNDH; Yniswenddor 1841 TAS, 1840 TM;; Yniswen-dorth 1841 Census; Ynyswaindorth 1790 PR; Ynis-Wendorth 1776 BFE; Ynis Bendorth 1570 AMR;

Ynyswendraeth (loc. dial. *Swendorth*) is the current name of a farm located north of the village of Penderyn, just off the A4059 road towards Ystradfellte. In its present written form, the name could be translated as 'white beach island'. This would be totally inappropriate for the name of a farm in the Brecon Beacons National Park, but literally correct if one assumed the elements to be ynys 'island', gwen 'white' and traeth 'beach'. *Yniswendrath* (1854) represents the local dialect pronunciation of *traeth*, but the 1841 Tithe Map and Schedules record *dor* 'door' as the final element. This is probably a scribal error indicating an unfinished word, because the 1841 Census has *Ynyswendorth*, showing Welsh *torth* 'loaf' to be the final element, lenited to *dorth* following a feminine noun. The final element remains as *torth*, (*dorth*) back to 1570, its earliest form.

The second element has also changed over the years. *Gwen*, feminine 'white', mutated to *wen* following a feminine noun, was *wain* (*gwaun*, 'meadow') in 1790, but this may have been a short-lived 'corrected' form. The 1776 example is *Ynis-Wendorth*. The earliest form however is the most revealing showing that the element was *ben*, the mutated form of *pen* 'head, top, end'. The final two elements *bendorth* (pen and torth) giving 'top (of the) loaf', figuratively 'top (of the) hill'. The early 'top (of the) loaf' then became *wendorth* the 'white loaf', before finally changing to *wendraeth* 'white beach'.

The first element *ynys* occurs very often in Penderyn place-names and means 'river-meadow' rather than 'island'. When *ynys* occurs inland, in the countryside, it is invariably located on the side of a river or stream. It is very rarely surrounded on all sides by water. This ynys is a 'river-meadow'.

The original *Ynysbendorth*, literally 'top (of the) loaf river-meadow' actually refers to a river-meadow that belongs to a farm at the top of a hill, and this is an accurate description of the incline top location of today's farmhouse. The 1840 Tithe Map shows the presence of a stream near the *ynys* (field no. 738).

Coincidentally, *Ynyswendorth* was a local farmer's pronunciation heard in a 1974 recording (RMR), rather than a written contemporary *Ynyswendraeth*.

For *torth* as a place-name element cf. *Craig y dorth*, Monm., *Mesur y dorth*, Pembs, *Rhiw'r dorth*, Carms. etc.. For *loaf* used figuratively as a hill cf. the *Sugar Loaf*, Carms. and Gwent. (see CVPN pp. 102-103).

1841 TAS Yniswenddor (51 acres)

Landowner – Morgan Morgan Esq. Occupier – Elizabeth Jones

738, Ynis (river-meadow) 739. Coed cae (grazing enclosure) 740. Cottage & Garden 741. Godre'r Coedcae (bottom of the grazing enclosure) 742. blank 749. Waun (meadow) 750. Wern (alder marsh) 751. Cae bach (small field) 752. do

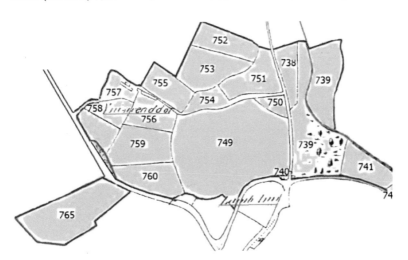

Sanitised 1840 Tithe Map of Yniswenddor with a small brook flowing through no.738 'Ynis', towards Nant Cadlan. ©DMJ

Gwyn (white do) 753. do 754. Wern (alder marsh) 755. Erw bant (yonder acre) 756. Cae dan ty (field below the house) 757. Homestead &c. 758. Cae (field) 759. do Cenol (middle do) 760. Coed cae Lloi (calves' grazing enclosure) 765. Waunfach (small meadow)

Ynys, pen, torth; 'top (of the) loaf river-meadow'

Ynysyfelin   Former Hamlet

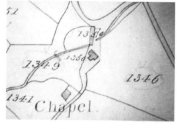

Ynys-y-felin 1905, 1884 OS6"; Ynisyfelin 1876 Daniel Humphreys, Weaver, Merthyr Telegraph; 1841 Census UP; 1813 OS; Ynisyfelin Factory 1859 Merthyr Telegraph; Unis y Velin 1786 Tredegar NLW; Ynys y felin 1783 PR; Ynys y Felin 1763-64 WP; Yniss Veline 1726 Tredegar NLW;

Ynysyfelin 1840 TM. 1341 Cae Ty Cwrdd, 1346 Ynis dan y felin, 1349 Cae Bach Tafarn, 1350 Buildings Garden.

Ynys-y-felin was the name of a hamlet in Cwm Taf Fawr. The final element is Welsh *melin* 'mill'. The mill referred to was *Pwll Coch*, see Melin Pwll Coch. The 'factory' recorded in 1859 above was a woollen factory. *Pwll Coch Mill* had originally ground corn, but by 1714 the mill had changed from a corn grist mill to a tucking mill, and later, by the 19th cent., to a woollen factory (*Vaynor* p. 167).

Ynysyfelin c. 1905

The 1840 TM opposite shows Bethel chapel (1341. Cae Ty Cwrdd 'meeting house field), the tavern's field (1349. Cae bach Tafarn 'tavern's small field'), the river-meadow below the mill (1346. Ynis dan y felin) and the location of the mill (1350. Buildings Garden. Owners & Occupiers Ann Williams and Gwenllian Williams). The 1841 Census shows Ann Williams and Gwenllian Williams of 'Independent Means' at 'Ynisyfelin'.

The first element *ynys* 'river-meadow' refers to the mill's location on the banks of a stream that empties into the nearby Taf Fawr river. *Ynys-y-felin* is 'river-meadow (of) the mill'.

Ynys, y, melin - 'the mill river meadow'.

Ysgol Gynradd Gymuned Penderyn Primary School
School
Ysgol Gynradd Gymuned Penderyn Community Primary School 2020 School Website; Ysgol Gynradd Gymunedol Penderyn 2018 Estyn; Ysgol Gynradd Penderyn/Penderyn Primary School 1995 Welsh Office; Penderyn County Primary School 1966 SM School Report; Penderyn Public Elementary School 1920 Kelly's; Ysgol Pontbrenllwyd 1903 Seren Gomer; Pontprenllwyd B School 1896 Inspector's Report; Ysgol Pontbrenll-wyd 1874 Logbook, (2003) YPP; Llwyn'r Eithyn, Ysgubor Fawr 1840 TM.

The present school is called *Ysgol Gynradd Gymuned Penderyn Community Primary School*. The 2018 Estyn report names the school using the adjective *gymunedol* for the noun *gymuned*, while the 1995 Welsh Office form does not include '*community*', *gymuned* or *gymunedol*. In the 1960s it was a *County Primary School* and in the 1920s, a *Public Elementary school*. In 1903, the school was known as *Ysgol Pontbrenllwyd*, due to its location within the hamlet, while a School Inspector's Report dated 1896 named it as *Pontprenllwyd B School*, with the letter 'B' representing *Board*.

The school started as a '*Board School*' following the 1870 "Foster's" Elementary Education Act which gave local authorities powers to set up 'School Boards'. These 'Boards' were responsible for erecting adequate school buildings and the appointment of competent teachers. Members of the first *Ponbrenllwyd School Board* were named as Jenkin Rhys, Esq. Ysgubor Fawr, Landowner, George Williams, Manager of Hirwaun Brickworks, John Aubrey, Tŷ Mawr, Hirwaun, Ironworks Official, Evan Edwards, (Ifan Torfoel), Manager of the Foel Silica Quarry and William Powell, Maesydderwen, Hirwaun, Quarry Owner. Previously, schools had been known as 'National Schools' (Church of England) or 'British Schools' (Non-conformist). The 1870 Education Act put the responsibility for children's education in the hands of local authorities rather than religious or charitable bodies. School Boards were abolished in 1902 by Balfour's

Education Act which established Local Education Authorities.

Pontprenllwyd Board School or *Ysgol Pontbrenllwyd* was opened in 1874 on the side of the Hirwaun to Brecon Turnpike road in *Llwyn'r Eithyn* field, no. 168 on the 1840 Tithe Map and the 1841 Tithe Schedules for *Ysgubor Fawr*, (YPP).

Ysgubor Fawr   SN 948085
Former Estate, farm, residence

Ysgubor-fawr 1952, 1905 OS6"; Ysgibor fawr 1841 Census D20; Skyborfawr 1829 HB iv, 71; Ysgibor Vawr 1777 PR; (Tyr) Skipor Fawr 1617 HPP 56; Tyr Skibor vawr 1609 RISW GGF 1/84

Ysgubor Fawr is the name of a small farm located between Pantcefnyffordd and Pontbrenllwyd. The earlier estate included farms such as Pantcynfarth and Erw'r Crydd (1609 RISW), as well as leasing quarries, private properties, a public house etc., but over the years the size of the estate diminished due to the sales of land and properties as well as extensive quarrying activity at Cwar Mawr and Cwar Aberaman. In 1841 Thomas Williams owned *Ysgubor Fawr* at 154 acres (as well as Pantycynferth at 173 acres), but by 1919 *Ysgubor Fawr* had been reduced to 50 acres (AL).

All the forms are consistent with the earliest examples including an additional *tir* element signifying 'land, ground, territory, etc.'. The other elements are *ysgubor* 'barn' and *mawr* 'big, large, great', lenited to *fawr* following a feminine noun. *Ysgubor Fawr* is 'large barn' from earlier *Tir Ysgubor Fawr* 'land (of the) large barn'.

Ysgubor fawr, 2017 © *DMJ*

1841 TAS Ysgubor Fawr (154 acres):
Landowner – Thomas Williams Esq. Occupier – Himself.
136. Nawer (nine acre) 137. Saither (seven acre) 139. Waste 140. Coed cae Eithin (Gorse grazing enclosure) 141. Cae Derw (Oak tree field) (142. Cottages, Gardens & Barn 143. Ton (lay-land) 144. Homestead Roads &c. 145. Cae Oflaen y ty (field in front of house) 146. Cae penbyr (short end field) 147. Erwpenllydan (wide end acre) 154. Cnifon? y Gerhin? (Cerrynt? the road shearing (place)) 155. Cae brynchwith ucha (upper brynchwith field) 156. do isha (lower do) 157. Quarry 158. Caer Odyn (the kiln field) 159. Wood 160. Neredd (half acre) 161. Quarry 162. Waste 163. Neredd y Gath (the cat's half acre) 164. Cae Der (dâr ? oak? Field) 165. Do ffynnon (well do) 166. Plantation 167. Cae Tycwrdd (church house field *Siloam*) 168. Llwyn'r Eithin (the gorse bush) 169. Ynis Ucha (upper river meadow) 170. do Isha (lower river meadow) 172. Plantation 173. Coedcaer Pant Crew (craw? grazing enclosure of the pigsty? dingle) 175. do Eithin (Eithin 'gorse' grazing enclosure) 176. Cae Newydd (new field)

Shoni Sgubor Fawr.
Historian Gwyn A. Williams calls Shoni Sgubor Fawr "a red-haired giant from Penderyn" (When Was Wales? p187) . Shoni, whose baptismal name was John Jones, was a pugilist, mercenary, rioter, ballad singer and a one-time 'hero of China', a notorious district of early 19th century Merthyr. In 1844, both he and his musical pal Dai'r Cantwr, were transported to Van Diemen's Land, Australia, for life and twenty years respectively, as a result of their involvements with the Rebecca Rioters.

There is no documentary evidence for *Shoni*'s presence at the Penderyn *Ysgubor Fawr* farm or estate. There is however evidence gleaned by a reporter at Carmarthen County gaol in February 1844 on the morning that *Shoni*, Dai Cantwr and Lewis Henry were to be transferred to Millbank Penitentiary prior to their transportation. In his report he gives "a brief outline of the lives of the first two prisoners" stating that "Shoni's father lived at Scybor-fawr (hence Shoni's nickname) in Breconshire but Shoni was born in Merthyr" (The Welshman 9/2/1844). *Ysgubor Fawr*, Penderyn could well have been the Breconshire location of *Shoni*'s nickname.

PS. A letter from Ishmael Jones in Australia, printed in the Merthyr Guardian, January 1853, stated that "Shoni Scubor Fawr and Dai'r Cantwr are both liberated and doing well".

Ysgubor, mawr; 'large barn'

INDEX